THE PEOPLE'S

Eric Midwinter's lifelong interest in comedians began 70 years ago when he saw Albert Modley in a Manchester pantomime. He thus brings untold memories, as well as his noted skills as a well-known social historian and commentator, to the task of describing and judging the major age of the comedians. The author of over fifty books, many of them dealing with social life and leisure activity in the 19th and 20th centuries, he prepared a dozen or so 'lives' of comedians for the *New Dictionary of National Biography* (2004), and, in *The People's Jesters*, he revisits, updates and widens his critically acclaimed 1979 study, *Make 'Em Laugh; Famous Comedians and Their Worlds*.

Books by Eric Midwinter ~ from Third Age Press ~

A Voyage of rediscovery: a guide to writing your life story (2nd edition 2001)
Encore: a guide to planning a celebration of your life (1993)
The Rhubarb People (1993)
Getting to know me (1996)
Best Remembered: a hundred stars of yesteryear (2002)
As one stage door closes . . . The story of John Wade: jobbing conjuror (2002)
Novel Approaches: a practical guide to the classic novel (2003)
500 Beacons: the U3A story (2004)

Photographs and playbills from
the Patrick Newley collection

'Stage' illustration on page 1 by Peter Ross

The front cover is designed from the poster for a charity show at the Manchester Hippodrome in the late 1930s; it features several of the comedians profiled in this study (Eric Midwinter)

THE PEOPLE'S JESTERS

BRITISH COMEDIANS

IN THE

20TH CENTURY

Eric Midwinter

Third Age Press

Third Age Press

ISBN 1 898576 25 4
First edition

Third Age Press Ltd, 2006
Third Age Press, 6 Parkside Gardens
London SW19 5EY
www.thirdagepress.co.uk
Managing Editor Dianne Norton

Layout and cover design by Dianne Norton
Printed and bound in Great Britain
by intypelibra

Contents

ACKNOWLEDGEMENTS

Although this study is based primarily on close on 70 years of watching, listening and reading, there are several books that must be mentioned as having been particularly helpful. These include Geoffrey J Mellor, *They Made Us Laugh* (1982) and R Wilmut, *Kindly Leave the Stage* (1985), both remarkably useful texts, brimming with enthusiasm and expertise; the exceptionally perceptive and glitteringly presented John Fisher, *Funny Way to be a Hero* (1973), something of a bible for students of comedy; Roy Hudd's *Cavalcade of Variety Acts; a Who's Who of Light Entertainment 1945-60* (1997), a veritable cornucopia of information from that engaging personality, Roy Hudd; and, less modestly, Eric Midwinter, *Make 'Em Laugh; Famous Comedians and Their Worlds* (1979)

Another invaluable asset was the timely publication in 2004 of the *New Dictionary of National Biography*, which, more eclectic than its distinguished predecessor, very properly includes notices of the lives of many comedians. This source has been remorselessly utilised, for, without exception, the detail and insight of these essays is of a remarkably high standard.

I want also to express my appreciation to my friend, Patrick Newley, the show business equivalent of cricket's *Wisden* when it comes to sheer knowledge and the show business equivalent of cricket's John Arlott when it comes to thoughtful understanding. He read the typescript and alerted me gently to untold errors of fact and countless infelicities of observation. It has been a pleasure to have his generous assistance; it is a pleasure to acknowledge this major debt with many thanks.

Nor is that all. All the illustrated material, both photographs and bill and poster matter, has been kindly provided by Patrick Newley, yet another cause for my genuine appreciation.

1. THE COMING OF THE COMEDIANS

Comedians are difficult to avoid. They are found on stage, on film, in advertisements, in clubs and cabaret, on radio and television and on their offshoots, such as videos, DVDs and cassettes. However misanthropic, humourless or intellectually snobbish a person may be, he or she is bound to cross paths with a comedian at some point. If a little less ubiquitous than in the previous generation, comedians are interfused with social life in Britain.

One utilises the word in its modern connotation, that is, comedians as comic entertainers, normally employing the spoken word. Until about the time of the 1914-1918 war, 'comedians' were chiefly comic actors, the converse of 'tragedians', and were found on and around the legitimate stage. During the music hall period, the title of 'comedian' was also used to describe singers of comic songs, the major component of the music hall bill.

The term came more to be employed for talking 'comics' at much the same time and as part of the progression from music hall, in its traditional convention, to variety. Comic entertainers, alone, in duo or in sketch format, grew in vogue, normally performing in spoken prose, with occasional ditties, unlike the chorus song formula of the old music hall. They were abundant during the dominant years of variety, roughly from the end of the

Great War to the mid or late 1950s. Indeed, it might be argued that, since as well as before that juncture, comedians have not existed in the same profusion. It is true that, even with the death of variety and the reduction in influence of its fellow medium, radio, comedians have found other fields to till since the 1950s. Nonetheless, it is arguable that there are, in regard of national eminence, less of them and that, particularly on television, their role has been partly superseded by comic actors, by what, pre-1914, would, ironically enough, have been known as 'comedians' in the ancient sense.

This study will examine comedians in this newer meaning, as from about 1920, with a few glances back to their derivations in Edwardian and late Victorian times and with, by natural weighting, some concentration on the variety and radio period. Although there will be some cross-reference to outside influences, in particular, the often strong American impact, this is primarily a scrutiny of British comedians. Its purpose is to identify and analyse the themes of subject matter, characterisation and style of these scores of working comedians over that phase of time and, by extension, right up to the present day. However, no excuse is offered for this being, in chief, a wholesale luxuriating in nostalgia, an attempt, that is, to revive remembrance of great performers and the fun and laughter they brought to millions of people over a couple of generations.

For the function of the comedian is a straightforward one. It is to make people laugh. One might spend overmuch time inspecting the physiological and psychological annals of how and why there is human laughter, but this is a social study, its premise a taking for granted that laughter is, by and large, a life-enhancing reaction and emotion. Artistically, too, there is a wide range of comedy, from the alcohol-infused belly-laughs of the clubroom to the more subtle humour of a Molière or a Shaw. Although this text will have a considerable amount to say about differing styles and also depths of comedy, its main focus will remain simply on comedians making people laugh and giving them a good time.

That said, all that laughter had and has a purpose. It was covert, largely unconscious and unexpressed, but, in overall effect, it was most purposeful. To begin with a negative element, the laughter was rarely, if ever, subversive. Comedy may be seditious, deliberately aimed with satirical force at the overthrow of some form of authority, but British comedians never envisaged that type of approach.

It is sometimes argued that the old-time music hall had a fiercer, sharper edge and that this amounted to a working class critique of the establishment. Albert Chevalier would sing *My Old Dutch* ('We've been together now for 40 years...') in front of a drop scene depicting the gates of a workhouse, for his separation from his bride of 40 years standing was not, as is sometimes thought, through her death, but through the harsh poor law ordinance that split asunder married couples on entry into the workhouse. In fact, the dormitory principle, male and female, made marital co-habitation difficult, whilst, given that most of the residents were relatively young, there was a rough and ready birth control mechanism at work, as the poor law authorities did not wish to encourage additions to their budgetary burdens.

Moreover, despite these strict edicts, the poor law authorities found themselves obliged to provide lots of 'outdoor relief' to the 'aged paupers' in their care. Indeed, towards the end of the Victorian era, many were receiving a weekly subsistence almost equal to the five shillings (25p) that would constitute the first old age pension in 1908 – something similar, in proportion to the average worker's wage, as the old age pension is today. Only about a quarter of elderly paupers were, in fact, incarcerated in workhouses and workhouse hospitals – a similar percentage of the older population as one might find in residential care nowadays.

Be that as it may, Albert Chevalier's song may be interpreted as an assault on the strictness of that workhouse precept. On the other hand, there is not much evidence that its rendition led to rumblings of discontent. Pity was probably the sentiment most typically engendered by its performance by 'the Coster Laureate.' What the music hall most adeptly offered was social comment. Gus Elen's *If it wasn't for the 'ouses in between* makes sardonic noises about chaotic urban development, while Marie Lloyd skitted at the problems of rented accommodation and surreptitious 'flittings' in *Don't Dilly Dally on the Way*. It may all have had the effect of keeping an issue in people's mind, but it is more likely that the issues were in people's minds already. What they enjoyed, either wreathed in smiles or shedding tears, was that comforting feeling of identity with the subject.

Equally, there were pro-establishment choruses. The Great MacDermott defiantly sang

'We don't want to fight, but by jingo if we do' in 1877 at the London Palladium. The idea of Jingoism was, then, first heard of in connection with a comparatively short-lived political crisis with a Russo-Turk background. Again, the moderate judgement must be that the song appealed to a public opinion already resolved and that it reinforced rather than inflamed the emotion.

Part of a 1938 London Coliseum bill featuring the likes of George Robey, Forsythe, Seamon and Farrell and Renee and Donald Houston, all mentioned in these pages

If anything, the comedians of the post-1918 dispensation were even less disposed than their predecessors in the music hall to take a lively interest in political affairs of a fundamental interest. There were two main reasons for this. First, with few exceptions, they were not revolutionary in personal thought; if anything, and as far as may be judged in such matters, the bulk of comedians have been of a small 'c' conservative nature or of apolitical personality. On the whole, the status quo served them well enough and they took it for granted. Many of them made their way from small, sometimes impoverished, beginnings; they were, in fact, self-made men and, in much tinier numbers, women. They did not look to rock political and social boats.

Second, they worked in a world controlled either by commercial interest or by safe public corporation. For example, between the two world wars, neither the capitalist sway of the theatre nor the Reithian autocracy of BBC radio would have tolerated any anarchic or dissident material. They would simply have not been employed, had they been that way inclined. Thus, by personality and by opportunity, there were few signs of incipient revolution among British comedians.

This did not mean that the comic material they presented was totally benign. Much of it, if by no means all, was acutely questioning of authority – but little of it was basically subversive. For example, the wonderfully sustained success of the *ITMA* radio programme throughout World War II was founded in an impudent critique of wartime bureaucracy. However, it was done affectionately, not malevolently. It invited listeners to laugh maybe with a little fondness at these institutions. By so doing it helped to divert any latent anger or mistrust. The jokes about foremen on *Workers' Playtime* or the cracks about any one of rank in wartime shows devoted to service personnel were of the same brand. They defused malign thoughts with laughter. As the 20th century drew on, the authorities came to understand more subtly how such soft-hearted patter was, in fact, beneficial. There was much more leeway in such matters in the second than in the first of the two World Wars.

This mode of laughing at troubles and despairs and this kind of, in the vernacular, 'taking the Mickey' out of those in command was, therefore, a safety valve, channelling any dormant rage through the flushing system of laughter. It is in this sense that, by accident or by design, the British comedian adopted the role of demotic jester. Just as the monarch's wit had leave, within certain boundaries, to insult and make fun at the expense of the king, so did the comedians contrive to lighten the load of the people. The comics pointed up the foibles and weaknesses of everyday life, personal and collective, private and institutional, and the public laughed both at themselves and at these aspects of the public weal.

Whether this was – and is – a good or a bad thing will depend on one's ideological viewpoint. Some might assert that the jester, by reducing important issues to laughter, weakens the case for perhaps necessary change. Others might claim that, in the pragmatic terms of day-by-day existence, laughter is essential to assist all humans to cope with the slings and arrows of outrageous fortune. 'If you can't laugh', people ordinarily remark, 'where would you be?'

Thus, almost surreptitiously, the comedians pursued this social purpose.

Victorian Derivations

A reference to the medieval jester reminds that the comedic role undertaken by the more modern comedian was by no means novel. There were, of course, plenty of derivations for the Ken Dodds of today. This account does not retreat into the past much further than the beginning of the Victorian era, with conjoined industrial and urban development speedily under way. The growth of manufacturing industry and of manufacturing towns was busily constructing the frame of reference for modern life – and the immediate predecessors of present-day comedians were already enlisted in the never-ending battle for laughs.

A cluster of entertainments gathered in and around newly urbanised Britain. These included the 'free and easy' amateur talent concert in the back room of the pub. This later gave rise to the 'singing saloon', sometimes with paid performers. Local theatres developed, some of them located in pubs, while there were supper rooms and night houses, principally in London, catering for a male audience who fancied itself as bohemian. The Vauxhall Pleasure Gardens in London or the similar amenities offered by the Eagle tavern on the City Road are other early examples in the metropolis. Improvements in road travel, especially with the turnpike trusts of the late 18th century and the prodigious efforts of road builders like John Macadam and Thomas Telford, encouraged the role of itinerant entertainers. From 1830 the advent of the railways transformed the whole concept of mobility for the nation and very much eased the passage to and fro of travelling entertainers.

The novels of Charles Dickens, themselves a runaway success in part because of an industrial construct that cheapened the printing process and accelerated the rate of transportation, illustrate the theme in picturesque fashion. This is especially true in his earlier novels, several of them, like *Nicholas Nickleby* or *The Old Curiosity Shop*, cast in a 'picaresque' mode, that is, with leading characters taking to the road for their adventures. Probably Vincent Crummles' fit-up theatre company in *Nicholas Nickleby* is the most affectionately recalled instance, but, in *The Old Curiosity Shop*, Little Nell meets up with Mrs Jarley's travelling waxworks, Jodlin and Short, the Punch and Judy showmen and other itinerant entertainers, working fairs and racecourses.

On more permanent sites we find, in the same novel, Dick Swiveller acting as 'Perpetual Grand' of the 'select convivial circle called the glorious Apollers', an example of the 'singing room' model. In *Bleak House* the room where Nemo's inquest is held in the Sol's Arms hostelry is more commonly deployed for a twice weekly entertainment, led by a gentleman 'of professional celebrity', Little Swills, the comic vocalist. That later tale indicates the shift from the amateur endeavours of Swiveller and his colleagues to the renditions of the paid singer. In *Hard Times* Sleary's circus is used as the counterweight of colour and imagination against the stern aridity of Gradgrindery, the dominance of 'facts' and the factory system. Even Fagin's local, the Three Cripples, in *Oliver Twist*, has a chairman and a blue-nosed pianist, an aspect picked up in Lionel Bart's musical version, *Oliver!*

The choice of Charles Dickens, the laureate of London and of bustling urban existence, has a further resonance. While supporting the middle-class Victorian concept of 'rational recreation', whereby libraries and parks and museums and concerts might be provided to woo the people away from the sordid vices of intemperance and indolence, he disapproved of the emphasis on grey seriousness. He yearned for 'sound rational amusement', preferring that noun to 'recreation'. It was not a lightweight preference. Much as he admired the function of recreation as educative and conducive to good behaviour, he believed that there was 'an innate love' among ordinary people for colour and excitement, not least in an urbanised and industrialised world, where work was soul-deadening and everyday life often a grim round.

He wrote of some 'rational recreation' as having ' a shyness in admitting that human nature when at leisure has any desire whatever to be relieved and diverted; and a furtive sliding in of any poor makeweight piece of amusement, shamefacedly and edgewise.' In eclectic and liberal vein, he also strongly felt that such amusement should be shared among the generations and sexes, one reason for this being the urgent need, in Dickens' view, for adults to retain their link with childhood.

This idea of a communal bond of good entertainment was of a piece with Charles Dickens' basic hope that a generous-spirited humanity was the chief, perhaps the only, remedy for the follies and miseries of humankind. His novels preach that text, towards the end, it has to be said, with increasing pessimism, whilst his famed Public Readings were determined and, ultimately, debilitating attempts to contribute something to the pool of high-class communal amusement. His love of the theatre and of pantomime – he edited the memoirs of Joe Grimaldi – bring the great novelist ever closer to this study. His recognition of the 'innate love', indeed, the essential necessity, of the populace for laughter and brightness is the key to the rise of comedians to supply that ingredient in the human condition. Little Swills was the forerunner, first, of the music hall chorus singer and, second, the stand-up comic.

The Father of Comedians

The honour of being fondly regarded as the grandfather of modern comedians is Joe Grimaldi. Charles Dickens edited his reminiscences in 1884, long after his death in 1837, the year of Queen Victoria's accession to the throne. He was then 59, having been born in London in 1778, and was thus an entirely pre-Victorian, more or less Regency figure. The Grimaldis were an Italian family of clowns and acrobats, his father, the flamboyantly improper Giuseppe, having married Rebecca Brooker, a dancer and bit-part actress. Joe Grimaldi, in the oldest of stage traditions, was flung in at the deep end, playing in a Drury Lane pantomime aged only three. He continued to play at the Drury Lane and Sadler's Wells theatres, sometimes at both at once, necessitating a horse-drawn or pedestrian dash between the two. In 1799 he married Maria Hughes, daughter of one of the proprietors of Sadler's Wells, but she died within a year. He married a Drury Lane actress, Mary Bristow, in 1802. Their only son, another Joseph, showed some theatrical promise, but succumbed to alcoholism at an early age.

Joe Grimaldi first played Clown in panto-mime in 1800, 'Clown', in this case, reflecting one of the particular quartet of characters that comprised the traditional panto cast. He was Guzzle the Drinking Clown, although, in an innovative shift, he was accompanied by Gobble the Eating Clown, portrayed by the leading London clown, John Baptist Dubois. We shall delve deeper into these conven-tions when the influence of pantomime on modern comedy is analysed in the third chapter. Henceforward, Grimaldi developed a versatile range of 'clown' roles, includ-ing some 'savage' parts, such as 'the Wild Man', soothed by the gentle sound of music. However, his major fame was founded in the continuum of pantomime clowns he played at Sadler's Wells and also at the Covent Garden theatre.

Before this time, the clown had been some-thing of a dolt. He had been a village idiot, stupid, countrified and put upon. Joe Grimaldi changed all this. It was as if Wur-zel Gummidge had become Max Miller. He evolved the notion of the clown as spry and sharp, cleverly outwitting others in a high-spirited round of thieving, gratuitous violence and general disrespect. It was a metropolitan concept. This was a Clown for the towns and cities of Georgian licence, noted for exactly such excesses of incivility and larceny.

With appearances in provincial towns, as far afield as Dublin, he also contrived to develop a national repute, hitherto not the easiest of achievements, given the paucity of theatres and the restrictions of transport. It might even be said that he was the first of the demotic comedians. As everyman's jester, he burlesqued the styles of that gaudy age, with his sartorial ridicule of Regency beaux and belles or with his parodies of the arte-facts of the hour. He became famous for his adaptations of everyday objects into noble constructs – wholesale cheeses for coach wheels; coal scuttles for military boots; his much admired Vegetable Man, appropri-ately debuted at Covent Garden, with local produce utilised.

In terms of the future, however, it was his comic songs, interspersed with expressive dialogue, rather more than his more circus-oriented clowning, that paved the route towards music hall. *Hot Codlins*, first sung in 1819, and still performed until recently, was the most famous of these numbers. Even more important for the future was that he brought a degree of respectability to the theatre, in particular to pantomime, that it had lacked. There was still a long way to go before the theatre was to slough off its dubious – and, in many ways, deserved – reputation, but Joe Grimaldi's influence was a factor. His appeal to the lions of society, from Lord Byron to William Hazlitt, was also important, in that he helped to make thea-tre visiting highly fashionable. The allure of Grimaldi to classes high and low created a powerful theatrical phenomenon – and it is precisely that element of cross-class charm that intrigued Charles Dickens, arch exponent of the integrated culture.

Joe Grimaldi was a big, muscular figure of a man, with a huge, looming countenance. Dressed in striped and multi-coloured clothing, his cheeks were anointed with scarlet crescents against a pallid background, the customary clown's make-up that he helped to make conventional. His was an aggressive demeanour, his facial contortions highly expressive and his bodily animation wildly demonstrative. Titanic, agile and thrustful, he dominated the stage and the audience. Quilp, the satanic and villainous dwarf in Charles Dickens' *The Old Curiosity Shop*, is often compared with Mr Punch, but, given Dickens' evident fascination from his childhood with Grimaldi, one is moved to wonder whether the great novelist was also celebrating the great clown.

That grandeur of attack would mark off many of the famous comedians who would inherit the Grimaldi mantle, while the element of grotesquerie would inform a singular branch of comedic talent. One might watch Ken Dodd today and recall Joe Grimaldi.

Disabled and ill by the mid-1820s and an imprudent manager of, for the day, the exceptional sums of money he earned, Joe Grimaldi died in London in 1837. The pantomime deviser and theatre producer manager, Charles Dibden, wrote that Grimaldi was the founder of 'a new school for clowns'. This was an assertion that was to prove true in the general as well as in the particular.

Dan Leno

This is probably the moment to linger over the life and career of Dan Leno, the man who most triumphantly carried the comic baton of Grimaldi through the music hall period and

was judged by no less an expert than Charlie Chaplin as Grimaldi's pre-eminent successor. In that the standard music hall approach, as we shall further examine in chapter two, was the chorus song rendered in appropriate character, Dan Leno's technique, with its emphasis on spoken prose, was of a different order. He used his songs sparingly, although they did signify his characterisations. He usually employed them to begin and end his act, a device much favoured by comedians of the coming generations. Thus, like his eminent predecessor, he was an innovator of some stature, the forerunner of modern comedians in many dimensions.

The sharp-features of Dan Leno, a genius of the old music hall and a progenitor of many modern comedians

It is a tragi-comic story. Like Grimaldi, Dan Leno was born into the business. He was the child of the not terribly well-known duo with the not terribly enthralling bill matter of Mr and Mrs Johnny Wild. He was born to a childhood of poverty in North London in 1860 and at the age of four he joined his parents on the music hall stage. His real name was George Wild Galvin, but his father, John Galvin, soon died, and his mother, Louisa Dutton, married William Grant, an Irish theatrical who used the stage name, Leno. He joined his mother and step-father, principally in provincial music hall in the north of England, where, aged twenty, he became the world clog dancing champion. It was about this time that he became generally known as Dan Leno and had the metropolis in his sights.

It was in and around London in the 1880s that he eschewed the clog dancing and the vocals and turned his attention to spoken monologues. What he did was to create a gallery of studies of commonplace humanity. He buttonholed rather than, like Grimaldi, overwhelmed audiences. It was if he allowed them to listen in to his wheedling, coaxing tones, as he stumbled on and endeavoured to explain one or another of the daily problems of life. There was the fireman, the shop-walker, the gossiping Mrs Kelly, the masher, the downtrodden husband and a host of others, their battered lives related in mundane style – and then lifted with an infusion of the surreal. It was as if each of his characters started out on a humdrum errand and soon found himself in a bizarre predicament, one that he would attempt to surmount with persuasive shows of dignity.

What must be underlined is the dangerousness of the approach. The fusion of the matter-of-fact and the fantastic is incredibly difficult to achieve on stage. The peril of falling between the two stools is only too obvious. Audiences will accept the believable and enjoy it being guyed; they will suspend belief and enjoy the fun of the otherworldly. Dan Leno's achievement was to merge the two and make it hilarious.

Audiences found this mix, portrayed with such humane accomplishment, irresistible. They found it deliciously entertaining, although it was reported that the laughter, whilst constant and full-hearted, was 'not noisy'. The enjoyment was more thoughtful than rowdy. Again, the targets were life's known adversities; again, their nastiness was deflected by the comedic treatment.

Most tellingly, he starred, almost always as a very three-dimensional dame, in the Drury Lane pantomime from 1888 to 1903, a remarkable tribute to his continuing ability to dominate the London light entertainment scene. He was often partnered by the solid frame of Herbert Campbell, large and stationary where Dan Leno was little and dynamic. It is interesting how many famous comedians were, like Dan Leno, to build a reputation in panto.

Of slight build and with sharp-edged features, he was the physiological opposite of the hefty Grimaldi. A restless, quick mover, his costumes always smothered him. Whether he was the lovesick swain, the beefeater, the bandit or the shop assistant, his cuffs eternally overshot his hands and his trouser bottoms consistently engulfed his feet. His collars ascended above his chin; his sizeable hats all had large brims, while, if bare-headed, his dark locks lurked out of control. If, as in the famous shop-walker characterisation, he wore a moustache, it took on a horizontal range of some hirsute distance, outdoing the handlebar moustache of, say, Jimmy Edwards. From within this cumbersome apparel and assorted properties shone an expressive face, the lustrous eyes framed by the archly expressive eyebrows, and the lips ready, should there be a temporary lull in the buffets of destiny, to dissolve into a shining grin. The ever perceptive John Fisher has rightly called him 'the archetype of the modern stand-up comedian'.

He married the young singer, Sarah 'Lydia' Reynolds, in 1884, just as he was on the cusp of his metropolitan conquests, and, as his earnings soared regally from £5 to £250 a week, his large family and he lived a life of some luxury. Known as 'the Funniest Man on Earth' and, because of Edward VII's delight in his antics, 'the King's Jester', he managed – and this is another constant among top comics – to combine the democratic appeal with the almost medieval Yorick-type role. There was another continuum. The great comedians tend to attract fashionable and intellectual regard. Where Hazlitt and Byron had adored Grimaldi, Max Beerbohm was an ardent and lyrical admirer of Dan Leno.

The compound of the humdrum and the eccentric that formed his act grimly sought him out in death. Poised on the verge of international as well as national fame, his behaviour grew odd and, aged 43, he died in 1904. Unbeknown to the thousands who mourned him, he was a victim of syphilis, the scourge of several noted Victorians and Edwardians, among them allegedly Winston Churchill's father, Lord Randolph Churchill, also reduced, at the height of fame, to an enfeebled wreck.

Dan Leno would not be the last major comedian whose life would end in sad and premature tragedy. Nonetheless, he had lit the torch for the 'speaking' or patter-comedians of the 20th century. In his ready adoption of everyday characters, bowed down by fate's wilful guile, he would offer something to Robb Wilton or to Al Read, perhaps particularly something to Frankie Howerd. However, in his brilliant tour de force of adding that weird, almost ethereal element, he perhaps looked more acutely forward to Billy Bennett and Max Wall on stage, the Goons on radio and *Monty Python's Flying Circus* on television.

Onwards

Joe Grimaldi and Dan Leno are, then, chief among the individual progenitors of the profusion of comedians that invested the 20th century. There were to be hundreds of them, laying siege to the citadels of British humour. Grimaldi and Leno were the founding fathers of a lively and prodigious dynasty. They were innovative in the manner of genius, in that they were both of and before their time. They attracted adulation when they performed in their prime; but there was little in, for example, the humour of the 1990s that could not be traced back to their antics and word-play.

There were, of course, institutional as well as personal influences. It is time to turn to one of the major examples of these; namely, the music hall.

Another 1938 London Coliseum programme, with great comics like Robb Wilton, George Lacey, Tommy Trinder and Elsie and Doris Waters on show — and the famous golfer, Henry Cotton, heralded for the next week . . .

The Advent of Music Hall

The BBC's *The Good Old Days* programme from the Leeds City of Varieties theatre, the long existence of the London Players' Theatre and sundry other activities kept alive in the public consciousness some notion of the old music hall. Although the device of the grandiloquent chairman has been rather overdone, the predominance of the chorus song was, in most of these nostalgic versions, a genuine reflection of those past theatrical events.

Certainly by the 1850s the varied mix of concerts and singing, usually associated with licensed premises, had taken more definitive shape. With publicans very much in the van, purpose-built theatres began to be erected as 'music halls'. The 1843 Act for the Regulation of Theatres was a factor. It abolished the monopoly, established a hundred years before in 1737, whereby the few 'royal patent' theatres – the Theatres Royal – were the only ones to offer what is still referred to as 'legitimate' drama. One effect of this had been to nourish any number of burlesque, circus-style and other types of minor theatre, with music and spectacle the keys. The 'burletta' had words but there was the legalising cover of continuous music, while the 'melo' in melodrama originally stems from the need for musical or 'melodic' accompaniment to stay within the bounds of the law. Moreover, the reforming statute established a licensing system for a range of theatrical entertainments and it was from henceforward that, for instance, a tavern concert room might apply for a license for singing and music, along with the permit to sell drink, tobacco and refreshments. The main provisions for the supervision of the music halls fell under a statute of 1751 for the regulation of disorderly houses.

In 1848 Richard Preece opened the Surrey Music Hall on Southwark Bridge Road, London, and this might be termed the first of the new-style old-time music halls. However, it was Charles Morton, an ebullient and capable businessman, who was 'the Father of the Halls'. He took out a license for the Canterbury Arms, Lambeth in 1849 and later opened the Oxford Music Hall close to Oxford Street, London, in 1861. New premises were built and old properties were refurbished and, in the last ten or fifteen years of the 19th century, there was a general switch to the kind of deluxe houses, of a brand familiar to present-day theatre-goers, from the somewhat primitive haunts of 50 years before.

There was legislation from 1878 by which the municipal authorities issued 'Certificates of Suitability' to music halls. This obliged music hall owners to meet the demands of safety. Many small, old halls closed, some because their walls could not tolerate the weight of an iron safety curtain. These certificates also had the effect of limiting the consumption of alcohol, eventually cutting off the bars directly from the auditoria. All in all, music halls, as buildings, took on a more sedate and wholesome quality.

As with other elements in the national economy, there was a shift to multiples and syndicates. Sir Edward Moss and Oswald Stoll were among the businessmen whose names became synonymous with theatre owning across the country on the grand scale. Their theatres were as familiar in many towns as were the high streets staples, such as Boots or W H Smith or Woolworths. In 1912 music hall and, indeed, pantomime, fell under the jurisdiction, like the legitimate theatre, of the Lord Chamberlain. This appeared to leave the rumbustious content of music hall open to harsh censorship, but the wily theatre owners were pleased to have the gracious imprimatur of respectability brought by the Lord Chamberlain's sanction. Theatre censorship remained in the reins of the Lord Chamberlain's office until 1968.

Although the story of the music hall has been romanticised as a warm-hearted and friendly development, growing organically as a hearty manifestation of English broad-mindedness, the truth has more of a dour economic ring about it. Peter Bailey, scholarly historian of the music hall, has claimed that 'there is an obvious analogy here with the transformation of industrial manufacture: the caterer's conversion of the pub sing-song into modern show-business can be likened to the shift from domestic to factory production.' The music hall was the coal mine or cotton mill of entertainment.

The performers, high and low, were as carefully regulated as any other branch of the labour force, even if, as with those other branches, there was occasional friction, as witnessed in the 1907 strike organised by the Variety Artists' Federation, that is, trades union. Audiences could be and were more sternly supervised in the all-seater halls, with rowdy conduct, in the main, gradually erased. It is worth noting that, by and large, it was a period when public behaviour was on the mend and the large crowd, as at a football match or at a seaside resort, for example, was no longer feared, as it might have been in the pre-Victorian era.

There was certainly gaiety and a two-way discourse, with the 'all together now' chorus a mainstay, but the change from the music hall's origins was marked. Where there had been an often fully participant group in a tavern cellar, with beer on tap and a chop supper to hand, there was now tiered seating, with refreshments at a distance and, most significantly, professional entertainment. We have already observed how the social commentary of the music hall lyrics served more as a prophylactic against embittered resentment than an incitement to revolution. The historian, Gareth Stedman Jones, insists that the music halls supplied 'a culture of consolation', rather different from the socially conscious engagement indicated by the radical view of the genre.

It is important to stress how strongly the owners fought to sustain respectability. They were opposed by temperance and moral crusaders, among whom Mrs Ormiston Chant, particularly in the 1890s, was to the fore, so much so that she is often now likened to Mary Whitehouse, the implacable, self-appointed censor of television in the late 20th century. Faced with the ire of nonconformist prudery, sometimes reflected through the actions of local councils, the music hall managers were anxious to show a sober-sided countenance to the public.

The People's Jesters

Respectability was the key to obtaining audiences that represented a cross-section of the population. The notion that music hall custom was primarily working class and male – and thus raucous – has been challenged by the research of students of the theatre such as Dagmar Hoher. This may have been the case in some of the popular London halls that have influenced the painting of a generalised picture of music hall clientele. More broadly, however, it seems that there had long been an influx of middle class and especially lower middle class customers into the music halls, with shopkeepers and traders well represented. Women and children were also among these theatre-goers. Single women, often arriving in groups from work, and middle class youngsters, music hall song-sheets among their scores for piano practice, were numbered among them.

The pantomime and the seaside concert party built the bridge. Weaned on those jollities, the middle classes, women and children were ready for the music hall, provided it was not too vulgar and boisterous. Differential pricing, as in the legitimate and musical theatre, facilitated this phenomenon. By the end of the 19th century some large theatres had as many as six differently priced areas, often with separate entrances. Prices for admission might range from as low as 3d or 6d (2.5p) to 5s (25p), with boxes at a guinea (£1.05p) or more; one's income and sense of social status then determined exactly where one chose to sit.

It was on a par with what had happened in many other parts of the British social economy. The differential accommodation of cricket grounds and racecourses, as well as the 'paid' and 'free' pews in church, the 'saloon' and 'public' bars of pubs, or the 'classes' on the railways, together with the 'select' and 'cheap' ends of seaside promenades – these are all examples of how the 'integrated culture' of Victorian life contrived to offer the same staples of leisure provision to all classes.

Perhaps the most pertinent illustration is the Savoyard urban folk-operas of Gilbert and Sullivan, with Richard D'Oyly Carte their efficient theatre manager. This total theatrical experience amounted to the world's first light entertainment industry, properly so called, in that, quite consciously, the highly successful attempt was made to woo the world and his wife, plus their children, from all classes and on an international basis to boot. It has been said that the middle classes and respectable artisan classes were 'weaned from the church to the playhouse.' W S Gilbert was wont to deploy culinary metaphors in this regard, viewing his work as supplying 'the gastronomic mean.' He claimed, for example, that 'tripe and onions' and 'sweetbreads and truffles' alternatively dismayed or satisfied the stalls and the pit, but that 'a plain leg of mutton and boiled potatoes is the most stable fare of all.' The music halls strove likewise to provide a diet of mutton and potatoes for all their customers.

Apart from scores of independently run and usually quite small 'free halls', still frequently with publicans at the helm, there were 415 large music hall theatres in Britain by 1870, 31 of them in the London area. The London region had, it has been estimated, no less than 347 'halls' of all types by about 1880. By 1910 there was some increased concentration of the larger range of theatres, with 317 in total, including 63 in London and most of the others located in the large provincial cities. In 1891, when the famous Manchester Palace, capable of holding 3000, was opened, there were a score of other music hall theatres within the city's environs, with, additionally, some 500 public houses with music licences for singing rooms that held, on average, about 50 people. That means there was about one such establishment for every thousand of the population.

Such was the degree of penetration of the music hall phenomenon across and among the populace, and its chief offering was the comic or tragic-comic song, with audience participation in the choruses. This standard act had three elements. There was the performer, recognised in his or her own right at some level of stardom. There was the character adopted by the performer. This might, as with Dan Leno, vary, or, more usually, as, with, say, Gus Elen, remain permanently the same. There was the song or, more usually, repertoire of very similar numbers, which were closely, indeed, exclusively identified with the character and with the artist. Marie Lloyd and *Don't Dilly Dally on the Way* is a prime instance.

In some ways, it was an inflexible technique, but, in an era without swift and instant means of communication, it was an uncommonly potent device. It took time for singer, prototype character and song to impress itself on the national psyche. For upwards of 60 years it formed the major component of popular entertainment. Who were the leading lights and how did they contribute to the 20th century dispensation of comedians?

Marie Lloyd

Where Joe Grimaldi was the leading light of pre-music hall comedy, Marie Lloyd was the shining star of the music hall itself. She was its purest, most golden essence, undisputed as the queen of the halls. Matilda Alice Victoria Wood was born in Hoxton, London in 1870, the eldest of the large family of John Wood, an artificial flower maker and waiter who was something of an influence on her

early career. She hit the ground running, making her debut, aged fourteen, and a star at sixteen, earning £100 a week. Whilst struggling with illness and money problems in her later years, she remained top of the bill until her death in 1922, aged 52, in Golders Green, having fallen ill on stage at the Alhambra Theatre, London. Poignantly, her life-time spanned the music hall phase almost exactly.

A well-shaped, busty brunette, with a chirpy, toothy grin and dark, flashing eyes, Marie Lloyd dressed sumptuously and elaborately, presenting a picture of effusive glamour. Her vocal technique, precise, clear and fluting, was superb. She could be heard and understood in the largest hall, while, at the same time, capable of a soaring range of modulations that made her the most versatile interpreters of music hall lyrics. Her earliest success was with *The Boy I Love is up in the Gallery*, but she soon switched to socially apt numbers, saucily delivered. These most famously included, *Then You Wink the Other Eye* (1890) *Oh! Mr Porter* (1893) *Everything in the Garden's Lovely* (1898) and, of later Great War vintage, *It's a Bit of a Ruin that Cromwell Knocked about a Bit* and the much-sung *Don't Dilly Dally on the Way*. Marie Lloyd entertained troops and munitions workers most energetically throughout the 1914-1918 War.

Of something about medium height, Marie Lloyd came to represent the mythic persona of the cockney sparrow, valiantly fighting against the odds stacked against the working class woman and cheekily sexual in approach and spirit. The ambiguity of Marie Lloyd's lyrics, and the sheer naughtiness of her presentation, left audiences delighted and gasping. The motifs – 'a little of what you fancy does you good' – 'every little movement has a meaning all its own'

– passed into the vernacular language and have remained there. Even *Oh! Mr Porter*, a seemingly innocent account of a missed train, took on a wayward significance, the phallic aspect of the train not lost on knowing audiences, among whom the euphemistic use of rail destinations for stages on the sexual route and the allusion to the 'punched ticket' were then common. This lewd undercurrent, tricked out with an armoury of spicy gesture and expression, made for vintage comedy. That interplay of virtuousness and awareness has been a constant in the saga of comicality – but no one ever mastered that clever little art-form as preciously as did Marie Lloyd.

It is true that some of her later songs spoke of East End distress, of unpaid rents and marital violence. Some attempt has thus been made to make of her a feminist icon. It is a complicated issue, not least in that she sang even these songs with joyous gusto, more in the manner of putting on a brave face – and encouraging her fellow Cockney womenfolk to do likewise. She naturally faced the officious challenge of Laura Ormiston Chant and other members of the Social Purity Alliance, as a consequence of which, the legend runs, Marie Lloyd performed *Come into the Garden, Maud* as a smutty song before a municipal music hall committee, the ultimate in her ability to make the pure impure and vice versa.

To be fair to Mrs Chant, her concerns were about domestic assaults and the associated peril of marital rape, and about the attachment of prostitutes to music halls, with the allied risk of the spread of sexually transmitted disease to wives. She was smart enough to realise that sexual arousal, fuelled by drink, was, in some part, the result of Marie Lloyd's provocative displays. Nonetheless, she assuredly disapproved morally of sexual arousal of itself, even without deleterious outcomes.

Here we come to the nub of the problem.

The Victorian concept of 'domesticity' cast the female in the role of 'home goddess', with the wife the affectionate superintendent of the domestic hearth, temperate in desire and chastely passive in disposition. John Ruskin and the poet Coventry Patmore delineated this convention ('The Angel in the House') lucidly, while much Victorian fiction and drama, such as the heroines of most of Charles Dickens' novels, exemplified the situation clearly. In so far as Victorian marriage espoused this view, there can be little doubt that many men turned to the music hall, more especially in the person of Marie Lloyd and her spirited female compatriots, for the sort of heated erotic buzz absent from their own bedrooms. It was the forward, open wantonness of her frontal attack that was so libidinous: Marie Lloyd's act was more about indirect male, than direct female, sexual proclivities. We shall have occasion to return to this theme when the subject of women comedians is explored in chapter thirteen.

As for Marie Lloyd herself, and in a sobering counterpoint of stage glitter and real-life drabness, she had a largely hapless private existence. At seventeen she married Percy Courtenay, who eked out a living on the fringes of horse racing, but they were later estranged in an atmosphere of threats and unpleasantness; she then married the singer Alec Hurley, but this alliance also fractured, as she became involved with the much younger Bernard Dillon, a Derby winning jockey, who also fell into bad ways, including drink and domestic violence. It was a marital pattern strangely akin to that of Gracie Fields.

There is a sense in which the genius of Marie Lloyd is too singular to be prototypical of the music hall era. She was, of course, the greatest of chorus singers in what was predominantly a period of chorus singers and, like all the supreme artists excited adulation among commentators on the high culture. However, she was a little out of step with the trend towards 'respectability' and was, for example, omitted on those grounds by Oswald Stoll when he arranged the very first royal command performance, in 1912 at the Palace Theatre. The valorous Marie Lloyd organised her own show at the London Pavilion Theatre as a 'command performance by order of the British public', one of the most conspicuous examples of a 'people's jester', just as, in 1907, she had wholeheartedly supported the successful Variety Artists' Federation strike against the Stoll and Moss theatre chains, when they had sought to drive music hall performers into even tougher contracts, at a point where many of them were lamentably over-worked and underpaid. It is much to her credit that the extremely well-paid Marie Lloyd was so sympathetic towards her colleagues.

Hegel wrote that 'the Owl of Minerva flies at Dusk', a warning that the height of success often arrives in the prelude to collapse. He was thinking of political entities and historical evolution, but he could have been commenting on the music hall, for, by the time it became recognised as a reputable British institution, in receipt of the regal accolade of George V, it was already in decline.

Other Stars in the Music Hall Firmament

Vibrant women, like Marie Lloyd, their acts the counterpoint to Victorian and Edwardian submissiveness, even if that may have had its soothing attractions, were very common among the leading lights on the music hall stage. Indeed, Marie Lloyd's daughter, also Marie, and several of her sisters, enjoyed the-

atrical careers of this type. Highly regarded among the female stars were Vesta Victoria (*Daddy Wouldn't Buy Me a Bow-wow*); Katie Lawrence (*Daisy Bell* – 'on a bicycle made for two'); vivacious Lottie Collins (*Ta-ra-ra-boom-de-ay!*); Victoria Monks (*Won't You Come Home, Bill Bailey?*) Ada Reeve (*She Glories in a Thing like That*) Gertie Gitana (*Nelly Dean*) and Marie Kendall (*I'll Cling to You* – 'Just Like the Ivy'). Then there was the impactful figure of the Australian chorus singer, Florrie Ford (1876-1940). Her roster of tunes reads like the agenda for some sing-along in the local pub. It includes *Oh! Oh! Antonio; She's a Lassie from Lancashire; Has Anyone Here Seen Kelly; Flanagan; Hold Your Hand out, you Naughty Boy; Down at the Old Bull and Bush; Pack up Your Troubles* and *It's a Long Way to Tipperary*.

According to the music hall historian, Richard Anthony Baker, the publisher, Bert Feldman, bought the rights *Tipperary* from Jack Judge and Harry Williams in 1912 for five shillings (25p). Later he relented and paid both men £5 a week for life – it was selling 10,000 copies a day by 1914 and by 1918 no less than 8m copies had been retailed and *Tipperary* had been translated into seventeen languages.

Of particular interest and for future reference was the male impersonator. This typology pressed into another dimension the concept of the brazen female and offers another gloss on the erotic appeal of music hall women. Often in tight-fitting costume or, principal boy style, with an extravagant show of imperious thigh, they struck a defiant and confident pose, usually guying the man about town, the military or naval type and other West End characters. They invariably played the role of the handsome young man with the roving eye, rather distinct from the more East End portrayals of Marie Lloyd and company.

Vesta Tilley, 'The London Idol', was something of a doyenne of this set, with *After the Ball; Following in Father's Footsteps; Jolly Good Luck to the Girl who Loves a Soldier* and *The Army of Today's Alright* among the favourite melodies, each of them an anthem to the worldly men she so immaculately portrayed. Millie Hylton, Fanny Leslie, Bessie Bonehill and Fanny Robina were others of the same sprightly ilk, while Ella Shields, with *Burlington Bertie* and *Show Me the Way to go Home* and the effervescent Hetty King, with her dude numbers like *Piccadilly* and naval airs like *All the Nice Girls Love a Sailor* had even more famous and more enduring reputations.

It is important to stress the success women had on the music hall stage, for, post-1914, the mantle of comedy fell more and more into masculine hands. At the same time, there were, of course, plenty of men making robust careers on the halls. Apart from Dan Leno, there were the likes of Charlie Coborn, he of *Two Lovely Black Eyes* and *The Man that Broke the Bank at Monte Carlo*; James Fawn, noted for his *Ask a Policeman* song, with its intimation – 'if you want to know the time... every member of the force has his watch and chain, of course' – that corrupt officers stole watches from corpses; Jack Pleasants, with his dim-witted rendering of *I'm Shy, Mary Ellen, I'm Shy*; Mark Sheridan, who popularised *Here We Are Again*; *I Do like to be beside the Seaside* and *Who Were You with Last Night?* and Harry Champion, the energetic Cockney performer of *I'm Henery the Eighth, I am; Boiled Beef and Carrots* and *Any Old Iron*

The names, and, even more, the song titles, give some impression of the music hall style. At the risk of some invidiousness and from among a glittering array, it might be useful to trace the careers of two or three of these male notables in more detail, before and also as a means to attempting to analyse the change from music hall to variety.

Marie Lloyd, for all her support of her profession, was remorselessly critical of its members. During the music hall strike of 1907 she suggested that the not very talented Belle Elmore should be encouraged to stay on working, on the grounds that she was guaranteed to empty the theatre; and when she was allegedly butchered by her husband, the notorious Dr Crippen, Marie Lloyd dismissed the murder as legitimate theatrical criticism. There were just two of her colleagues she would deign to watch. One was Dan Leno and the other was George Formby, Senior.

Of course, he was never known as 'Senior', until after his death when his son sprang to stardom. The older Formby, not unlike his son in features if with a differing approach to comedy, was born as James Henry Booth in Ashton-under-Lyne in 1880. His puny frame and already weak chest were much harmed by an early apprenticeship amid the heavy tackle and sulphurous fumes of a blacksmith's forge in a Manchester iron foundry. He endured the miseries of these conditions from the age of twelve, seeking solace and a few extra pennies around the 'free and easies' of that northern industrial city. Curiously enough, he then sang, rather like his son, to his strumming of a banjo, although this never figured much in his mature act. In his late teens, he was spotted by Danny Clarke, of the famous Argyle Theatre, Birkenhead. He appeared there with his name changed from Booth to Formby, a coastal place between Liverpool and Southport, and found work around the Wigan – he brought 'Wigan Pier' into enduring prominence – and St Helens areas. He married Eliza Hoy, a Wigan girl, the mother of the ukulele-wielding son and a woman who lived to be a centenarian.

In this she was the healthy converse of her sickly husband, whose struggles with bronchitis make up one of the sadder legends of show business lore. With oxygen cylinders in the wings and with a brave face set against adversity – his whispered asides of 'coughin' better tonight', 'coughin' summat champion' and 'I'll have to get a bottle' for long remained standard catch-phrases in the north of England. He died in 1921, during a pantomime at the Newcastle Empire, aged just 41, vowing his children should not go on the stage.

George Robey, probably the best example of a comedian who bridged the music hall and variety stages with some aplomb

George Robey, of whom more shortly, gave 'the Wigan Nightingale' his break with a £35 a week panto engagement in Newcastle-upon-Tyne in 1907, whereafter he broke into the metropolitan scene, joining Yorkshire's Jack Pleasants as the comparative rarity of a northerner among that largely cockney conclave. Wistful in manner and naturally pallid of countenance, with his checked muf-

fler, his large boots and his short-sleeved jacket, the older Formby crept on the stage and proceeded haltingly. His chief songs, lugubriously offered, with many a hesitant comment to the orchestra, were *I was Standing at the Corner of the Street; Looking for Mugs on the Strand; John Willy, Come On; Since I Parted My Hair in the Middle; One of the Boys* and *I'm such a Hit with the Girls.* He bantered gently with the musical director: 'getting ten pound a week for wagging a little wooden stick – why, for half that money I'd wave a telegraph pole.'

The song titles give an indicator as to the style. Here was a naive provincial, subdued, gauche and tentative, who had somehow persuaded himself he was cutting a dash, as one of the boys and being a hit with the girls. On bills on which there would usually be several turns, including male impersonators, eager to convey the swagger and assurance of the predatory male, this was a carefully observed conceit. It was a complex approach. He essayed to persuade himself and his audiences that he was a dashing blade, despite the woebegone evidence to the contrary. The audiences could obviously see behind the flimsy mask of assurance, whereas the persona of George Formby the elder never quite understood. Only Tony Hancock has emulated him in that most difficult of comic processes, compounding self-delusion and insecurity in equal proportions.

Another popular and distinctive star was Gus Elen. He was born in Pimlico in 1862 and christened Ernest Augustus Elen and it was only after a varied career in and out of show-business that he finally settled into his mainstream routine as a Coster singer in the Albert Chevalier convention. He was in his thirties before he became a well-paid and well-known artist, with authentic costermonger costume and trappings. Unlike some of his contemporaries, he avoided any undue sentiment, rather underlining the gritty realities of cockney life and hymning the cockney's efforts to cock an independent snook at authority. From *Never Introduce Your Donah to a Pal* and *It's a Great Big Shame* – both wry takes on sweethearts and wives – to the social commentary of *If it wasn't for the 'ouses in Between* and *'E dunno where 'e are*, the latter a cautionary tale about the sudden acquisition of riches, Gus Elen waxed sardonically on the mundane facts of urban existence.

A tall man, with features capable of adopting a somewhat watchful, even suspicious, expression, his slow, clear tones were gruff and occasionally harsh, although the pitch was resigned, not irked. It was a very competent piece of acting, for, offstage, Gus Elen was a well-spoken man of domestic virtue, charitable habits and inoffensive hobbies. He made a brief comeback in the 1930s and, along with extensive recording coverage, this helped to keep his name in the lights of memory. He died, aged 77, in 1940. The sharper edge of his knowing observation probably encouraged some of the post-music hall brand of comics to indulge in something akin to satire. At least, there would be, for instance, in the work of Billy Russell, 'on Behalf of the Working Classes', or of the great Robb Wilton, a challenging note about the perfectibility of the human condition and human institutions.

Another late Victorian and Edwardian favourite, Little Tich, was both the forerunner of a curious genre of comedians and the representative of a long tradition of what used to be called 'freak' entertainers, usually associated with the fairground. Born Harry Relph in 1867, he had strangely webbed and six digit hands, while he never grew beyond 4 feet 6 inches in height. He came from an extensive Kentish family and began entertaining in childhood, soon adopting the pseudonym of Little Tich, a reference to the chubby Tichborne claimant who was in the news. What is interesting is that 'Titch' or 'Tich' was then the nickname for a fat child, whereas, under Harry Relph's influence, it became an indication of smallness.

From about 1890 he starred on the English and French stage, being particularly noted for his lengthy 28 inch boots, footwear that became the identity card of his act, as famed as Charlie Chaplin's cane or Harry Tate's moustache. As an eccentric and double-jointed dancer and as well as his acrobatic 'big boot' dance, he developed a number of often mimed characterisations, ranging from the Gas Inspector to Little Miss Turpentine. The essence of his act was the frenzied nature of his singing and the agile nature of his dancing, with his catch-phrase 'oo'er' the accompaniment to what seemed to be the painful standing on his fingers, as he leaned and swayed at impossible angles.

Like Marie Lloyd, and many another in the showbiz fraternity, his private life was a fractured and rarely cheerful affair of three marriages and several other relationships. Like George Robey, he was a man of civilised tastes, with a participatory taste for painting and music and languages. He died, aged 60, in 1928, following a stroke. There are two lines of comic inheritance. One is the 'midget' style of child impersonators, which will be discussed in the chapter on speciality comedy; the other is the fashion for eccentric dancing, of which Max Wall, Nat Jackley and Billy Dainty would be exponents in the variety generation.

However, the comic entertainer who possibly most effectively personifies the switch from music hall to variety, and thus the move to the 'modern' comedian, is George Robey. His real name was George Edward Wade and he was born in 1869 in – like so many music hall stars – London. Unlike, however, many of his colleagues, he came from a well-to-do home and was, from childhood, a most cultivated and well-travelled person. An eclectic personality, his interests ranged from football and cricket to classical music and aesthetics. It was probably this middle class background, together with a child-centred rather than a narrowly institutional education that gave him the massive assurance to take the music hall by storm. Despairing of the tedium inherent in the sort of clerical work to which his father, a civil engineer, set him, he quickly applied himself to concerts of all kinds, sparing the family blushes by a change of name. From his London debut in 1891, he sprang to the top of the bill in double-time. His amazing confidence was fuelled by ceaseless energy. Like others of his ilk, he was ferried around London, visiting as many as five or six theatres a night and performing ebulliently in each.

He still retained sufficient ardour for a staggering regime of philandering, interposed with two marriages, one, of not too successful a nature, to the actress, Ethel Haydon, and a later life and more enduring alliance, to Blanche Littler, of the famed family of theatre impresarios. As time went on, he diversified into legitimate acting, including representations of Falstaff, operetta and, most notably, revue – his partnership with Violet Lorraine (*If You were the Only Girl in the World...*) in *The Bing Boys are Here*, that most typical of Great War shows for the soldiers on leave in London, still lingers in the collective memory. George Robey was another of those music hall and variety comedians who commanded the respect – Neville Cardus; Laurence Olivier – of cultural greats outside his immediate line of professional activity.

He was knighted in 1954, and he died later that same year in Sussex, aged 85.

His chief act was a strange combine of burlesque clown and florid actor. He rushed on to the stage, rather after the manner of Ken Dodd, and his charismatic presence achieved an immediacy of authority. 'The Prime Minister of Mirth' sported a bald wig, a red nose, a short crowned bowler hat, a collarless shirt, a clerical jacket and highly prominent eyebrows that appeared to have something close to a linguistic property. There were other character studies, chief among them perhaps the Mayor of Mudcumdyke, another predecessor to Robb Wilton in his role of Mr Muddlecombe JP. His songs were anthems to what he termed 'honest vulgarity', including *Fancy That!; The Simple Pimple; Bang went the Chance of a Lifetime; Archibald, Certainly Not!; Oh, How Rude!* and *I Stopped and I Looked and I Listened*. He was also a superb panto dame.

His vigorous longevity, the very fact that he was playing theatres and broadcasting almost to the end of the variety, let alone the music hall era, meant that he was a powerful influence on the new generation of comedians. In terms of technique however, what was most pronounced was George Robey's emphasis on the spoken word. This was where the aspect of the orotund actor-manager enters into the equation. George Robey cosseted language in a loving manner; there would shortly follow several comics – from Will Hay to Les Dawson – who would have something of the same affection for the nuances of English.

There was much of Mr Micawber in George Robey's announcements; where Micawber would say 'in short' before the simple explanatory word or phrase, Robey would say, 'in other words'. Always, like other fine comic operators such as Max Miller, hinting at simmering lewdness, and always, like a former-day Frankie Howerd, shocked by the noise and morality of the onlookers, he would swing from grave silences to outbursts of disgusted rhetoric, interspersed with more flights of double entendres.

'Desist' was his famous and famously unheeded command. 'Desist', he would cry again authoritatively, visibly shaken by the peals of unbidden laughter. 'Let there be merriment by all means', he would assert, 'but let it be tempered with dignity...' and so on in another roaming sentence or two of high-flown latinate nouns and verbs. 'Kindly temper your hilarity with a modicum of reserve' was his best-known admonition. It is not the least of the marvels of his act that his listeners could and did understand and enjoy this flamboyant usage of their native tongue.

Above all, with George Robey the songs shrank a little and the spoken word blossomed. This was his main gift to the future. Here was a brilliant performer who broke up his patter with songs, as opposed to the music hall standard of maybe interspersing some patter among the songs. The new brigade of comedians would be, like George Robey, talkers, not singers.

The Switch to Variety

The gradual change to variety from music hall was, of course, not one of a fundamental kind. To some degree, the terms were interchangeable. Although the music hall was consistent in its custom of the chorus singer, the style and message of the songs and of their vocalists varied considerably. There were romantic and patriotic and dramatic ballads as well as the main line of comic tunes. Occasionally, there would also be mimed clowning or involved acrobatics, as there would be in variety. The post-1918 shift in the focus of popular music had its effect. The coming of modern dance melodies and the interplay of musical comedy brought another dimension to the variety stage, with male and female vocalists offering musical play and dance-hall numbers. There was also the influence of revue, where, sometimes with the semblance of a plot, the same artists would appear throughout in different scenes and guises.

A major social change concerned refreshments. The music hall had usually involved the taking of food and drink in the auditorium, something not allowed in the 'legit' theatre. As, legally and culturally, the two theatrical vehicles grew closer in character, refreshments were entirely confined to the outer limits of the bars, except for some interval sales – in both sorts of theatre – of cups of tea and ice cream, The upshot was that the whole idea of going to a music hall became much more like going to a theatre to see a play, substantially the position the major light entertainment circuits, like the Stoll and Moss combines, wished to achieve. One of the defining aspects of variety, then, was that the experience was more akin to an ordinary visit to the theatre than had been a trip to the old-style music hall.

The brave new world of the post-war years brought the technical input of cinema, wireless and recording on a much more sophisticated and ubiquitous scale. All these elements competed with the old-time music hall, but, above and beyond that, was the sheer modernism of outlook, changed and liberated by the Great War, bringing with it a sense of the outdated nature of pre-war forms, such as the music hall. Several of these elements will be surveyed in later chapters.

Nonetheless, the major alteration lay in the comic style, in particular, with the patter of comedians, alone, in twos and in sketch format. Because of the legislation in respect of the theatre, dialogue or anything that looked like the flimsiest of playlets was expressly forbidden, although some managements did deliberately flaunt such anomalous laws. It was only after 1907, when agreement was reached between the music hall and legitimate theatre managers on this topic, that this matter was harmoniously resolved. On the other hand, the comic who stood and jabbered forth a string of stories and jokes was more or less unknown. As we have observed, it was only with the likes of George Robey that something of this fashion began to emerge. Crucially, it was at a time when it became legal to conduct a spoken discourse outside of the so-called legitimate theatre.

Apart, then, from the social and cultural reasons, the chief difference between pre-1918 music hall and post-1918 variety was the deployment of comedians, as we would recognise them today. It is often said that 'variety' is hard to define. However, at its simplest, it speaks for itself. It was just very much more varied than the music hall of previous years. The twice-nightly show, introduced earlier in the provinces than in London, was fairly standard by 1914 and the variety formula followed that pattern. Some of the old music hall programmes had been lengthy, with maybe thirty turns over several hours. Now variety offered a couple of hours of diverse entertainment, running the gamut of, for instance, a dancing act, a 'second spot' comic, a circus type act, such as a juggler, another comic and, to finish the pre-interval bill, another and longer speciality act; this would be followed by repeats of the dancers, perhaps the first or second comic again, a musical act and then the top of the bill, often a comedian, but sometimes a singing or instrumental act, in which case the comic would be deposed to penultimate spot. For some time it was also common to close the show with an acrobat or something of that sort; just as the dancers allowed time for late arrivals, first, from the street and then, second, from the bars after the intervals, the gymnast or tumbler was supposed to cushion the rush for the buses while the top of the bill was performing.

One way or another, the comedians played the role of cement in the edifice of variety. As funny as Marie Lloyd and company had been, with their robust songs and jolly patter, the monologue and dialogue of the new breed of comics was of a different manner and attitude, even if the genuine stuff of personality was still the key to their success or failure. These are the comics with whom this text is concerned. In the next two chapters it is intended to examine two subsidiary channels that offered theatrical opportunities to comedians, namely the Christmas pantomime and the summer holiday show.

'There'll never be another' — Max Miller, probably the finest stand up comedian of the peak variety age

3. SEASONAL FRUITS: CHRISTMAS CRACKERS PANTOMIME

Apart from the strong and obvious contribution of music hall, there were two other tributaries that flowed into the river of modern comedy. These were pantomime and seaside shows, both of which predated the era of the 20th century comedian, and both of which have struggled to survive into the 21st century. It is true to say that, for many people, their most likely annual visits to the light theatre would be at Christmas or whilst on holiday in Britain. Importantly, it is still true to assert that, for most people, their first visit, as children, to any theatre would have been to either a seaside entertainment or, more likely, a Christmas show, normally a panto. It follows that, for many of the performers working in light entertainment, their employment, especially during the period from about 1890 to 1960, would have revolved around a summer and a Christmas booking. If one could find a lengthy seaside sojourn of maybe sixteen weeks, together with a long-running pantomime of up to thirteen weeks, then one's bread and butter was satisfactorily supplied and the rest was the additional luxury of jam. It should be added that something of this basic income might have been achieved with touring outfits of both dispensations.

The Beginnings of Pantomime

At superficial sight, the chief difference between the Christmas show and the summer entertainment lay in the comparative youthfulness of the latter. It is possible to trace panto back to the ancient concept of misrule, through misty Italian clues, even to Roman times. It is possible – but it is not altogether helpful. The summer seaside shows are self-evidently the construct of the urban holiday resorts for newly urbanised middle and later working class folk, a direct consequence of industrialism. In terms of a widespread and cross-class entertainment, pantomime, for all its purported lineage, was also cultural fodder for the urban populations of the late 19th century and afterwards.

It was a sop to the moral conscience for scholarly allusion to be made to the transvestite revels of antiquity, but, in reality, it was the majestic thigh of the female principal boy that caught the keen eye of the Victorian male theatregoer. This particular feature actually owed more to the burlesques and extravaganzas of the then London theatre. These were frothy confections of music and dance that contrived to evade the stricter terms of the theatre licensing regulations. The main exponent of these light-hearted and slightly erotic entertainments was J R Planché (1796-1880), operating at the Olympic Theatre, London. The major attraction was the lovely and junoesque Lucy Eliza Ventris, practitioner of the art of the female 'boy'; it was she and actresses like her who really guaranteed that modern pantomime would be characterised by handsome, thigh-slapping principal boys.

One advantage of pantomime, and a trait that would be recognised and acted upon by the providers of other kinds of entertainment, was its family appeal. At a time in Victorian Britain when the theatre was widely regarded, sometimes not without cause, as a sink of immorality and disorder, the respectable middle class gentleman would take his wife and children to the pantomime. It should be emphasised that it was not as sometimes later happened, an autonomous children's entertainment, one to which parents took their offspring for their offspring's enjoyment. The ideal was that it should be a genuinely shared family diversion. It was only in the last quarter of the 19th century that the concept of child-centred activities, in the wake of Lewis Carroll, developed, along the lines of stories, games, clubs and allied child-based processes, such as clothing designs.

Charles Dickens' love of pantomime, and his adoration of Joe Grimaldi, has already been noted. His contemporary, the novelist, William Makepeace Thackeray, wrote of pantomime; 'lives there a man', he dramatically said, 'with a soul so dead, the being ever so blasé and travel-worn, who does not feel some shock and thrill as the curtain rises' on a pantomime stage. The historian and politician, Lord Macauley, wrote firmly that 'no man, whatever his sensibility may be, is ever affected by Hamlet or Lear as a little girl is affected by poor Red Riding Hood.' As with

the music hall, the pantomime did have the bonus of some high-class cultural support.

Nonetheless, the pantomime did undergo what nowadays might be called a make-over during the later decades of the 19th century. In effect, this amounted to a major shift of emphasis. Initially, the Harlequinade had formed the substantive part, briefly prefaced by an introductory piece. This short prologue was about the characters in some fairy-tale or classical legend or mythic fable. There would be two young sweethearts, an unwanted and grotesque suitor and a feeble papa – and the good fairy would transform them into Harlequin, Columbine, Clown and Pantaloon. Slowly, the 'nursery tale' opening grew longer; slowly, it reached the juncture whereby the Harlequinade was the epilogue, not the introduction. The 'transformation' scene was retained as a plot device, as in Cinderella's coach being formed from a pumpkin. By the 1880s the Harlequinade vanished almost altogether, to the dismay of the conservationists.

However, the stock repertory of characters had been enshrined forever. There was the Columbine of the principal girl; the Harlequin of the principal boy, invariably played by a statuesque young actress; the 'heavy', often a father, but not quite as enfeebled as Pantaloon, and the comic figure, sometimes with designs on the principal girl and jealous of the principal boy. To take a familiar example, there would be Dick Whittington, Alice Fitzwarren, her father, Alderman Fitzwarren, and Idle Jack. Good and evil (always entering stage right and left, dexter and sinister) would also be represented, with, in this same case, the Good Fairy and King Rat.

The chief metropolitan locations during most of the 19th century were the Drury Lane and the Lyceum theatres. Lord Mayor's Day, in November, and Boxing Day were the traditional opening nights, but there were also Easter and even summer productions. J R Planché, H J Byron, Francis Burnand and Edward Blanchard, alone responsible for over a hundred panto scripts, were the leading writers. Rhyming couplets were in vogue and the remorseless pun was in fashion, for instance:

And as my youthful feathers all unfurled seemed to make a bold-stir in the world.

But suddenly the future seemed to frown; fortune gave me a quilt and I'd a down.

Frank Randle, doubtless creating chaos in panto at the Hulme Hippodrome, Manchester, along with Joseph Locke, making an interesting combine . . .

The heritage of the circus and of burlesque was on show in the most extravagant of spectacles. Augustus Harris, at Drury Lane, produced a version of *Ali Baba* in which each of the forty thieves had twelve assistants and the company numbered over 400. There were menageries, castles, sea-going vessels and magnificent parades, such as a procession of all the Shakespearean heroines. William Beverley, at the Lyceum, provided exotic scenes, up to twenty of them, each with their own title, such as *The Silver Cascade of the Lily Bell Fairies in the Land of the Cloudless Sky.*

The titles were as long as the sets were luxurious. The minds of poster designers must have been exercised by, for instance, *Harlequin and the Tyrant of Gobblemupandshrunkthemdown,* or *The Doomed Princess of the Fairy Hall with Forty Redblood Pillars.* The sub-title, as with the Savoyard operas of Gilbert and Sullivan, was obligatory. There were instructional pantos, typical of the Victorian mentality, featuring the life and success of, for instance, James Watt. Over 400 stories have been identified.

As the format altered and became moulded, the number of story-lines dwindled and a group of favourite plots emerged, most of them still utilised today. They reflect the literary culture of the Victorian age, when the reading of the family novel was a major part of leisure and when there was sufficient awareness of popular literature for its heroes and heroines to be heralded on the popular stage. *The Arabian Nights* tales, first translated into English about 1839/41, supplied the plots of *Aladdin*, *Sinbad the Sailor* and *Ali Baba*, while *Red Riding Hood* came from the canon of the Brothers Grimm, first translated into English in 1823. The enjoyment of fairy tales, with their bonus of a pointed moral, became very common in the Victorian era, owing something to the so-called 'discovery of children', the sense of childhood being a discrete stage and not merely pre-adulthood à la little men and, ominous title, 'little women'. The Danish tales of Hans Christian Andersen (first translated into English in 1846) were very popular, while there was a surge of interest in the *Contes de ma Mère L'oye*, that is, '*the tales of Mother Goose*', collected by the Frenchman, Charles Perrault. They were available in English from the 18th century but were very much popularised in the late 19th century.

Via Charles Perrault came, as well as *Mother Goose*, the Persian *Sleeping Beauty* and the Italian *Puss in Boots* to the pantomime stage, while his '*Cendrillon*' became our *Cinderella*, a French mistranslation ensuring that Princess Crystal ends up wearing a glass slipper. The present-day version of the *Cinderella* panto dates from 1864, and the sympathetic character of Buttons, by no means the horrid suitor for Cinders' hand, was established by 1914. Nonetheless, there are commentators who would trace the linage of a fable such as that of *Cinderella* back into the mists of antiquity. Originally, it has been suggested, Cinderella was the dawn threatened by the night clouds of the Ugly Sisters and rescued by the sun of Prince Charming.

Of rather more sociological and timely note, all the pantomime plots reflected the cross-class convention that was also the Victorian mainstay of the popular novel and the light musical theatre. In short, the hero and heroine usually came from either side of the tracks, to use the American reference point

of life on each side of the socially divisive railway line. Aladdin, Colin (the owner of Puss in Boots) and Jack, he of the beanstalk, are working class, being respectively laundry-boy, mill hand and agricultural labourer – and they all eventually gain the reward of marriage to a princess. Cinderella, from the kitchen, and the impoverished and alleged thief, Dick Whittington, manage to overcome the odds to marry Prince Charming and the upper middle class Alice Fitzwarren.

A key to the continuum of pantomime, that strange British theatre phenomenon, has been cross-pollination. No theatrical institution has been pronounced dead or dying more frequently than the pantomime. It is true that there are only about a hundred professional pantomimes today, whereas a hundred or so years ago there may have been as many as a thousand. Paradoxically, it has been the killers that have proved to be the life-savers. Each new medium of entertainment – the music hall, variety, radio, film, television, pop music, soap opera – has been predicted as sounding panto's death-knell, only for its personages to be recruited to the pantomimic cause. For example, Marie Lloyd and Dorothy Ward, from the world of music hall, were very popular principal boys. Obviously, the Buttons or Wishee Washee type of roles would be taken by well-known comedians of the day, while the tradition of the comic song, complete with song-sheet, with maybe children brought on to the stage, borrowed from the audience participation of the music hall typology.

Another act of salvage was to be found in the industrial towns and cities, where there would be block bookings for one or another of the local employers. For many years, when its work-force numbered well over 20,000, the Trafford Park based Metropolitan Vickers engineering firm used to book a complete week at the prestigious Manchester Palace pantomime, matinees included. It was a great boost for the panto business. The cast would visit the works the week before, partly to drum up trade, partly to pick up references to obnoxious foremen or surly managers that could be introduced into the script.

Possibly the most important 19th century development, one that, as much as any other element, came to identify pantomime firmly in the public consciousness and carry that conception deep into the 20th century, was the addition of the 'dame'. In contradistinction to the male impersonators of the music hall era whose ideal was one of smartness and glamour, the men who acted the part of dame opted normally for the monstrously unsightly image. It was in 1812 that Joe Grimaldi introduced the modern 'dame' in his role of Queen Roundabellya. By 1870 the 'dame' had become a much-loved and regular character in pantomime. Although 'clown' remained in some fashion, much of the broad comedy element of pantomime now devolved on to the 'dame'.

The 'dame' provided another chance for the male comics of music hall to find good employment; in turn, the comedians of the variety stage and afterwards inherited that niche and made excellent use of it. It is time to look more closely at the music hall and variety comics who achieved success as 'dames'.

A Lineage of Dames

*Norman Evans and others

In the wake of Grimaldi, Dan Leno and George Robey flooded a tide of dames, with usually one or two outstanding in and representative of their generation. Some, like George Robey and, later, Les Dawson, often,

even normally, appeared in male guise, just donning the wig and apron for the festive season. Manchester-born Wilkie Bard (William Augustus Smith, 1874-1944) acted the dame in pantomime, being an especial hit as Widow Twankey. In music hall he was also known for his railway guard, his policeman (lying in a hammock warbling, *I'm here if you want me*) and his *Truly Rural* number. Unruffled and – noted for his tongue-twisting lyrics – decorous of address, and deliberately ponderous in feminine figure, Wilkie Bard made famous the ballads *I Want to Sing in Opera*, *The Leith Police Dismisseth Us* and *She Sells Sea-shells*. Others adopted the 'dame' characterisation the year round. One such was G S Melvin, reverting to a time when the usage of initials was all the fashion, from G H Chirgwin, 'the White-eyed Kaffir' singing on the music hall stage or A J Balfour being prime minister to H G Wells writing his novels or W G Grace playing cricket. G S Melvin, another who found himself as a child on the music hall stage, developed a series of presentations that served him well, until his death in harness, aged 69, in 1946. As panto dame, he was ideally placed to intersperse these cameos within any plot. There included the girl guide; the cyclist, singing *I Like to Jump upon a Bike*, and the hiker, whose *I'm Happy when I'm Hiking* was adopted as the anthem of the rambling fraternity in the inter-wars years, when the hiking epidemic was at its virulent height.

In between the singing and the business with the cycle or the knapsack, he gossiped away merrily in the tradition of Dan Leno's Mrs Kelly. Lanky, angular, sharp-featured and invariably bespectacled, he took on something of the image of an animated giraffe. With his concentration on outdoor pursuits, he caught something of the homespun fun of the 1920s and 1930s and was one of the most popular dames of that era.

Another such was George Lacy (1904-1989), with the tight, curled wig, the high-necked dress and the fancy bonnet. He played dame in sixty or more pantomimes and was very affectionately regarded. His 'Mother Goose' was an especial treat. That eponymous role is, of course, the premier 'dame' showcase, one that, for instance, John Inman, who was to find fame in TV's *Are You Being Served?* series, very much made his own for many years in the later decades of the 20th century. Jack Tripp was another who, in those post-WWII years, won great respect for his consummate 'dame' performances, while many will recall the 'dames' of Clarkson Rose, who was also the welcome star of many seaside shows. Having been his understudy, some of Sid Field's movements were added to Jack Tripp's routines.

Then there was Norman Evans (1901-1962), whose popularity was sustained well after World War II. Especially as Widow Twankey in *Aladdin* or as an eponymous Mother Goose, some, the author included, would regard him as the premier dame of the 20th century. The son of a church organist and himself a Methodist lay preacher, he was for several years a salesman and am-dram enthusiast before springing to affluence and fame. He starred at the Palladium and the Coliseum, as well as at locations closer to his native Rochdale, where he was something of a protégé of Gracie Fields. His work was not entirely in womanly attire. On stage and eventually on television, he introduced a shy Sooty-like little bear puppet that had to be cajoled into yielding up the hiding place of his jacket in order to provide the finger movements for a cornet solo, before diving back again, embarrassed by the applause. Norman Evans also offered a marvellous mime, around and behind a white screen, of a dentist faced with a painful extraction and a reluctant victim.

FOR RELEASE APRIL 1950

The famous NORMAN EVANS WITH JIMMY JAMES IN "Over the Garden Wall" *and a Great supporting Cast including* DAN YOUNG

A flyer for a film starring Norman Evans, among the very greatest of panto dames — and with a part for Jimmy James, destined to be regarded by many as the true genius of British stage comedy

Nonetheless, it was as a female impersonator he is most affectionately recalled. He was in his 30s before he really made the grade, but he was almost immediately a bill-topper. There was his 'Auntie Doleful', consoling a sick neighbour with constructive advice – 'don't you think yer should have your bed moved downstairs; they'll never get a coffin round this landing.' Most famously, there was his Fanny Fairbottom, lovingly revived at a later date by Les Dawson, in the *Over the Garden Wall* routine, during which a conversation was negotiated with the invisible next door neighbour.

Red-wigged, mob-capped and, allowing for frighteningly flexible expressions, toothless, Norman Evans listened wide-eyed, 'oohing' and 'ahhing' and ' 'as she-ing?' at the latest tit-bits of news of the street and the mill. The silently mouthed explanation owed something to the lip-reading in the textile work-place, where the roar of the looms made ordinary conversation difficult: 'she's 'ad it all taken away', Norman Evans would mouth. A stern watch was kept on the amatory coalman who was spotted shouting 'Whoa' to his horse from the bedroom window of a slattern neighbour – 'it doesn't take 35 minutes to deliver two bags of nutty slack'. The domestic pet was eternally a nuisance – 'I could smell that tom-cat i't'custard a'Sunday'. The knowledgeable audience would wait for the slip on the wall with consequent damage to a jutting bosom: 'that's the third time on that same brick', came the gravelly voiced complaint.

In touring revue and pantomime, he would frequently be joined by the diminutive Betty Jumel (1901-1990), an effervescent entertainer, also of north-western origins, playing opposite Norman Evans as, for instance, Humpty Dumpty and teaming up with him in variety. There was a 'cod' brass band sketch, with Betty Jumel as overwhelmed base drummer and Norman Evans as harassed conductor in a spirited rendition of *The William Tell Overture* or, very tellingly, in a duet of *The Merry, Merry Pipes of Pan*, he the heavyweight, flustered soprano, she the moustachioed tenor, their sheet-music reduced, under stress, to imaginary portions of fish and chips.

Not for the first or last time, one might point to largely working class audiences with a cultural reference that embraced such light classical music.

Norman Evans was able to transfer this wealth of observation to the dame role in pantomime. He was the northern matriarch,

fussy, petty-minded and autocratic, yet with a certain dignity and always able to evoke a little sympathy. His kitchen scene was a gem. The cooking was amusing enough, but it was the unexpected entrance of the king or baron that caused embarrassment and led to a nervy, discomfited game of billiards with scones and rolling pin on the kitchen table. In the wartime winter of 1944/45 Betty Jumel and he starred in *Humpty Dumpty* at the Theatre Royal, Leeds, and, with a twenty two week run, Yuletide to Whitsuntide, they established a never to be emulated record traditional panto season.

★Old Mother Riley and others

In these years the man who raised or lowered, according to perspective, the dame art-form to the ultimate was Old Mother Riley. There was no relaxation from the effigy. He was listed on the posters and in the comic, *Film Fun*, as Old Mother Riley; from shortly after the creation of the model, he never appeared in any other guise; it was rumoured that he turned up at the theatre already dressed for the role, so that even the back-stage people only saw Old Mother Riley, although a counter-rumour claims that this was as a cover for his understudy, if Mother Riley's original was beset by drink.

'He' was Arthur Towle. Arthur Towle was born in Boston, Lincolnshire in 1885 and was soon infected, in spite of family disapproval, with the theatrical virus. He was sweeping the local stage aged eight and was in a pantomime at ten. Seaside busking and concert party work ensued and then he toured with the Musical Cliftons, Danny and Vera, from whom he learned the essentials of his trade. It was on show-biz donkey-drawn safari with them in Ireland where, in 1910, he had the chance of writing and playing dame in a Dublin pantomime, at which he met the thirteen year old Kitty McShane, whom he married in 1916. Just as George Hoy had spotted the place-name 'Formby' on a railway truck, so did Arthur Towle notice in Ireland a van marked 'Lucan's dairies'. This referred to the estate and village of the Lucan family and thus he became Arthur Lucan. It would be a neat quiz question that asked what linked the Charge of the Light Brigade (in which the then Lord Lucan had some command), Old Mother Riley and the notoriously murderous peer who disappeared with a finality that variety magicians must have envied.

It was now that Arthur Lucan began the creation of the harridan Old Mother Riley, with the greying locks, the bonnet, the bombazine dress, the washerwoman's shawl and the black boots. Kitty McShane joined her husband as daughter Kathleen, Kitty and Bridget in sketches such as *The Match Seller*, in a successful joint career that brought broadcasting fame from 1941, when they shared their own programme, *Old Mother Riley Takes the Air*. Equally, they found further sources of income and national recognition in the production of no less than fifteen low-budget, crudely made but profitable films, usually with 'Old Mother Riley' in the title. Incidentally, it was in *Old Mother Riley's Ghost* that Arthur Lucan was actually seen for the only time in mufti; this was when the 'ghost', a crook dressed as a Riley lookalike, was unmasked.

The stage and radio sketches normally began with Old Mother Riley fretting over the absence of Bridget: 'where's me darter; where's me darter', she would yell. 'Here oi am, muther', Bridget would announce herself, in sweet Irish brogue, as the band struck up *When Irish Eyes are Smiling*. The mainstay cameo was *Bridget's Night Out*. Anxiety mounted as mother awaited daughter's ever so late arrival home from date with dubious suitor. The resultant row rocketed to a crescendo of intemperate tirade, accompa-

nied by the crash of flung crockery. It was a masterpiece of clever timing, with the temperature rising and with, night after night, not a bowl or saucer thrown out of sync.

The language, as in all Old Mother Riley's main pieces, had a drive towards free association that James Joyce, another artist who took his inspiration from Dublin, might have acknowledged. The confusion and elaboration of speech was remarkably sustained. 'Good evening blackguards, bodyguards, coalyards and fireguards' might be the bellicose greeting, whilst the mawkish self-pity might be manifested in such a statement as 'I've got one foot in the grave, one foot in a bedsock and I'm kicking the bucket with the other'. Kitty McShane, the dark, smiling, pretty colleen, would meet the fretful, cantankerous onslaught with a frisky, affected charm – 'shame on you' was the constant maternal rebuke – although, as the years drew nigh, her characterisation did become less credible. With spiky arms and legs, Arthur Lucan added the circus techniques of considerable physicality, jumping, legs flying outwards and elbows shooting sideways, so that the whole performance was a combine of characterisation, story-line, language, slapstick and something close to acrobatics.

Unluckily, the stage and off-stage relationships resembled one another all too desperately and the legends of both are part of theatre lore. Kitty McShane led her husband a dance in what could only be laughingly described as private life, so much so that there were hints of physical abuse as well as general henpecking, gross extravagance – Arthur Lucan ran into severe tax problems – and extramarital jaunts. Just as a tiny measure of this unhappiness, there lies in the Savage Club archives Arthur Lucan's note asking for his football pool coupon to be sent to him care of the club, to avoid the bitter disapproval of his wife. Indeed, such were the backstage rages that, after Kitty McShane left the act in 1951, some theatre managements banned her from their premises.

The tale is told of the Western Brothers being involved in a motor accident. They awoke in adjoining hospital cots, bandaged, splinted and sore. They lamented their lot – and then one said to the other reflectively, 'well, at any rate, it's better than going on after Lucan and McShane.' (However, the ageless Dominic Le Foe, for so many years the priceless chairman of the London Players Music Hall, offers a much more authenticated version, in which he was intimately connected, whereby the punch-line was Kenneth Western's reply when asked how he felt: 'bloody dreadful, but not so bad as I did at the Glasgow Empire'. Both editions, fictional or factual, have a moral.)

Arthur Lucan soldiered on, and, having swept a stage of one theatre aged eight, he collapsed in the wings of another, the Tivoli, Hull, and died in his dressing room. Unbeknown to the customers, his understudy played both performances that evening. It was 1954 and he was 68. His wife, after some attempt at a re-jig of the act with Roy Rolland, died aged 66, ten years later, a victim of alcoholism. Rather like the George and Beryl Formby relationship, the Lucan and McShane partnership is, sadly, one of those where the line between the public and the private domains becomes murky and it is difficult to analyse the performance without some reference to the fraught domestic situation.

The analogy of the strife of Old Mother Riley and her daughter with the travails of Steptoe and Son, the televisual creation of Galton and Simpson, is self-evident. There is no doubt that the later duel is the better observed. Were it deemed 'literature' rather than an emanation of the lowly telly, it would be studied in schools and colleges, for it is a classic text of intergenerational torment with a closely-knit couple unable to sever the link despite the angst. It is of a higher standard than the Riley/Bridget study, in part because the battle was drawn out over many episodes rather than concentrated in one or two brief sketches, but more because both characters are fully developed. They are three-dimensional constructs, whereas the 'Bridget' figure was more the two-dimensional 'straight man', so to say, of the normal double act.

Indeed, Old Mother Riley is an excellent example of one of the problems of this kind of study. Classification is arbitrary. Arthur Lucan might have found himself falling under scrutiny in the chapters on double acts or on sketch comedians or on regional comedy, as well as among the famous dames. Whatever the category, Old Mother Riley, with the assistance of film and radio, became an emblematic figure of the 1940s, a name that may still be used as shorthand for the slovenly washerwoman.

Another female impersonator whose stage persona became his chief billing was Mrs Shufflewick, aka Rex Jamieson, originally Rex Coster. Where Old Mother Riley became popular, Mrs Shufflewick remained something of a cult figure, just if abbreviated reward for a talent developed against a canvas of oppressive life-chances. Rex Jamieson was unceremoniously dumped in the entrance of a police station in Southend in 1924 and collapsed fatally in a Camden Town doorway no more than 58 years later in 1983. Ominously, his show business vocation began with his membership of a wartime concert party in the Middle East, his colleague and drinking partner that legendary toper, Tony Hancock. The Windmill, dates with the Norman Evans revues and, of course, dame roles in panto offered him a bright career, but during the 1960s he became a self-destructive and rather seedy drag act, depressed by his puniness, his bisexuality and his sense of professional failure. He was salvaged in 1972 by the quietly efficient and effortlessly knowledgeable Patrick Newley, whose management brought some decency and respect into his chequered existence. Unlike the rather secretive nature of Arthur Lucan's stage personality, Rex Jamieson wandered about in casual clothes with Mrs Shufflewick's accoutrements in a carrier bag.

From out of the carrier bag emerged raiment of clashing colours of damsons and scarlets, a fading flowery hat and a trademark fur boa – 'untouched pussy, practically unobtainable in the West End' – while the demure wearer spoke in tones of refined if reduced gentility. Had she not once been the variety star 'Bubbles Latrine and Her Educated Sheepdogs' who had years before been married to a pheasant-plucker? Tiny, pithily bird-faced, and with a clipped southern accent, Mrs Shufflewick optimistically sought pleasure but was ceaselessly baffled by the outcome. Although 'Broadminded to the point of obscenity' and 'If I'm not in bed by half past eleven, I'm going home', she invariably ended up stark naked, apart from her hair-net, on the top of a 29 bus. Some commentators saw elements herein of Nellie Wallace, of whom more will be revealed in the chapter on women comedians, whilst it is possible to witness some of that heritage of raw desire and injured dignity in Paul O'Grady's Liverpuddlian beldam, Lily Savage, a later leader among drag acts.

✱ Danny La Rue and others
We are trespassing on the blurred frontiers between 'dame' and 'drag', which, like so many aspects of popular comedy, are not clearly marked. It is sometimes said that the dame always insists, in performance, that he is a male dressed as a woman, whereas the drag artist excels and rejoices in the actuality of the imitation. Arthur Askey was never in two minds about this; he was booked as Arthur Askey and, whatever the dame's part and the costume, he remained unconquerably 'Big-hearted' Arthur. Sometimes the attack is altered by the venue and the audience. The demands of being a panto dame and playing a very adult nightclub, maybe with a largely gay clientele, obviously call for a different script and approach.

Another variation that touches on the dame/drag dilemma is the distinction between the consciously grotesque and the avowedly smart. There is often a class and generational element involved. Old Mother Riley was working class and ancient; Mrs Shufflewick was edging towards suburban fancies and flirting with middle age. One may trace, then, a more sophisticated branch of British 'damehood', including some female impersonators who presented themselves in attractive if flamboyant gear.

Douglas Byng, born in 1892, was of this school. He served the usual apprenticeship in concert party work, before developing his risqué style that went well in cabaret and the luxurious, London-based revues of C B Cochran and Andre Charlot. His shrilly trilled Cowardesque songs, like *Doris, the Goddess of Wind* or *Sex-appeal Sarah* ('...my body gets barer, each time I appear on the screen; oh, I've played such rare pranks with Douglas Fairbanks; really risky, but never obscene...') were eked out with saucy patter. As Nell Gwynne, he reported telling the Merry Monarch 'Charles, if you must dance, stick the maypole up yourself...and dance round it.' These kinds of characters, including Boadicea and Mexican Minnie, gave him the opportunity to wear often fetching costumes.

He was in much demand as a panto dame, a role he performed with enormous authenticity. It is said that, during the interval of *Sleeping Beauty*, he was once asked to make a charity appeal to the audience. He retorted severely that, as far as the paying customers, especially the children, were concerned, he was asleep for a hundred years, and he would not destroy that illusion. Nonetheless, one of his most spirited cameos was a one-man panto, in which he played all the parts and which included the audience participation number, *Who'll Come to Roll Mother's Pudding?* – '…Daddy is out in Australia; Granny has papered the tin; so if you're all good, you shall all have some pud: now who'll stick the first currant in?'

The heir – or heiress – to and the supreme exponent of that tradition is the dazzling Danny La Rue. Daniel Patrick Carroll was born in Cork in 1928 and, after experience in the rather equivocal *Soldiers in Skirts* all-male revues of the post-war era, he developed his very accurate impersonation of the aggressive, pushy glamorous lady. Statuesque and imposing, and exquisitely gowned and coiffeured, it is a most glittery effect, and yet, in so doing, he somehow contrives still to enjoy being the jocose impostor. As a scarlet-clad Miss World, he details his vital statistics as '38, 26, and I couldn't half make you jump'. His perpetual aside is 'I know what you're thinking – I wonder where he puts it?'

From knowing cabaret he graduated to family entertainer, ranging from Lady Cynthia Grope, a wicked take on the Conservative woman of the age, the 'hoary toastess', and the Japanese Geisha girl to the extravagant lead in a modernised Christmas story, *Queen Passionella and the Sleeping Beauty*. He also added to his act, by way of light and shade, sentimental ballads, like *On Widow Kelly's Doorstep* or *When I Leave this World Behind*, songs of a vintage that completes a conscious and conscientious linkage with his music hall forebears.

In pantomime he was formerly a not so ugly sister in *Cinderella*, selfish and assertive, nevertheless. Later he made a formidable and showy Widow Twankey in *Aladdin* and what was impressive was the fashion in which he interpreted the needs of the genre, keeping the children busily amused with his silliness and antics, but not forgetting the adult need for some of George Robey's 'honest vulgarity'. His whole and quite complex personality has been devoted to an appreciation of what it means to be a top-class present-day entertainer – and one always has the engaging feeling that he has some sense of this disposition as being the product of a century and more of show-business history. That frank appreciation of those past glories is uppermost in his stage deportment. In response, his many fans would be right to believe that Danny La Rue might have topped bills for all of those hundred or so years.

Pantomime and Comedy

Once embarked on the panto trip we are likely to find ourselves wandering down many incidental by-ways. Even while concentrating on the dame character we soon find ourselves exploring other avenues, but the pantomime has remained central to the continuity of the character and the guarantee of the income of the performers undertaking the part. It is sometimes said that the dame role may be traced back to Noah's Wife in the medieval morality plays, apparently played as a shrew and possibly played outrageously by a man. From our standpoint, the quintessence of this phenomenon is described by a gamut that stretches from Joe Grimaldi's Queen Roundabellya at the commencement of the

19th to Danny La Rue's Queen Passionella at the end of the 20th century.

If the dame flourished as the spine of British pantomime, many other comedians found starring roles therein as well. The most eclectic of theatrical genres, pantomime gaily recruited from all sources. There is scarcely a comedian who did not find himself signed up as a Simple Simon or an Idle Jack, and, as we stroll down the gallery of British comics, such examples will be pointed out, along with the double acts that played supporting roles or the burlier, more cumbersome types that found themselves playing the barons and emperors.

The sheer bulk of pantomime, as a quotient of the theatrical fare made available to the population over the last 150 years, cannot easily be gainsaid. It provided comedians with a training ground, a regular beat and a substantive showcase. Now for a literary transformation act: from the excited bustle and smell of orange peel of a wintry, often dark and rainy, visit to the pantomime, let us switch to the, one hopes, warmer clime of the British seaside resort and join the crowds, be-frocked, be-sandaled and with open-necked shirts, sauntering along the promenade to the concert party.

The First Resort

Whereas many aspects of light entertainment claim, truly or falsely, venerable derivations, no such legends or myths pervade the, in historical time, brief saga of seaside shows. They came with the territory of the seaside resort, itself an urban manifestation and reflex response to industrialism. Within a lifetime, ordinary men and women saw their leisure jump from one or two free days a year, via an annual long weekend from Friday to Wednesday, to a wage-less wakes week and finally the chance of a holiday with full pay.

A Victorian health fetish for briny seawater had seen one or two places assume the attraction of an inland spa town, like Bath, Buxton or Tunbridge Wells. Suddenly this expanded to meet the demand of mass holidays, when, particularly in the textile towns of Lancashire, entire communities would decamp on holiday. The trains obviously were the key to this act of bulk transportation. Brighton, already well-established and with regal connections, expected 50,000 visitors a year in the pre-railway era; with the coming of trains that shot up to 73,000 a week. By the end of the 19th century 3m people, inclusive of day visitors, travelled by rail to Blackpool.

The stringent regime of the cotton industry actually paid the workers some dividend in this regard, for, rather than a dribble of holiday-making, it made sense for the mill owners to shut down completely for a week's maintenance and repair. Elsewhere, with manufacturing still often piecemeal and a trifle unsystematic, it took time for the notion of the complete break to register as a possibility. Oldham and Darwen were among the first towns to benefit from the shut-down scheme. Entire communities went to the seaside, often on a regional basis, with the midlands industrial towns favouring the Welsh and southwest coastal fringes, Londoners gravitating to Margate and Southend and so on. Even as late as the 1950s variety artists arriving in northern townships in summer would note with disappointment the absence of smoking chimneys, indicator of a very quiet week at the box-office. There were no paid holidays, so the holiday club, based on chapels, shops and pubs, was the chief device for the necessary saving. In Oldham the total invested sprang ten times from £23,000 in 1882 to £228,000 in 1906. It has been calculated that 126 such excursions were organised in Burnley alone in 1906, 65 of them to Blackpool. During the Burnley wakes week something like 70,000 weekly tickets would be bought for Blackpool.

The railway companies, appropriately enough, were the first to offer holidays with pay. This was during the 1870s. As a week's holiday would cost, including travel and entertainment, about £8 a head around the 1900s, this meant for, say, a family of two adults and two children a weekly outlay of 15s (75p) a week out of a wage of less than £5, quite a substantial saving. By the 1940s about 12m workers, that is, half the work-force, had paid holidays In 1951, just about the peak of the 'variety' period and the hay day of stand-up comedians, there were 27m holidays taken at home in Britain, something of a zenith before the flight to Spanish sunshine and sangria. Blackpool, originally an obscure watering-hole, abruptly became the monarch of the holiday resorts. With the Tower, plus, later, Reginald Dixon at the theatre organ, the Golden Mile, the Pleasure Beach and a host of indoor attractions, as well as the spectacular free show of the tumultuous waves, its siren call lured a host of visitors, while the brainwave of the famed Illuminations served to drive the season deep into the autumnal months. By the turn of the 19th century Blackpool received 100,000 paying guests a week or 1.5m a season and between a third and a half of the town's dwellings were utilised for digs; there were 4000 officially registered 'lodging house keepers'.

Blackpool may well have been the king of the coast, but there was a jostling throng of pretenders to the crown. By 1911 no less than 145 resorts were officially recognised around the sandy and rocky beaches of Great Britain. In the wake of a thirst for camping and caravanning came the purpose-built holiday camps, associated with the name of Billy Butlin. From the 1940s and then in the post-war period, the 'instant community' of the holiday centre, with food and entertainment self-contained within the complex, made for a safe gamble for those blessed but with one week's holiday and thus fearful of being caught in an unfriendly, unfamiliar and windswept locale. The strict regime of school, factory and office life, coupled with the stern discipline of military service in the Second World War, braced the populace for the hearty briskness of the holiday camp regulo. 'Wakey Wakey' was the reveille call of the army barracks, the alleged cry in the holiday camp and, aptly, the ignition key for the cheery *Billy Cotton Band Show*, itself a feature of summer holiday entertainment – on the island of Jersey, for example – as well as a successful radio then television programme.

The demand for entertainment in what were basically urban adjuncts to the sea was immense. Initially, the response was individualistic, with a mix of showmen and women that might have been found at any large Victorian gathering, like the fairground, the market, the procession or the racecourse. So, as people strolled and frolicked on the sands, there were vendors of ice cream, toffee, monkey nuts, ginger beer, toy windmills and balloons, along with quack doctors and the still to be found fortune-tellers, plus a modicum of itinerant musicians, wrestlers, singers, orators, acrobats and the favoured Punch and Judy show.

As the crowds grew larger and more regular, and as promenades and piers, as well as bandstands and indoor theatres, were constructed, there was a more systematic provision of entertainment. By the 1850s the first groups appeared on the sands of Britain. These were the minstrel shows; far from having some mythic origin, they were, of course, a newfangled American invention. The famous Christy's Minstrels appeared at Southport in 1860, while the Mohawk Minstrels and the Moore and Burgess Minstrels were chief among the many such black-faced troupes. Singing the songs of Stephen Foster and his ilk, they gave a start to several music hall favourites, among them Little Tich, G H

Elliott, G H Chirgwin and Eugene Stratton, who came to England with Haverley's Minstrels, singing Leslie Stuart tunes, like *Little Dolly Day Dream*. The minstrels dominated the resorts for 30 years.

Then came the concert parties. The first is usually thought to be the Marguerites, formed about 1890 by a group of concert singers, keen to augment their earnings by performing at yacht and houseboat parties in the more select resorts, as well as at stately homes. They discreetly wore masks with their evening dress to preserve their anonymity, for such goings-on might have imperilled their reputations as serious soloists. It was Clifford Evans, fascinated by the French pierrot costume of loose blouse and pantaloons with ruffs and pom-poms, who introduced the pierrot shows. His first was at Bray, near Dublin, in 1890, but he made his name with his company at Cowes on the Isle of Wight, where he gained from the fashionable patronage of the Prince of Wales, later Edward VII. Where the minstrels blacked up, many of the pierrots whitened up, using a rather unappealing compound of zinc and lard.

Will C Pepper followed suit with the White Coons at Hove and later Clacton. The choice of places like Cowes and Hove, both mainly middle class in custom, points to the moderate style of the concert party, as opposed to the more raucous tones of music hall and variety. Then Edwin Adler and W G Sutton energetically built a chain of some 20 pierrot 'pitches' at coastal sites, while Will Catlin formed the Royal Pierrots, with Scarborough his first base. With the open air shows vulnerable to the unpredictable fortunes of the British climate, he next led the way in building enclosed premises, with his 'Arcadias' at Scarborough, Llandudno and elsewhere. Will Catlin's son-in-law, Billie Manders, made a

home for himself at the Amphitheatre, Rhyl, where he organised the Quaintesques concert party for 29 summers, and in which was included, with a backward glance at the last chapter, considerable female impersonation. In many places the compromise was struck of the audience basking in the deck chairs, but, as the well-known notice ran, 'if wet in the pavilion'.

Another feature of the open-air theatres was the habit of standing around the outside of the enclosure, just as everybody had done in the olden days when the minstrel shows busked on the sandy beaches. Holidaymakers would perhaps stand for a few minutes as they promenaded in the afternoon or early evening. The entertainers would cajole this crowd into contributing to a voluntary collection. This was the last vestige of 'bottling', so called because, in summers of yore, an actual bottle was used – it was ceremonially broken in the presence of the entire troupe after the show to guarantee that the collector had not deceived his comrades.

For the most part the world of minstrels and pierrots had been exclusively male, but soon women were included, while another change was the deployment of blazers and boaters or yachting caps, sometimes just for the second half of the show. George Royle launched the first of his much-loved Fol de Rols companies – another first for Scarborough – in 1911, and he maintained them for years at places like Hastings, Torquay and Eastbourne. Their motto was 'the show that any child can take its parents to', a gentle indication of the friendly, unaggressive style of the concert parties. Many of them worked inland in the winter months, with J B Priestley's 'the Good Companions', formerly the Dinky-dos, a fictional example – that exuberant novel was published in 1929. The most famous non-fictional example was the Co-optimists, who were considered good enough to appear in the West End.

Concert parties became and remained common all around the coast. The bigger resorts fielded several versions, while many seaside resorts built theatres and hosted variety shows and revues of top-class calibre. There were circuses, too. Eventually, Blackpool and Great Yarmouth had the last two purpose-built circus venues in the country. The pier pavilions and floral halls of the medium sized and smaller holiday places hummed with the songs and laughter of scores of concert parties. The mood was cheerful. Here were families removed and escaped from the drudgery of school, work and kitchen for a week; they needed no bidding to enjoy themselves. All they required was the catalyst of a decent jolly show.

The writer, from about 1937, spent time most summers in or near Rhyl, and haunted Will Parkin's open-air show, forced by the pressure of childhood economics into hanging around the outside of the enclosure and, he thinks he remembers, contributing a few coppers to the collection box. Here he watched 'second spot' comics like Hal Blue and Tony Dalton telling slightly lavatorial tales and participating in varied sketches and concerted items, many of which he remembers and some of which he still relates.

Needless to say, comedians, as well as singers, had their major part in this form of entertainment. Although, of course, most comics played both summer concert party and variety dates, for, quite simply, one without the other would not have totted up to a reasonable income, one may discern some difference of approach. Put another way, some comedians were more attuned to one medium than the other. The seaside show was a quieter, more relaxed experience and appealed, by that token, to the quieter,

more relaxed comedian. The extremes of the range, in terms of location, might be defined by comparing the second house on Saturday night at a packed, noisy, drunken Glasgow Empire, nicknamed by Ken Dodd 'the House of Terror', with a pleasant, sunny Wednesday afternoon, with a few dozen placid holiday-makers in deck chairs on the front at Frinton.

That comparative thought gives us the opportunity to look at one or two of the comedians who relished that kind of situation, as compared to those whose eyes gleamed at the thought of taking on and beating the tough audiences of the industrial cities.

Arthur Askey et al

Of course, you could throw a stick at a bunch of entertainers from the period and you would be certain to hit one with concert party experience. Especially in the initial part of careers, such a relatively amiable induction into the profession was not too threatening. It still had its challenges, however. Whereas the music hall and variety stage called for a ten minute spot that could be honed and sharpened and deployed at all times, the concert party was more of a collective endeavour, with everyone involved in sketches and other ensemble items. Moreover, the programme had to be changed, so that, over a week, the holidaymakers might be able to enjoy two different shows.

As one example of the scale of this kind of employment, the Fol-de-rols employed, at one time or another, Arthur Askey, Richard Murdoch, Cyril Fletcher, Jack Warner, the Western Brothers, Elsie and Doris Waters, Avril Angers, Reg Dixon, David Nixon and Leslie Crowther, most of whom we shall encounter in sundry guises later in the text.

As one would predict of the prototype, many of them would be described as 'light comedians', often administering a line of soothing humour along with a smile and a friendly song. In some ways they were not unlike the sentimental branch of the old music hall acts and, of course, several of them were exactly that.

Randolph Sutton (1889-1969), from Bristol, charming and well-mannered, was one of these – just, having made his music hall debut at the London Pavilion in 1915. He was famed for his rendition of *On Mother Kelly's Doorstep*, a song that Danny La Rue would later include in his repertoire, but he also sang – and successfully recorded – *When are you going to lead me to the altar, Walter, Give Me the Moonlight, Bye Bye Blackbird* and *My Blue Heaven*. He had a long career in variety and at the seaside as well as in the recording studios.

Arthur Askey is an excellent example of the 'light comedian' who found the taste and early training for show business in the world of seaside concert party. He was born in Liverpool in 1900 and christened Arthur Bowden Askey. The son of the company secretary of one of the sugar firms in that port of West Indies linkages, he was schooled at Liverpool Institute, later to be the alma mater of a Beatle or two, and worked in the city's education office. However, holidays in Douglas, Isle of Man, where there were usually four concert parties, and Rhyl, where the Jovial Jesters then reigned, together with short ferry trips to Rock Ferry on the Wirral to watch the concert party in the Olympian Gardens, inspired Arthur Askey to start his own troupe, the Filberts. A young church chorister who had sung for World War I wounded (sometimes in premonitory duet with a youthful Tommy Handley) he could warble and chirp refreshingly. Tiny, but with his 5ft 3inch body full of bounce, with red hair, large-framed glasses and a huge half-moon smile, he turned professional in 1924 and soon became a concert party favourite. His first job was with the *Song Salad* show, which played at Ventnor and elsewhere. He married May Swash in 1925, the beginning of a lengthy partnership; he moved to London and strove away at the usual series of Masonic evenings and other functions. Then he gravitated to the summer shows that had, in the first place, stimulated his theatrical ambition.

After bookings at Margate and other resorts – he completed, all in all, a stint of fourteen summer seasons – from 1938 to 1945 he was a regular star of the Sunshine Concert party at Shanklin on the Isle of Wight – and it was his initial success there that led to his being so triumphantly recruited for broadcasting duties, an issue to be addressed in the next chapter. Sufficient for the present to assert that the broadcasting authorities were then keener on good cheer than the sharper, more dubious edge of the fast-talking variety comics, like Max Miller. Many of those with concert party experience were similarly drafted, among them Leonard Henry, a regular with the Margate Jetty shows, and Ronald Frankau, whose the Blues concert party played venues like the Wellington Pier, Great Yarmouth.

Arthur Askey's had verve rather than iron in his comedic soul. Hyperactively dancing and chatting, there was a childlike flavour about his performance that registered well at the seaside, where family audiences were the normal format and where adults, escaping the rigours of paid work and housework, were ready to jettison stern responsibilities and join their offspring in amusement arcades, on donkeys and in sand castle construction. Arthur Askey evolved a set of silly songs, many of them about small creatures like the seagull and the moth or, most eminently, the bee, 'the busy, busy bee; sting if you like, but doannnt sting me!' These he gaily burbled, skipping hither and yon in dapper fashion. Even when he was being, to employ the regulatory word of the period, 'rude', he was rude after the manner of the saucy infant, not the knowing adult, with the seagull depositing excrement in the parson's eye or the frequent mention of 'coms', which, for the uninitiated, was an abbreviation for 'combinations', a mysterious item of female nether wear.

Arthur Askey was reputedly a kindly off-stage figure, whose wife offered him the inestimable gift of, to quote her husband, telling him when he arrived home about the bargain she had bought, rather than asking him how he had fared at the Royal Command Performance. He maintained his good humour in civilian life when not on active service as an entertainer and included in his armoury a vast resource of tales about theatrical digs. He was also in demand in pantomime. Here he played dame, but with – as was explained in the preceding chapter – but a few curtseys to female impersonation. He reasoned, sensibly, that the customers had paid to see Arthur Askey and, apart from a wig and a bonnet, Arthur Askey was what they received. He died, aged 82, in 1982. Thus he survived the Nazi menace. He was the first person to record the somewhat banal and prematurely optimistic war song, *We're Gonna Hang out the Washing on the Siegfried Line* and, in dire consequence, was placed on the German black list for execution that was drawn up at the time of the planned invasion of England in 1940.

Curiously, there was a repeat of this phenomenon in the next generation of entertainers, with television now the medium, not radio. Visitors to post-war Torquay, Babbacombe or Eastbourne may have enjoyed the antics of Bruce Forsyth, milking the audiences for all he was worth, organising games and distributing token prizes of packets of crisps or balloons, dancing a little, gagging a little, playing the piano a little. With this kind of panache and without developing any major comedic persona as such, he soared to be a superb television compere and presenter of games shows. Tall, angular of frame and countenance, his stock in trade was instant command of an audience and, at need, its individual members. From ITV's *Sunday Night at the London Palladium* to the BBC's *The Generation Game* and beyond, with affable energy and a flair for the telling catch-phrase – 'I'm in charge'; 'Nice to see you – to see you nice' – he turned his summer show talents to television, just as Arthur Askey transferred his to the 'wireless'.

In those same post-war year, the holiday camps, especially the Butlin holiday centres, would also offer something of the same opportunity to budding young 'light' comedians, often those, like Bruce Forsyth, with some all-round musical skills. Des O'Connor was such a one, who found his mètier as part unassuming vocalist, gently deprecatory storyteller and unthreatening chat show host on TV.

Another example of the quieter type who found the concert party less uncomfortable than the steely variety stage and also found fame through radio was Gillie Potter. Baptised, doubtless by his father, a Wesleyan minister, Hugh William Peel, in Bedford, in 1987, his was an unlikely background for music hall. Nonetheless, as Arthur Askey's experience in a Church of England choir reminds, the similarities of church and theatre are ever present, and there is an 'am-dram' tradition dating at least from the medieval miracle and mystery plays. He found his way via acting, including being George Robey's understudy, and service with the Royal Fleet Auxilary in the 1914-1918 War, towards concert party work, notably with Reuban More, who ran shows at seaside resorts like Boscombe and at inland places like Guildford.

The boater, which had become the conventional headgear for male concert party members, became Gillie Potter's standard wear, as, complete with flannel trousers, blazer, umbrella and even notebook, he created his contemplative posture of mock-erudition. He was the public school alumnus, 'the Old Borstalian', given to scholarly homilies. 'Good evening, England', he would begin in his highly cultivated accent, 'this is Gillie Potter, speaking to you in English'. Many of his lecturettes centred on Hogsnorton and the impoverished but genteel Lord Marshmallow and his family, the denizens of Marshmallow Towers, plus other inhabitants, among them Sir Stimulant Maudlin-Tite and the local rector, Canon Fodder. Allusive and mannered, it was tailor-made for radio – there are even hints of *The Goon Show* in the word-playing format – but the content did date rather.

Gillie Potter, with his wife, Beatrice Fanny Scott, thus sought early retirement in the sedate clime of Bournemouth. His academic interests did, in fact, range over heraldry, church history and genealogy, while, like many another comedian, his politics were decidedly right-wing, on the xenophobic extreme of patriotic, so that, all in all, his 'old boy' pose perhaps came fairly naturally to him. He died, aged 87, in 1975.

The present writer discovered that Hogsnorton was not entirely mythical and decided to seek out the original in rural Hertfordshire. After several false trails, he was about to give up, when he spotted what appeared to be an ancient rustic yokel scything grass by the wayside. He asked him whether he knew where Hogsnorton might be. 'Have you ever heard of Gillie Potter?' was the questioning response. After some explanation, the aged mower told his story. He was not a local Hertfordshire countryman, but an ex-merchant navy man, a native of Kendal, only recently come to the south-east from the Lake District. Arriving in London by train in 1940, preparatory to joining a ship at London docks, he had been addressed by a fellow-passenger. It was Gillie Potter and the young sailor recognised the voice from the radio. He had no change to tip the porter he expected to engage to carry his luggage and he wondered whether the sailor would lend him sixpence – quite a sizeable sum out of merchant navy wages – for the purpose. Slightly overawed, the youth agreed, and Gillie Potter very carefully copied down his home address, so that he could return the loan. 'I'm still waiting', continued the now ancient mariner, '...and if you go down that cart track, second on the left, you'll come to Hogsnorton' – which was no less than the truth, for Hogsnorton was nothing more than a dog-leg in a muddy lane, with two semi-detached cottages gracing the corner.

Sandy Powell and others

Not only did the concert party entertainer have to squirrel away plenty of material to fulfil his or her manifold duties, there was also the issue of becoming identified with one resort. Of course, this was very good for business, but there was some pressure to find even more material, although, as with pantomime audiences, there was a yearning and fondness for the familiar. Clarkson Rose (1890-1968), for example, made Llandudno's Happy Valley and other resorts the home of

PALACE THEATRE - WATFORD
Box Office Tel: 25671

Commencing Monday 21st June 1976
FOR ONE WEEK ONLY

DON ELLIS presents

MUSIC HALL STARS IN
OLDE TYME MUSIC HALL

SANDY POWELL	KIM CORDELL
CAN YOU HEAR ME MOTHER	STAR FROM TV's STARS & GARTERS

TONY RAYMOND & BETTINA

THE PETT SISTERS

GAY & ROGER HOWARD

DAVID O'BRIEN DUO

DON 'CHAIRMAN' ELLIS	BILLY WELLS
THE VOICE OF THE STARS	FAMOUS LONDON COMEDIAN

7.30 NIGHTLY	PRICES: MONDAY to FRIDAY £1.00 85p 70p SATURDAY £1.25 £1.00 85p WED. & SAT. MATINEES ALL SEATS 50p	MATINEES WED. and SATURDAY at 2.30 p.m.

G. & M. Organ, Theatrical Printers, Wrington, Bristol.

Sandy Powell, features at the Watford Palace . . . as well as his records and 'wireless' work, he was one of the hugest hits of the seaside shows and became known as 'Mr Eastbourne'

his Twinkle concert party for over forty years, just as Arthur Askey kept a similar watch on the Isle of Wight. Clarkson Rose was also another noted panto dame.

One example is Sandy Powell, in turn yet another to combine radio and concert party appeal. He was born in Rotherham in 1900, the son of Lily Powell, a minor starlet in the music hall firmament, and began life as an impressionist. He then developed a burlesque style, his chief mainstays being his 'cod' conjuror and his 'cod' ventriloquist, often in concert with his wife, Kay White. Well before Tommy Cooper, his tricks would go awry to his barely concealed dismay. As an equally inefficient 'vent', with a distractingly collapsible soldier-boy dummy, he wore a large moustache to mask his absence of technique. Sometimes he would report the dummy's whispered answer – 'he says he's alright', in reply to the query, 'how are you today, my little man?' Sometimes he would alter the answer; when the dummy attempted to mutter 'Wolverhampton' in response to the question 'where do you come from, my little man?', he would plaintively suggest 'couldn't you make it Leeds?' There were many verbal mix-ups over, for instance, 'Vegetarian' and 'Presbyterian'.

Late in his career, he found, abroad in Australia and in British clubland, that there were customers too young, too intoxicated or, it has to be considered, too unintelligent, to realise that he was performing skits. They thought they were watching an inefficient ventriloquist. His Delphic put-down of one such inebriated heckler has classic proportions. 'I can see your lips moving', cried the confused onlooker; 'Aye', said Sandy Powell, 'but only when the dummy's talking'. Bespectacled, unhurried, expansively smiling, he enjoyed a long career. His allegiance to

Eastbourne, where he died in 1982, was such that he became known as 'Mr Eastbourne', having presented himself in summer show there for so long.

As well as his radio fame, he was also one of the first variety artists to make a killing with records. In the 1930s he cut *The Lost Policeman*, originally a concert party and variety sketch. He was offered either a straight £60 fee or a £30 advance and subsequent royalties of penny halfpenny a sale. 500,000 were sold – and he followed that with a further 80 records, selling 7m altogether, quite a substantial heap of 1.5ds. He portrayed the goalkeeper, the boxer, the gangster, the nudist and many other eccentrics, but the policeman remained the best seller. Sandy Powell's slow, sombre conversation with 'Little Percy' had as its solemn refrain 'Our 'Erbert's fallen in the river', with the policeman intent on the correct procedure and reluctant to indulge in any moist life-saving exercises. The prolonged interview relied on such tried favourites as 'how long's your father been in his present position?' – 'three months' – 'Three months; and what is it he's doing?' – 'six months'.

The guying of the forces of law and order, from Shakespeare's Dogberry and Verges, the watchmen in *Much Ado About Nothing* to Gilbert and Sullivan's policemen of 'unhappy lot' in *The Pirates of Penzance*, is familiar game. The music hall and variety performers knew an easy target when they saw one. We noted James Fawn's sly dig at the corrupt officer in the old-time song, *Ask a Policeman* and Wilkie Bard's lazy policeman; soon there would be Charlie Penrose, with his uproarious, if eventually slightly tedious, *The Laughing Policeman*. Best of all would be Robb Wilton's police sketch and Will Hay's filmed version of maladroit constabulary, also entitled *Ask a Policeman*. As Peter Sellars' Inspector Clouseau, in the Pink Panther cinematic series, would testify, it was an inexhaustible seam.

The lengthy career of the ineluctably affable Sandy Powell is at once a sublime illustration of the variety of the variety star and the chance for yet another admission about the problems of pigeon-holing comedians. He took out his own companies – *Sandy Powell's Road Show* – on the variety circuit; he was an early master of radio comedy; he made a fortune out of records, in his prime days a fine underpinning of a stage career; and he was a welcome pantomime artist, normally as a dame in the Arthur Askey mode, that is, scarcely more than beaming Sandy Powell with a few feminine accoutrements rather than a full-blooded female impersonation. He is credited with making popular the 'look behind you' audience participation panto technique, with the paying customers invited to assist him in guarding some valuable item, such as a bag of gold, left at the side or back of the stage. He is also credited with the allied technique of the 'oh, yes it is/oh, no it isn't' exchanges with the audience on some vital question. Those are two splendid memorials to this droll comic, apart from his work at the seaside and his lampooning of two other variety specialities, the magician and the ventriloquist.

Although more vigorous and abrasive in style, Dave Morris (1895-1960) had something of the manner of Sandy Powell, with his straw hat, his giant cigar, his pebble thick spectacles and is amiable grin. His origins were in Middlesbrough, where his father was a tailoring cutter, but he adopted Blackpool as his spiritual home. Undeterred by ill-health, in part the consequence of being gassed whilst serving with the Green Howards in the Great War, he bestrode the piers and promenades of the Golden Mile like a comic emperor. Blackpool was, of course, the biggest date in summertime show-business, attracting high-class acts of the like of George Formby and Gracie Fields, but, after his own fashion, Dave Morris developed a close association with the grand north-western resort.

First, for many years on North Pier before and during the Second World War, and, next, at the Palace Theatre for another long stint, 25 seasons in all, Dave Morris was the equivalent in Blackpool of Sandy Powell's 'Mr Eastbourne'. His apprenticeship had been a long one, involving winning a talent competition at the Middlesbrough Empire when he was aged thirteen, joining the Stable Boys, one of several troupes of youngsters that flourished at the time, and then into variety as a single act. He was active in panto – his Mayor in *Goody Two Shoes* was widely admired, and he too made a success of radio, chiefly as 'the Wacker' in the *Club Night* series. Based on a fictional working men's club (Bernard Manning and Colin Crompton would, for there is little new under the sun, revisit the formula in television's *Wheeltappers' and Shunters'* Club in the next generation) its catch-phrase, ''as 'e bin in?' is still sometimes heard in common parlance. Joe Gladwin, later to play Norah Batty's long-suffering husband in *Last of the Summer Wine* and to advertise Hovis bread against the background of a sloping, cobbled Dorset street, played his stooge, Cedric, while characters like Pongo Bleasdale might also have been found at the club. In is earlier incarnation, Dave Morris had been assisted by Billy Smith, in, for instance, his strong man and embittered landladies sketches.

Dave Morris was as breezy and brash as the town with which he enjoyed a reciprocal affection. He was full of bustling aphorisms and explanations: 'a fine regiment – they always blanco their pyjamas before retiring' – 'Rita Hayworth has been married five times: she hates men but she loves wedding cake' – and, at the entry of the dame, Phil Strickland, in *Goody Two Shoes*, the strangled cry of 'Crippen was Innocent!' For over 50 years, he entertained and, with never a hint of Pagliacci, he was as wholesomely good-humoured off stage as well.

A further example of the good-natured northerner with a lengthy seaside connection was Albert Modley, billed as 'Lancashire's Favourite Yorkshireman'. He worked in the lineage of Tom Foy, who, in the days of music hall, acted out the role of the gormless northerner, helpless but with a fool's wisdom: in check suit and hard-topped bowler, he would nervously mutter, 'she did laugh at me. Well, you couldn't blame her; I'll bet I'd laugh if I met me.' Albert Modley had show-business roots. His father, 'Professor' Modley graduated from his own gymnastic act to train wrestlers and strong men for the stage. Albert Modley (1901-1979), after a childhood in Ilkley, soon wormed his way into the entertainment industry and became an accomplished pantomime comic. The author's first panto visit was to the Princess Theatre, Manchester, in 1937, with Albert Modley starring in *Mother Goose* – a child-like laugh out of place from the front row of the circle led to a kindly word from Albert Modley, still fondly recalled.

For 40 years, at Christmas and at summer shows, he did his classic 'tram' act, whereby, with the help of front cloth painted like a tram, he used his drum kit as the controls. They acted as brakes and steering wheels, while the percussion also provided the sound effects of bells and so forth. 'Just to be sure we get there', he would say, 'we're following another tram marked 'Duplicate''. His humour was always of this wholesome, daft quality. 'Me eyes are going funny; I keep running into pubs' – 'I flew down to London; ee, me arms are reet tired' – or, booking a return railway ticket, in reply to the inquiry, 'where are you going?', 'back here, o'course'.

He was to prove to be to Morecambe what Sandy Powell was to Eastbourne and Dave Morris was to Blackpool. He made his home there. For years he was chief comedian for Ernest Binns' *Arcadian Follies* on Central Pier and was made a freeman of the then borough. Geoff Miller, the variety historian, reports that Albert Modley believed that this entitled him 'to graze cattle on t' sea front and ride on t' buses for nowt'. Aptly enough, his last TV appearance was a small part in an Alan Bennett play about retirement to the seaside, for which Morecambe was the location.

There were many more comedians with both seaside and a pantomime dates prominently in their engagement books, and we shall have cause to meet up with some of them hereafter. The case has been made, in these two last chapters, that the panto and the summer show provided a nursery for the up and coming young comic as well as solid employment for the journeyman comedian.

In these two arenas comedians were building on by-gone conventions, if, in the case of the seaside shows, a briefer one than that of pantomime. The maturity of the variety phase in entertainment also coincided with the advent of three novel technologies. Each of these contributed to the evolution of British comedy and offered comedians other outlets, both for them to enhance their earnings and to advertise their wares, that they might be more widely known and thus more attractive to potential customers when back on the variety, pantomime and concert party circuit.

Each of this mechanistic trio has been mentioned. One was the recording industry, and dozens of comics were to make records. The next two chapters relate how the other two technical vehicles – radio and cinema – augmented the livelihood and the comic style of many comedians, especially in the late 1920s, the 1930s, 1940s and 1950s.

5. THE ADVENT OF RADIO

A preliminary word might be in season with regard to records, for they arrived prior to 'wireless' and then contributed hugely to its output, with Christopher Stone the first disc jockey, although that is an anachronistic usage. Incidentally, Christopher Stone actually performed a variety turn, whereby he played records on the stage and sat there listening to them with a patient audience in front of him.

The British introduction to commercial recording came through the Emile Berliner concern, a German firm. In 1897 William Barry Owen opened the British subsidiary of what came to be named the Victor Talking Machine Company. In 1899 he bought the painting of the dog with its ear cocked at the sound emitting from the trumpet-shaped instrument and one of the earliest and most enduring advertising slogans – 'His Master's Voice' – was born. Many music hall stars are thus immortalised on cylinder and record. The primitive recording conditions favoured solo rather than ensemble performance, for it was obviously simpler to track the single voice. Thus comic singers and monologuists were preferred, just as classical instrumentalists and singers, such as Caruso, were busy in the recording studios in preference to the orchestra or the choir.

As we have noted, comedians, such as Sandy Powell, benefited from this new craze, espe-cially after 1926, when electrical replaced acoustic recording and the whole process became more sophisticated. Sometimes – and the same is true of early films of many comics – the absence of an audience and the inflexible discipline of the nascent process makes for a stilted, cold performance. Gracie Fields was the first variety star to record her act with a live audience. This was about 1930 and, self-evidently, there is at once a warmer flavour. One can compare, for instance, the recordings of Max Miller alone in the studio with those live in a packed London theatre: predictably, the crowd lifts the whole style and tone of the act.

Some of the same technology that brought records to the people also brought microphones to the theatres. There has been much controversy about the help-mate of the mike, with the conservatives feeling that it robbed the performer of a natural intimacy with the audience and sometimes, especially in the early days of the technique and the mechanism, trapped the artist into a stationary posture. The absence of amplification had made for a rather brassy, extrovert style of presentation, with weightily pronounced vowels and over-precise, lingering consonants in the old music hall, although there had been exceptions, among them George Formby Senior, who had retained the attention of the audience by the sheer delight of his quiet appeal. In any event, the device of the microphone had a greater effect on singing, because it encouraged the 'crooning' style, associated with the mellifluous Bing Crosby or the modestly sentimental tones of Vera Lynn.

Records had a peculiar relationship with radio. In one sense, the one superseded the other and, indeed, record sales dropped when radio became popular. If one could listen to the tunes and stories on the radio, why bother buying the records? Then again, the appearance of the artist on radio or the actual playing of the record was a major commercial boost, although, again, this link became much more important over time for popular singers than for comics. Nonetheless, from the viewpoint of the enjoyment or study of former comedians, the archive of recorded material, much of it now re-released in improved and modern forms, is a godsend of immense value.

Radio Times

It is well-known that all radio listeners owe a debt to Guglielmo Marconi. It was he who spotted that there were functional and financial possibilities in what had hitherto been an academic exercise in fairly obscure laboratory experimentation. An entrepreneur of some boldness, he initially produced 'wireless' signals in 1895 and, crucially, he had, by 1901, increased the transmission distance from what originally had been little more than the space of the physics laboratory to 200 miles. As with so many inventions, it was the military and naval need that took priority. There was also a diplomatic function to be served and it should not be forgotten that much of the communication was by Morse Code; spoken communication was mainly confined to the parallel development of the telephone. It was not until after the end of World War I that farsighted experts began to visualise the civic deployment of the technique.

Manufacturers were eager to sell receivers more widely; listeners, many of them assembled together in 'wireless societies' (rather like the public reading of Victorian novels in mechanics' institutes and other venues in the 19th century) were equally eager to have something to which to listen. A critical date is usually deemed to be 1920 when the *Daily Mail* funded a broadcast of songs by Nelly Melba, and this opened up the world of entertainment and culture to the 'wireless' device. The licensing authority for the building and running of wireless station was, by a statute of 1904, the General Post Office, but there was considerable argument about which manufacturers of receivers should have such a permit.

As the controversy rumbled on and as continental broadcasting, whose output British based receivers could pick up, began to develop, firmer action was taken. An exclusive licence to broadcast in the United Kingdom was granted to a consortium of leading manufacturers in 1922. It was known as the British Broadcasting Company. It was in this very casual and reflexive manner that the grand concept of public service broadcasting was born. Some historians have pointed out how, at that time, both political wings in Britain approved of the compromise. The Labour Party disliked private enterprise and welcomed a degree of public scrutiny; the Conservative Party indulged its paternalist and authoritarian values, watchful of Johnnies-come-lately who might have a baleful influence on the populace.

A mesh of regional stations was erected, with London's 2LO at the centre, and with the rigorous and puritanical figure of John

Reith as managing director. In 1923 the first edition of the *Radio Times* was published and 2LO moved from the Strand to Savoy Hill. In 1924 the first Greenwich 'pips' were heard. A dominant feature still remained the sale of wireless receivers. This led to what has continued as the ongoing curio of funding public service broadcasting through the sale of individual licenses for the reception of programmes, while, for decades, the post office was central to this process and the Postmaster-General was the minister with responsibility for the BBC.

John Reith, a dedicated supporter of the establishment, gave the government welcome support during the General Strike of 1926. Some have suggested that it was, in part, as a reward that a royal charter was issued in 1927 that created the British Broadcasting Corporation. In finally ruling out the manufacturers from the administrative arrangements, the government fulfilled the ambition of those who sought a completely public service process.

John Reith was made Director-General and he ruled with a rod of iron cast in the forge of Calvinistic ethics. Censorship was harsh and there was no popular music on the Sabbath. Serious music was allotted nearly three quarters of the time prescribed for all music and improving 'talks' were high on the agenda. John Reith felt no embarrassment in asserting that 'the brute force of monopoly' was the necessary tool for guaranteeing that radio fare would be wholesome.

In looking back from the vantage point of nearly 80 years, one might be tempted to believe that such an austere regime would have been assailed with neo-liberal complaints. The truth is that its morality was not out of keeping with the overwhelming weight of bespoke respectable opinion. In the early 1930s there were 5m licenses purchased annually, but by 1939 this had doubled and more. Nine out of ten households had a radio. Because the BBC could be trusted to censor unmentionable items and keep the Sabbath holy, its exceedingly narrow focus exerted an exceedingly wide appeal. In the wake of the Victorian family novel, it was attractive to a middlebrow audience, with a broad swathe of decent middle class and aspiring artisan class listeners. In that primmer epoch, no man feared that his wife or children might switch on the wireless and be shocked. One sound testimony to this was the outstanding success of *Children's Hour* (named after the Longfellow poem, with its plea for 'a pause in the day's occupations'), which kept going from the early days until 1965.

Comedy Takes to the Air

The prospects for comedians on this new medium were hardly, therefore, propitious and the solemnity could become tedious, even for the most dedicated of earnest listeners. Commercial broadcasting, from continental stations like Radio Normandy (from 1931) and Radio Luxembourg (from 1933) could be clearly heard in Britain, with products and stars – the Kentucky Minstrels and OK Sauce, for example – indelibly intertwined. Luxembourg's take on childhood was in support of clubs such as the Ovaltinies (its 'happy girls and boys' lyric the work of child impersonator, Harry Hemsley) and the Cocoacubs. George Formby was one of several comedians who added to his formidable earnings with an advertising slot on Radio Luxembourg.

There was a further problem. The theatre managers were not too keen on loaning out their stars, fearing it might, as happened with records, deter the customers from visiting the variety halls if they could listen to the artists on the wireless. In time, it would become apparent that the reverse happened; hearing the acts stimulated a yearning to see them in the flesh. For their part, the comedians were bothered, not only about whether their lines would pass moral muster, but also about the consumption of dearly fought for material. Some of them had only one or two routines, at which they had worked hard and long to bring to some approach to perfection: one broadcast and the routine would be gone. Again, as so many pantomime comics had found, the desire for the familiar sometimes allowed the same material to be repeated over and over. Possibly the main stumbling block was contractual. In those first years of broadcasting, there was much squabbling about fees and what proportion of fees should go to artists and managements and where the BBC stood legally in the procedure. Ted Ray, for example, never broadcast until 1939 because of such quarrels. The details of those now arcane disagreements need not detain us, but it was only in the late 1930s that suspicions were quietened all round and amicable concord was agreed.

The upshot was that, at first, the BBC had to provide its own sparse ration of homely fun. The first comic character appeared three days after the BBC went on air. This was 'Our Lizzie', played by Helen Millais, who thus has the epitaph of being broadcasting's first such representation: "Ullo, me old ducks', she would cry, "ere I am again with me old string bag', before launching into a quavering rendition of *Ours is a Nice 'Ouse, ours is*. The earliest of the joint offerings was John Henry and his wife, Blossom, a down to earth Yorkshire couple. In a series of short sketches they discussed the comings and goings of everyday life, with particular reference to John's pal, Joe Murgatroyd: 'Joe and Emma always think alike: Emma thinks first, but they both think alike at the finish'. Blossom's stern command

'John Henry, Come on' (something of a steal from the elder George Formby's 'John Willie, come on') has the honour of being the first of many of the BBC's popular catchphrases that were assimilated into day-by-day conversation. Another family format (and, from *Mrs Dale's Diary* to *A Life of Bliss*, radio was to use the family formula lavishly) was supplied by Mabel Constanduros, with her creation of Mrs Buggins, a lady who went on to give useful war service to the BBC.

There were also cheery BBC concert parties, known as the White Coons and the Roosters, while the Kentucky Minstrels, with C Denier Warren and Scott and Whaley, interspersed a little light humour among the tributes to Stephen Foster and the solemnly intoned spirituals and Victorian hymnal ballads. Their long association with the BBC began in 1933. The concept of the series was evolving, with John Watts' *Songs from the Shows* (1931) and John Sharman's *Music Hall* (1932) as illustrations. Later there was the *Palace of Varieties* – somewhat paradoxically, this last offering was a nostalgic memorial to the old-time music hall, whilst *Music Hall* was a straightforward variety show.

In 1933 a rather grudging John Reith had acknowledged the need for a separate Variety Department. Until that point light entertainment had principally been the responsibility of Gerald Cook at the Outside Broadcasting Department, which, at least and with administrative justification, had brought variety shows direct from theatres like the Argylle, Birkenhead, under yet another misnomer, *Vaudeville*. An interesting and reverse example is Nan Kenway and Douglas Young, who were brought together as a radio double act, and then were recruited, not entirely without trauma, for the variety stage. Their catchphrase, much used in wartime in connection with advice and recipes on how best to cope with rationing, was 'Very tasty; very sweet', with a lascivious licking of the lips. It is still occasionally heard in normal converse even today.

Slowly, recognised comedians began to make their way on the air-waves. Sandy Powell introduced another famed catchphrase, when, pretending to broadcast from the North Pole, he hoarsely shouted 'can you 'ear me, mother', although an alternative tale suggests he was asked to say something by the producer for voice level and the filial query adhered. Robb Wilton, of whom much more anon, attracted happy attention with *Mr Muddlecombe JP*, a series of half hour Wednesday episodes devoted to that bewildered and irritated magistrate, which bridged the pre-war and early war years.

The 'Court of Not-So-Common-Please' derived from Robb Wilton's variety sketch, *The Magistrate* and he radiated confusion in the township of Nether Backwash, where, as chairman of the council, he was responsible for 'Public Futilities'. On the heated issue of a bypass, he had this to say: 'the passers-by who do pass by, if they had a bypass to pass by, would be able to pass by the bypass.' He captured the obfuscation of British institutional pettifogging to a nicety.

Over the years there were some comics who appeared to be bespoke 'wireless' performers. The balding, genial, ex-teacher, Stainless Stephen (Arthur Clifford Baines; 1892-1971) is an example. Born in Sheffield – hence his steely adjective – he served as a sergeant-major in the Lancashire and Yorkshire Regiment in World War I and joined in unit concert parties. He was 34 before he became a fulltime professional. It was army signals that gave him his motif of spoken pronunciation: 'This is Stainless Stephen speaking; semi-conscious...' Although, with something of a reliance on the infinite possibilities of the semi-colon, it had a limited focus, it served him and his listeners well enough until his retirement in 1952. This coincided with the end of the golden radio age and it should be the cause of no surprise that he billed himself as 'the Renowned Wireless Entertainer'.

Leonard Henry (1891-1973) was another who was principally a 'wireless' comic, in his case rather after the style of Arthur Askey. A mere 5ft 3inches, he babbled incessantly with a strong hint of cockney, his somewhat impudent face alert and slyly irreverent. Educated at Alleyn's School, he joined his father's concert party, the Mountebanks, at Southend, and gained experience by the sea and in revue. He wrote his own patter – 'I owe everything to my creditors' – and he burbled away happily on the radio as very much his natural mètier. Oliver Wakefield, 'The Voice of Inexperience', suited his bill matter exactly, in that his act was almost all to do with his intonation. It was that of an upper class, Woosterish burbler, stammering through his insouciant but dumb-witted patter on radio: 'laying the country to waste...looting...looting and...and...pillaging...from pillage to...pillage.'

It was, obviously enough, these more unassuming characters, highly dependent on word-play, who took most spontaneously to the airways, as opposed to the brash performers, reliant on costume, bravura and masterly contact with a live audience.

Climbing on the Band Waggon

The stern John Reith departed from the BBC in 1938 and with him went some of the hair-shirt attitudes. Conversely, there was an acceptance of the influence of American broadcasting, in particular, the work of George Burns and Gracie Allen, with its snappier approach and awareness of the potential of radio as a medium in its own right. One clear-cut change was the decision to deploy flagship programmes at regular times, an idea neatly encapsulated in the very title of *Monday Night at Seven*, later *Monday Night at Eight*, a well-liked magazine show and, for its time, very inventive. *Inspector Hornleigh Investigates* briefly outlined a mystery and listeners had to spot the criminal's error; *Puzzle Corner*, introduced by Ronald Waldman and the first broadcast quiz, set the listeners' posers, inclusive of – its original usage – a 'deliberate mistake'; Richard Goulden, in his roles as the night watchman ('seated one day by my old fire bucket') or Mr Penny, the antique shop owner, would provide another moral parable for the hour. There was, therefore, a kind of audience participation – at intervals in the programme, the criminal, the quiz answers and the optional advice would be revealed.

However, from a strictly comedic stance, the true breakthrough came with the launching in January 1938 of *Band Waggon*, the programme that made 'Big-hearted' Arthur Askey a household name. He was teamed with Richard Murdoch, whom he promptly nicknamed 'Stinker'. He proved to be the perfect foil and a consummate radio career lay ahead of him. Richard Bernard Murdoch had a loose tea-time affinity with Arthur Askey; the latter's father had been in the sugar business and Dickie Murdoch's father was a tea-merchant, albeit of rather wealthier stock than Askey père. That slight resemblance apart, they were opposites. They were born at opposite ends of the country, if not the social scale. Richard Murdoch was born in Kent in 1907 and was educated at Charterhouse and Pembroke College, Cambridge, where he found his feet in show-business with the Cambridge Footlights revue group, one of several light and satirical comedians from that star-lit stable. He married an Archdea-

con's daughter, Peggy Rawlings, in 1932 and in-between-whiles, he furthered his vocation modestly in revue and musical comedy, before the broadcasting call came.

He was 6ft 1inch in height, almost a foot taller than 'the silly little man' as he consistently referred to his partner; he was handsome, polished with a voice elegantly clipped in modulation, whereas the other was the homely one, whose own celebrated catchphrase 'Ay Thang Yew' (a convoluted 'I thank you') was supposed to have been borrowed from a jaunty bus conductor on Arthur Askey's route-ways. Arthur Askey has some reason for being hailed as the first radio comedian in the saga of British entertainment. He obliged with a remorseless chain of catchphrases over the years – among them 'Hello Playmates'; Before Your very Eyes'; 'Don't Be Filthy', and the enduring 'Read any good books lately?'

The essence of *Band Waggon*, with its regular Wednesday spot, was its pure radio-ness, for it relied both on the pace and thrust of the spoken word and on a imagined dimension that could not have been made manifest on the variety stage. For all that, Jack Hylton, the bandleader and impresario, bought up the rights to the show and toured it around the provinces, terminating with a run at the London Palladium. It was the first radio show to take that reverse direction and head for the halls.

The magazine element, already noted in *Monday Night at Seven/Eight*, was to the fore, and Syd Walker – 'what would you do, chums?' – did his rag and bone man's agony column on *Band Waggon*. There was *Chestnut Corner*, in which the two protagonists dealt in ancient gags, with Arthur Askey an adept in the art of demeaning his material. The hour long show included several musical numbers, and the melodic component was to be a feature of radio comedy more or less until the time of Tony Hancock and the more naturalistic format of situation comedy.

The cockney – although born in Salford, a typical accident of theatrical parentage – comedian, Syd Walker (1887-1945) contributed his rag and bone man's agony column. 'Day after day', he would warble, 'I'm on me way; any rags, bottles or bones'. He would introduce himself as 'it's your old china, Syd Walker, still seein' it through'. This compassionate totter would present a little problem and ask for the listener's advice about how to solve the query: 'what would you do, chums?', was the invocation, another phrase that echoed for years afterwards. Syd Walker, whose career ranged from Fred Karno touring companies to musical comedy, died during a pantomime run at the Grand Theatre, Croydon.

For all the bits and pieces, the chief device was that Arthur Askey, as the BBC's first 'resident' comedian, was assumed to have taken up 'residence' in a flat on the top of Broadcasting House. It was from and around this surreal condition that the central humour flowed in the scripts crafted by Vernon Harris – not that he received much credit, as the BBC wished to sustain the illusion that 'Stinker' Murdoch and 'Big-hearted' Arthur were simply enjoying a genuine if eccentric relationship. Arthur Askey's fiancée was reputedly the unseen Nausea Bagwash, the daughter of the equally invisible Mrs Bagwash who looked after the laundry, while Lewis the Goat,

a pair of pigeons, Basil and Lucy, and even Hector the Camel were mythically installed at the top of Broadcasting House. One thread was a weekly exercise in training in some skill, with Richard Murdoch as the instructor, very much a glance back and across at variety, where, for instance Sid Field was being taught golf by his stooge, Jerry Desmond. One example was Arthur Askey learning to be a waiter – 'do you serve lobsters?' – 'we serve anybody; sit down'.

The inventive clown and cult-figure, Max Wall, was one of several mid-century comics to make his name on radio in shows like Hoop-la (seen here with artist Maggie Hambling)

For all its triviality, the show was much enjoyed by listeners, not least because of the originality of its form if not its content. Moreover, it posted a sign of what radio comedy and comedians on radio might aim to do, other than presenting their stage act non-visually. It ran pre-war for a couple of series, some 40 episodes in all and enjoyed some success thereafter, and it certainly made an important contribution to the story of British broadcast entertainment.

ITMA

If the BBC were spurred on to include lighter moments following the departure of the austere John Reith, the onset of the 1939-45 War was an even more massive stimulant. After a faulty start and some press criticism, the BBC determined to concentrate on morale-boosting programmes as a complement to its essential news broadcasting. The Variety Department, evacuated first to Bristol and then, given the bombing of the south coast ports, to Bangor in North Wales, proceeded to enjoy its finest hour. It produced a regular diet of light entertainment between the end of *Children's Hour* at 6.0pm and the close-down at midnight, based on a major show every evening and a number of supporting minor variety and musical programmes.

This offered an unexpected opportunity to many comedians and scriptwriters to reach for the moon – and several did to legendary acknowledgement.

The success of *Band Waggon* had left the BBC authorities searching for a second such show, with the American impact of George Burns and Gracie Allen very much in their sights. The hope was to partner Tommy Handley, who had been broadcasting off and on since 1924 in programmes like the 1925 revue, *Radio Radiance*, with a Canadian

entertainer, Celia Eddy, but that never quite worked out. Tommy Handley combined with the script writer, Ted Kavanagh, from New Zealand, and the producer, Francis Worsley, to create *ITMA*, an original and perhaps unique piece of broadcasting history.

Thomas Reginald Handley was the son of a cow keeper operating in central Liverpool, a bizarre enough start in life, who was, as we have seen, a chorister like Arthur Askey. He became a professional singer and even did a musical duet with Jack Hylton for a short while. He also saw some active service with the Royal Naval Air Service in World War I and soon afterwards he launched his music hall sketch *The Disorderly Room*, written by Eric Blore, and which he persevered with for 20 years. His pleasantly light baritone voice was well suited to this piece, which was basically a 'song-chainer', a set of parodied popular songs, relating, in this example, a tale of army discipline. In 1929 he married the singer, Rosalind Jean Allistone and it is intriguing to remark that this lively, ebullient radio presence was essentially a very private man, not terribly assured about his capacities and, preferring the quietude of the domestic hearth and a good book, seldom seeking the noise and banter of show-biz partying.

There is some mild controversy about the derivation of 'It's That Man Again', with counterclaims on behalf of the American Republican Party, as it rubbished the latest of President Roosevelt's New Deal initiatives in the 1930s and on behalf of the Daily Express, as it scolded Adolf Hitler for yet another of his more lethal actions. It was Tommy Handley himself apparently who spotted the compelling acronym. It was the first age of the acronym; the coming war would breed a host of them and thus it was an appropriate title of some cultural resonance. The first pre-war *ITMA* episodes, tricked out with magazine style quizzes and other features, were unimpressive. It was as if the outbreak of war and the shift to Bristol set flowing the creative adrenalin. The vast bureaucracy of war became, in effect, the target, with earnest and over-weighty officialdom ripe for good-natured attack.

Barry Took has written that *ITMA* was 'a radio cartoon of daily life in the war years'. Tommy Handley accepted the portfolio of 'Minister of Aggravation and Mysteries' (agriculture and fisheries) and located in the 'Office of Twerps' (works). In later series he would serve a term, among others, as Mayor of Foaming-at-the-Mouth in 'It's That Sand Again'; as Squire of Much Fiddling, as manager of a factory; and, immediately post-war, as a planning officer and, in a low-cost brave new world, as governor of the island of Tomtopia. Between 1939 and 1949 there were 310 episodes, 170 of them in wartime. With its regular Tuesday, later Thursday, 8.30pm slot, plus repeats and overseas airings, *ITMA* gradually caught the public imagination to the point where 30m people, 20m of them on the home front, were tuning in on a weekly basis, the nearest to a complete national audience there has ever been.

There was much affection in the laughter that greeted the show. It was like a weekly therapeutic session in which the population gained some relief from the stress of the Citizen's War. It was neutral in terms of class, gender and age and thereby had a massive range of appeal. In 1942 *ITMA* became the first Royal Command radio show, when it was performed at Windsor Castle for the then Princess Elizabeth's birthday.

The three combatants, comedian, producer, writer, set themselves the rigorous goal of a hundred laughs a programme, all of which had to be earned in the eighteen minutes – that is, one every eleven seconds – of time available out of the 30 minutes, when the two standard music items and the signing in and off credits and tunes had been negotiated. This they accomplished by a helter-skelter of characters ostensibly visiting Tommy Handley in a rapid succession of quick-fire exchanges, building up a repertory of Dickensian names and memorable catchphrases, many of which echo down the decades. The opening and shutting of the door to whatever sanctum was inhabited by Tommy Handley became the most familiar of sound effects, and, in listening to recordings of *ITMA*, one is able to discern the studio audience tangibly predicting the arrival of the next identifiable catchphrase or punchline.

The reference to Charles Dickens is deliberate, in that, for the first time for three quarters of a century, the country rejoiced together linguistically in a cavalcade of funny names and sayings. Tommy Handley had been noted in variety for his quick and quirky delivery – 'this hotel's motto is 'short sheets make the beds seem longer.''

In *ITMA* he stood at the rostrum and conducted a weekly concerto of verbal brilliance. Few doubt that he was the finest reader ever of a light entertainment radio script. His masterly eye, his rhythmic – was that the singer in him? – pace, his insouciant timbre – they made for a devastatingly acute and consistent performance, added to which was his generous sharing of the laugh-lines with his colleagues.

The picture one saw in the *Radio Times* or in the daily newspaper of a craggy featured, cheerful man, with a jutting jaw and a trilby pulled down over his face, was the picture we imagined as he exchanged a rapid fire of puns and wordplay with the other members of the cast, although, truth to tell, the characters were recalled better than the players. The first to have a potent impact was Jack Train's

Funf, the German spy with the muffled voice ('This is Funf speaking') while that same clever impressionist went on to score a great hit with the inebriated Colonel Chinstrap, whose 'I don't mind if I do' is still occasionally heard in pubs and at drinks parties.

Maurice Denham supplied the coy tones of the obliging Lola Tickle, 'who always did her best for all her gentlemen'; Horace Perceval (Ali Oop – 'I go; I come back' and the Diver – 'don't forget the diver, sir'), Sidney Keith (Sam – 'gee, boss, sumpin terrible's happened' - Scram) Clarence Wright as the – 'Good morning; nice day' – commercial traveller and Fred Yule (Norman the Doorman, for whom everything was 'vicky verky') were others among dozens of supporting artists and scores of eccentric characters, each with his or her own oral tic and the identity tag of a catchphrase. A young Hattie Jacques (Sophie Tuckshop) did well on *ITMA*, while Joan Harben's Mona Lott's plaintive 'it's being so cheerful that keeps me going' is another aphorism heard today.

Overnight the voices and sayings would be incorporated into the daily conversation of shops, school playgrounds, and factories and among the armed forces. 'After you, Claud' ; 'No, after you, Cecil', the refrain of the exceedingly courteous Horace Perceval and Jack Train, was apparently adopted by bomber command pilots over their intercoms, while one could scarcely step into a department store lift without the lift boy mimicking the Diver's doleful 'I'm goin' down now, sir'.

There was an especial fondness for Dorothy Summers' charlady, Mrs Mopp, to the point where, of course, the term continues to be deployed as shorthand for cleaning ladies, while both her 'Can I do you now, sir?' and her 'Ta ta for now' or the acronymic 'TTFN' are still in common parlance. The repartee of Tommy Handley and Mrs Mopp was awaited with particular delight, whether it was the odd dish she had brought to tempt his palette in a country on strict rations, or his abbreviated response to TTFN, as in 'NWYWWASBE'. 'What does that mean, sir?', would ask the bewildered char in her broadly working class accent. 'Never wash your windows with a soft-boiled egg' would come the explanation.

Tommy Handley died suddenly of a cerebral haemorrhage in 1949 and, needless to say, *ITMA* died as abruptly, for there was no replacement possible. As his funeral procession moved slowly the streets, the mourners were packed as thickly as six deep, while 10,000 congregated around the crematorium. There were memorial services at both Liverpool Cathedral and, without precedent for a comedian, at St Paul's Cathedral, where 4000 crammed into the church and 2000 listened to the service outside. They mourned the passing of a comedian who, it has been asserted, was as much the icon of radio comedy as Charlie Chaplin was of silent film, but who had also played an immense part in a war-winning exercise.

War-time radio comedy

ITMA was king among princes, for there was a conscious BBC emphasis on comedy during the Second World War. The long-running lunch-time series, *Workers' Playtime*, 30 minutes of variety from war-related factory canteens 'somewhere in England', was a standard opening for many comedians, especially of the second grade. There was also the rather more painful *Works Wonders*, where the amateur talent at industrial sites supplied the entertainment.

The sociological range was immense. At one extreme there was *Hi Gang!*, 'brought to you from the heart of London', at a time when variety was chiefly disgorged from Bangor and hitting the air waves first of all in May 1940, at the height of the immediate post-Dunkirk peril. The sophisticated transatlantic mood was to the fore in the engaging personalities of the American actor, Ben Lyon, and his wife, the singer and first performer of *There'll be Bluebirds over the White Cliffs of Dover*, Bebe Daniels. There was music – Jay Wilbur's orchestra, the Greene Sisters and Sam Browne – and breezy chatter and a notable guest, sometimes from the world of sport, such as the brilliant footballer, Stanley Matthews. The third participant was Vic Oliver. Victor Van Samek (1898-1964) was born in Vienna and played classical violin, thus adding to the cosmopolitan mien of the show. Tall, bald and polished, his was more of a cabaret than a variety turn, although his jokes – 'she had a glass eye; I didn't know at first, but it came out in the conversation' – had the whiff of the music hall stage. He came to Britain, via violin playing in the United States, and, after meeting her while both were appearing in C B Cochran's show *Follow the Sun*, he rather improbably and temporarily married Sarah Churchill, daughter of Winston Churchill, not altogether with the great politician's approval. With its boisterous signature tune, *I'm just Wild about Harry*, *Hi Gang!* proved to be very popular and, with their offspring in tow, Bebe Daniels and Ben Lyon later had further radio success with *Life with the Lyons*.

At the other end of the cultural scale was *Happidrome*. This was a Sunday evening variety programme; the writer recalls a Sunday family stroll, reluctantly undertaken by his childish self, on a sultry evening. As one ambled through the streets, most houses with the windows open, it was possible to eavesdrop on the broadcast of *Happidrome*, such was the incidence of its reception. Apart from offering opportunities to comics on what was a straightforward variety bill, three comedians staffed the fictional theatre and gave the show its focus.

Harry Korris (Henry L Corris; born Douglas, Isle of Man, 1888, died 1971) was Mr Lovejoy, the manager of the Happidrome. Originally, and like many radio comics, he was a concert party performer, indeed, initially a pierrot with the Debonairs on his native island. He appeared for eleven years with Ernest Binn's *Arcadian Follies* at Blackpool, where he came to be known as 'The Falstaff of South Pier', another of those interesting cultural references that assumed, probably rightly, that everybody knew something about Sir John Falstaff. In 1913 he married the soubrette, Connie Emerson, and they did revues – *Gay Paree*, for instance – as well as summer show work together. He did some film work with Frank Randle, whilst his 'Happidrome' antics led to his taking the lead in the modest 1950 movie, *Mr Korris Goes to Paris*.

Since 1926 Harry Korris had worked with Cecil Fredricks, more of a 'feed' than a comedian, but a useful asset to *Happidrome* in the role of the stage manager, Ramsbottom. The trio was completed by Robbie Vincent, who created the part of the idiotic call boy, Enoch. 'Let me tell you', he would whinny, 'my teacher says I'm a soldier of heaven'; 'tell your teacher', Mr Lovejoy would ruefully reply, 'you're a hell of a long way from your barracks'. Or, 'let me tell you; I've got blue blood in my veins' – 'and what do you think I've got – dandelion and burdock?' Then there would follow the irked Wiltonesque closure: 'ee, if ever a man suffered.' The character of Enoch became as well-known and, in playground, work-place and Nissen hut, as much imitated as any *ITMA* creation. The threesome usually did a funny song at some point, and they always sang their plaintive

The Advent of Radio

signature tune, a parody of the Inkspots' favourite, *We Three*. The show ran consistently from 1940 to 1947.

Predictably, there were programmes targeted at the armed forces and there was now a Forces (later, from July 1945, the Light) Programme, as over against the rather more serious Home Service. Some of them were highly specific, like *The Forces Show,* which transmuted into *Calling All Forces* and, later from 1952, *Star Bill*, while there was *Shipmates Ashore* and, with Doris Hare of later TV *Rag Trade* fame, *Ship Ahoy*, aimed at the merchant navy, *Under Your Tin Hat*, with a civil defence audience, and *Ack, Ack; Beer,Beer*, its target the home-based anti-aircraft (AA) and barrage balloon (BB) units. Most of these offered broadcasting chances to comedians.

The author had several choice opportunities in the early 1970s of chatting to Charles Shadwell, then the landlord of 'the Green Man' at Trumpington, just outside Cambridge. He had formerly been the conductor of the BBC Variety Orchestra. Bespectacled, cheery and shorn of hair (Tommy Handley, in yet another interesting cultural cross-reference, compared his head to the imperial yarn by A E W Mason, recently filmed, *The Four Feathers*) Charlie Shadwell was known as 'the comedian's friend', for his distinctively high-pitched and ready laugh was a godsend, in that it spurred the studio audience into louder guffaws.

He explained how he had been the source of the early wartime show, *Garrison Theatre*. Having been, as a young man, the manager/producer of an actual garrison theatre in the 1914-1918 War, he suggested the format to the BBC in 1939, and a variety show with a service audience was the result. As with the slightly later *Happidrome*, it was deemed wise for broadcasting purposes to build in a kind of constant off-stage element for continuity's sake. This device made the name of Horace John Waters, better known as Jack Warner, born into a comfortable artisan home in Bromley in 1895, married Mollie Peters, a secretary and non-theatrical, in 1933, and died, in quite affluent circumstances, in Ravenscourt Park, London in 1981.

His early work had been in the motor trade and he had driven just about everything, from hearses to racing cars – he was also a driver in the Royal Flying Corps during the First World War – before becoming a professional entertainer when well over 30 years of age. His background covered much of the ground of the would-be performer from a non-Thespian clan: church choir, wartime concerts and the local amateur dramatic society. Initially, he was a cabaret turn, doing impressions of, most notably, Maurice Chevalier, where his command of French, picked up while working as a mechanic on the continent, was certainly helpful. Suddenly, in December 1939, he was converted to being the cockney comedian, playing the role of the British Tommy, aligned on the good-natured side of irreverence and creating a mild chaos among the clientele of the *Garrison Theatre*.

Troubles with his bicycle gave rise to the famous catchphrase, 'Mind My Bike'; there was the letter from 'My bruvver, Sid', also in the forces, with frequent use of the military censor's blue pencil ('the weather is blue-pencil awful'... 'not blue pencil likely!'); there were edifying chats on 'ills for rill mills (eels for real meals... 'de-da-de-da-de-da.'). Each week he gave a monologue on 'Necessary Occupations.' This was a skit on what in reality was an acutely necessary format of deferred occupations, when people were conscripted. The scheme had been formulated by the inspirational social entrepreneur, Michael Young, when, as a young man, he sought for Britain to avoid what had happened in World War I (and happened in Germany in WWII) of men in essential jobs being drafted into or volunteering for military duties. Naturally, such burlesque as 'I'm a Bunger-up of Rat-'oles', 'I'm a Caster up of Alabaster Plaster' or 'I'm a Shaver-off of Gooseberries' played well with the rude soldiery who made up Jack Warner's audience and were suspicious of those who avoided army service. Jack Warner also carried on a brash flirtation with 'my littel gel', the pert usherette, played by Joan Winters, Charles Shadwell's daughter, with her clipped sales cry of 'programmes, chocolates, cigarettes'.

Jack Warner's after-life as an actor needs little or no recalling. Although untrained for the legitimate stage and rarely seen on stage, his solid virtues made him ideal for film and television parts, and, as Mr Huggett and then, significantly, as the authoritative policeman, from 1955 to 1976, *Dixon of Dock Green* (having been resurrected by his originator, Ted Willis, from death in the Dirk Bogarde film, *The Blue Lamp*) he became a proletarian father-figure to the nation. Few comedians have adapted so successfully to 'straight' parts on film. A tall and good-looking man, he apparently possessed in real life the qualities he espoused on the screen – but, nonetheless, he sprang to fame as a chirpy private soldier-cum-comedian. On one of those Trumpington occasions, Charles Shadwell proudly flourished Jack Warner's Christmas card; it was of himself in the uniform of a police sergeant, with the simple inscription, 'bless you, Charlie.'

Three series of programmes were devoted to each of the three arms of the services. These, too, offered important opportunities to rising comic performers and they carried over into peacetime. It all began as *Merry-go-round*, with army, navy and air force taking turns about, but the three shows that emerged took on an existence of their own. The naval version of *Merry-go-round* graduated into *Waterlogged Spa* and *Just Fancy*. It was a vehicle for Eric Barker, a Surrey-born character actor and impressionist, and, in later editions, his wife, Pearl Hackney. Eric Barker served in the Royal Navy for over five years. His tentative self-encouragement – 'Steady Barker' – was yet another much-used catchphrase, whilst older readers may remember Jon Pertwee's anarchic Mummerset postman – 'it doesn't matter wot yer do, so long as yer tear 'em up.'

Charlie Chester, born in Eastbourne in 1914, was finding his way as a stand-up comic in pre-war days, but it was as a sergeant in the Royal Irish Fusiliers that he came into the limelight, as organiser of the *Stand Easy* army show. He built around him a team, including Arthur Haynes, destined for future stardom, a 'legitimate' actor, Len Marten and the musical talent of Ken Morris, with – 'when love descended like an angel' – the tenor, Frederick Ferrari, supplying a colourful ballad by way of intermission. The show began with a rousing gang chorus, ending. 'Stand easy and let yourself go – it's the *Charlie Chester Show*'. There were *ITMA* style criminal characters, such as Whippet Quick and Ray Ling, the Chinese fence, while the natives in the jungle beat out the newsy stanzas:

'Down in the jungle, living in a tent; better than a pre-fab – no rent'...or

'Sir Ben Smith just said; gonna give the white man black bread':

to the uninitiated, references to, respectively, the rapid erection of pre-fabricated dwellings to help solve the post-war housing crisis and to the minister of food's tampering with the constituency of the National Loaf.

Cheerful Charlie Chester, and most of his team, thereafter enjoyed good careers. Charlie Chester remained close to radio, with quiz shows and with over 20 years as presenter of Radio Two's *Sunday Soapbox* programme. He was also a song writer – *Down Forget-me-not Lane* and *Primrose Hill* – and his death in 1997 was much mourned.

The RAF contribution is probably best remembered. It was smarter and longer-lived than the other two, while one of its two stars, Kenneth Horne, went on to decorate the second generation of radio comedy with his beaming, expansive gifts. The son of a nonconformist minister and MP, a Cambridge tennis blue and, throughout his career, a Director of Triplex Safety Glass and other businesses, Wing Commander Horne allied with the experienced Squadron Leader Richard Murdoch, scarcely escaped from his seclusion on top of Broadcasting House with Arthur Askey. They ran the mythical Much Binding in the Marsh RAF station in Laughter Command, and, in post-war years, they accommodated there such civilian amenities as a country club and a newspaper office.

They were joined by the singer-cum-light comedian, Sam Costa, and by the versatile Maurice Denham, both recruits from *ITMA*. Maurice Denham – 'Dudley Davenport at your service, sir' – created no less than 60 Much Binding roles. He helped inaugurate the fashion of comic actors fulfilling the parts beforehand played by comedians, a fashion that was to be inherited by television in some abundance.

The catchy lyrics of the 'Much Binding' weekly song, still imitated today, and the by now obligatory but fresh-minted catchphrases – 'When I was in Sidi Barani'; 'Not a word to Bessie about this, Murdoch'; 'Good morning, sir; was there something?'; 'These sets take an awfully long time to warm up, Murdoch', to the accompaniment of Murdoch-sounded atmospherics – lifted the show out of the ordinary, so much so that, after *ITMA*, it remains perhaps the most affectionately recollected of wartime comedy series.

This takes us, in respect of broadcasting to the end of the war, with some needful overlap. It will be necessary to revisit the radio and its comedic influence in a later chapter.

6 · THE INFLUENCE OF CINEMA

The cinema was a mammoth example of the application of industrial precepts to the demands of popular leisure. The process itself was, of course, highly technical, while the incidence of cinema-going was very much wedded to the sort of urbanised culture that sprang from the Industrial Revolution.

The milestones of cinema's early journey may be quickly set down. Edwin S Porter's *The Great Train Robbery* (1903) is usually regarded as the first film story, inaugurating the era of silent yarn-spinning on film. The vibrant Al Jolson introduced the 'talkie' (more accurately, the 'singie', as only the tunes were audible) with *The Jazz Singer* in 1927. Experiments with colour brought the first technicolour movie, *The Toll of the Sea* (1922) but it was Douglas Fairbanks, Junior, with *The Black Pirate* (1926) who first made that genre profitable.

In Britain, as in the United States, the cinema enjoyed an astonishing degree of penetration. As early as 1916, still in the 'silent' era, British ticket sales had already reached 1bn annually, that is some 20m a week. By the 1940s the figure peaked at 30m a week, that is, a yearly sum of 1.5bn. Two-fifths of the population went to the 'flicks', as they were nonchalantly referred to, once a week and a third of people went twice a week, while 80% of adolescents went to the cinema at least once a week. At this point there were over 5000 cinemas in the United Kingdom, ranging in size from 200 to 4000, and in the heavy industrial conglomerations there was a cinema seat for every nine of the population. Leslie Halliwell, the famed film critic and reviewer, reckoned there were 47 cinemas within five miles of the town centre of his native Bolton. London withstood the destruction of 60 cinemas in the wartime blitz with hardly a dent in its film watching statistics. In 1938 the income from British cinemas was £5.4m; from theatres and music halls, it was just £1m.

In a sense, the impact of the cinema came closer to matching the immediacy of the radio than any other leisure mechanism, prior to television, in that, just as millions were tuned into *Happidrome* or *Hi Gang!*, so did millions, in any one week, watch, for example, *Gone with the Wind* in 1939. This was not lost on managements and agencies, and, although there were some of the same worries about contracts and about material as with the radio, comedians were soon attracted to the medium of cinema. One element that helped in the inter-wars years was the introduction in 1927 of a quota system, whereby a certain number of British films had to be shown. This was intended to protect the British investment in filming from its dominant Hollywood rival and it led to the making of rather slipshod, if inexpensive, 'quota-quickies'. Although few of these were ever noteworthy, they do offer modern day buffs a chance to see old-time comedians in action. Indeed, there is considerable film, silent and spoken, of past comedians. The rigidity of film production in its primitive days and the obvious discomfort of audience-less performances means that one is rarely seeing old comics at their most vital, but, nevertheless, it is good to have that visual record.

Charlie Chaplin and Stan Laurel

The cinematic review must begin with a strong argument that the music hall influenced the cinema, rather than the reverse, at least in its early days. For the most part, comedians made films that showcased their stage personae and, often enough, their material. With flimsy plots and conventional production, comedians from Max Miller (for instance, *Educated Evans*, 1936) and Arthur Askey (*The Love Match*, 1954, one of a dozen or more films that he made) to Tony Hancock (*The Punch and Judy Man*, 1962) and Morecambe and Wise (*The Intelligence Men*, 1964) starred in films that did little more than spread their theatrical or televisual characterisations thinly over the larger screen and the lengthier time of the feature film. Sid Field included in the somewhat mundane musical, *London Town* (1946) four of his marvellous sketches. As a record for posterity of his undoubted stage talent, it is highly valuable, but the critics panned the movie for its 'disastrous and expensive' failure to emulate the American musical film. Where the 'wireless' actively changed the nature and approach of comedians, films, for the most part, merely photographed them.

On the other hand, two British-born comedians, Charlie Chaplin and Stan Laurel, utilising their music hall experience, had a pronounced effect on the style of cinematic comedy. It was the happy outcome of a legal prohibition. Inducted into the business at a time when sustained spoken dialogue was forbidden outside the legitimate theatres, they were versed and expert in comedic mime. Thus they had the brilliance of technique to convey into the new industry of silent film with remarkable and compelling consequence.

There is an uncanny similarity about the burgeoning careers of these two great filmic English comedians. Both were born into the theatre trade, albeit Stan Laurel was more fortunate in his forebears. He was born in Ulverston, now in Cumbria, in 1890, the son of Arthur Jefferson, a theatre manager, and christened Arthur Stanley Jefferson. The father was not over keen on his son treading the boards. Charlie Chaplin was born a year earlier, in 1889, his parents, who were soon estranged, both music hall performers. He was named Charles Spencer Chaplin. He was born in Walworth, South London, and knew the bitterness of destitution, worsened by the occasional glimpse of music hall glamour. He endured the meanness of his father and the mental illness of his mother and he was no stranger to Lambeth Workhouse and the poor law system in general, acidic experiences that forcefully marked both his private and public lives.

Charlie Chaplin was apprenticed, from 1898, through the Eight Lancashire Lads, some touring legitimate work and William Murray's Casey's Court Circus, another vehicle for child actors. Stan Laurel, meanwhile, made his way in the northern music hall, before, in 1907, he joined the Fred Karno troupe. In 1908 Charlie's elder brother, Syd Chaplin, already a Karno employee, persuaded Fred Karno that his sibling should be enlisted. The

The People's Jesters

cross-references are again heavy; there will be a fuller exploration of the Karno enterprise in the chapter on comic groups. Suffice it here to say that, beset by the careful watch of the 'legitimate' managers on continuous dialogue outside their bailiwicks, Fred Karno had pioneered the notion of 'speechless comedians', miming with body language of extensive vocabulary. Stan Laurel was adept and spry as the eponymous Jimmy the Fearless, in the sketch of that name, while Charlie Chaplin graduated to become the convincing drunk in the *Mumming Birds* sketch, the most popular of the Karno products.

The 'eccentric' and 'grotesque' comics on the Karno circuit were not unlike the red-nosed clowns that were all the rage in the American vaudeville, the transatlantic equivalent of music hall, and Karno companies toured the United States with fruitful gain. Both comics were, therefore, in the United States just before World War I. In 1913 Charlie Chaplin was tempted by Mack Sennett's Keystone Film Company by the offer of $150 a week. In 1915 Stan Laurel — he adopted the new surname on the advice of his common law wife and stage partner, Mae Dahlberg — also added filming to his vaudeville exploits.

Both, incidentally, were also alike in that, perhaps in some sort of punishment for their obsessive attention to the filmic craft, they underwent chaotic private lives. Charlie Chaplin was notorious for his penchant for the nubile nymphet, finding eventual contentment with Oona O'Neill (1925-1991; they married in 1943), the daughter of the playwright, Eugene O'Neill. Stan Laurel had a string of disastrous marriages, including two to the same bride.

STARS TO FETTLE THEE
from the Mancunian Film Studios

Advertising Mancunian Films, the provincial studios where many comedians, like Jimmy Clitheroe and Tessie O'Shea, sought to become film stars

Returning to the professional arena, it was now that Charlie Chaplin began to outstretch his rival from the ranks of Fred Karno. By 1916 he commanded a salary of $10,000 a week and in 1917 he was contracted for $1m, making him one of the best paid people in the world, something unheard of in the often penurious haunts of show business. These were the years in which he developed the character of 'the little tramp'. The very titles of the beautifully etched two-reelers of this time — *The Tramp, The Immigrant, The Pawnshop* — are self-explanatory. Few will need to be reminded of the tight fitting bowler, the smirking face and the twitching moustache, the twirling cane, the three o'clock feet and, in deliberate satire on the then flickering images of rudimentary filming, the stuttering walk. 'The son of a bitch is a ballet dancer', exclaimed W C Fields, the American vaudevillian, not without something of irascible despair, for Chaplin's acrobatic routines, honed in the Karno factory, added an extra dimension that few could emulate.

Charlie Chaplin aspired to appeal to the intelligentsia as well as the populace, in the same way that Charles Dickens had striven to attract critical as well as popular acclaim. To this end, he endeavoured – another Dickensian device — to combine fun and sentiment in harmony, knowing that the key to intellectual applause would be tragic-comedy. For example, his routines with the blind flower girl or when he is reduced to eating his boots have some of this quality, as well as demonstrating his balletic, light-footed, circus-like expertise.

The Kid, with Jackie Coogan in the title-role and produced in 1921, was the first major presentation of this motif. It was followed by such successes as *The Gold Rush* (1924) *City Lights* (1931) and *Modern Times* (1936),

one of the last mainline silent feature films. Charlie Chaplin knew that he would have to embrace the world of the talking pictures, and this he did with the avowedly political *The Great Dictator* (1940), his heartfelt, dark burlesque of Adolf Hitler. It was perhaps appropriate that, as the present writer walked home, as a child, after watching this movie, the sirens sounded and bombs began to crunch.

Charlie Chaplin made one or two more full-length films, wherein drama and sentiment overwhelmed the comic elements and about which there is some critical controversy. Such argument does not reach back to sully the repute of his 'silent' output. Driven perhaps by his childhood rebuffs to be a self-important, suspicious and even mercenary adult; with his ostentatious wealth at odds with the impoverished configuration of his creation, and with his knighthood long delayed because of American prurience about his sexuality and panic about his left-wing politics, he still remains the original icon of film-making. 'I am a citizen of the world', he cried, and, for all the self-adulation of that slogan, there was the truth in it that the silent film needed no translation and formed an international language, a kind of visual Esperanto. Charlie Chaplin died in Switzerland in 1977, aged 88.

In most walks of cultural life there are just one or two genuine icons, like Pele in football, Walt Disney in the field of animation or Elvis Presley in popular music. In the world of film, Charlie Chaplin rates that degree of eminence. He is to the cinema what William Caxton is to printing or James Watt to the steam engine.

Stan Laurel's opening film ventures were less spectacular and salient. It was 1927 before, in *Slipping Wives*, he made his first film with the rotund Oliver 'Babe' Hardy, the beginnings of a joint image of the regulation fat and thin partners, suited and bowler-hatted, that still has a ready resonance to this day. They made over a hundred films together, 30 of them silent, but, even in their 'talkies', it is often the mime that remains the most expressive aspect of their performance. Critics usually regard their best work as the short 20 minute cameos they produced between 1929 and 1935, among them the classic *The Music Box*, involving the delivery of a piano up a steep incline to a house. They went on to make feature length movies, such as *Sons of the Desert, Way Out West, The Flying Deuces* and *Blockheads*, and they sometimes abandoned their conventional garb for the costumes of the foreign legion or the air pilot

Oliver Hardy, a genial actor from Georgia, was the first to acknowledge that Stan Laurel was the master planner, the comic genius behind their hilarious stratagems. Olly Hardy, content with his golf and his family, conceded that role to the obsessive perfectionist, Stan Laurel, who spent hours over editing and checking and trying out material. In essence, their comedy began in blandly ordinary situations, wherefrom disaster then spiralled, the anarchic ratchet towards chaos turned by the dignified chagrin of Hardy and the flustered nervousness of Laurel, until Oliver Hardy delivered the ultimate verdict: 'this is another fine mess you've gotten me into.' There has been little on stage or on film to match the harmony of this close-knit duo, the whimpering bathos and the uneasily twirled hair of the one and the elephantine smugness and the embarrassedly twiddled tie of the other forming a delicious compound of mellow humour. It was a hymn to an imperishable friendship, racked by constant social and domestic buffets.

They did a stage tour of England in 1947 and made their last film in 1952. Oliver Hardy died in 1957 and Stan Laurel in 1965. Although Charlie Chaplin will ever remain supreme as the highbrows' darling clown and cinema hero, there are many who actually find the playlets of Laurel and Hardy more endearingly amusing and barely a week goes by without one of their short films being repeated on our television sets. What is remarkable is that these two Englishmen, coming from the same Karno stable and at the same time, should create and set the standards for American film comedy from its onset.

In turn, they influenced British comedians. Laurel and Hardy obviously encouraged the interplay of the double act, on stage and on film, and on both sides of the Atlantic. Charlie Chaplin was, again obviously, the forerunner of the bathetic comedian, the one who hoped that audiences would weep for him or, at least, love him, as well as laugh at him. Most were to find that it takes a particular kind of complex genius to evoke genuine sympathy at the same moment as real laughter. The slide into mawkishness is the predictable hazard.

George Formby and Will Hay

Two English comedians contrived to produce films that were not mere representations of their stage act, but which had some pretence to being cinematically satisfying in their own right. Nonetheless, in background, style and personality, these two men, George Formby and Will Hay could hardly have been more different.

George Hoy Booth was born in 1904 in Wigan, the eldest of James Lawler Booth's (aka George Formby Senior) largish family, and, having left school at seven to train as a jockey, he was near illiterate all his life. On the premature death of his father in 1922, his mother encouraged him to adopt the paternal persona, although he had never seen his father, reluctant for his children to have stage careers, perform. As George Hoy, he made his debut at the Earlestown Hippodrome but soon renamed himself as George Formby. In 1924 he married the clog dancer, Beryl Ingram, who gradually took complete control of his destiny and the management of his burgeoning career. In a grimly prescient glance at their future personal life, they performed a honeymoon sketch, with George as the backward groom and Beryl as the forward bride. She helped switch him from the rather complex 'John Willie' of his father's carefully observed creation to the more straightforward toothily grinning, optimistic, naïve Lancashire lad, while, crucially, he became an adept of the banjulele, the pupil of Sam Paul, a pierrot banjo-player.

The infectiously rhythmic jangle of his surprisingly deft right hand became, on stage, record, radio and film, one of the landmark sounds of the 1930s. With something of Donald Duck about the countenance, he sang away in jaunty mood, the lyrics a musical version of seaside postcards and a melodic tribute to the Freudian potency of phallic symbolism. From the *Little Stick of Blackpool Rock* to the *Little Ukulele in His Hand*, these were hymns to the tense repressions and frustrations of communities where sexuality was blanketed by convention and fear. In choosing the window cleaner and Mr Wu the laundryman for his chief depictions, George Formby had spotted the occupations where voyeurism might be endemic. They were harmless enough and, delivered with the broadest of grins and with a characteristic jutting of the neck to underpin the obvious, they amounted, from his *Aunty Maggie's Remedy* to *His Grandad's Flan-*

nelette Nightshirt, a tuneful succession of what might be called 'single entendres.' All in all, he recorded 189 of these songs, not forgetting romantic exceptions like *Leaning on a Lamp-post*, one of the defining love-songs of the era.

The background of William Thomson Hay was very different. Will Hay was born in Stockton-on-Tees in 1888 into an engineering family of some respectability. He had a reasonable schooling and worked as a commercial correspondent in Manchester, where, in 1907, he married Gladys Perkins, a postmaster's daughter. Unlike the childless Formbys, they had three children, two of whom, Will Junior and Gladys, followed their father on the stage. Unlike the downtrodden George Formby, Will Hay seldom permitted his wife the upper hand – she is reported as complaining that it was not much fun being married to a comedian – and the marriage broke down in 1934. He formed a subsequent relationship with a Norwegian showgirl, the rather ambiguously named Randi Kopstadt. There was no Randi Kopstadt for poor old George Formby: Beryl Formby kept a beady eye on him. His pocket money was limited; his film heroines were changed constantly — and he only kissed one on screen — it was Googie Withers – a stolen shot when Beryl was temporarily off the set. On one occasion when Beryl was absent, George, according to another of these pretty starlets, asked her if she was interested in 'a bit of hanky-panky', scarcely the most sophisticated of romantic overtures and a reminder that George Formby was probably psychologically closer to his material than one might imagine.

Before World War I, Will Hay had embarked on a stage career, including some experience, like many another, with Fred Karno, and he now developed his character of the Schoolmaster Comedian. His first sketch, *Bend Over*,

The People's Jesters

was inspired by the anecdotes of his school-mistress sister, Elspeth, while from about 1920 he performed his mainstream playlet, *The Fourth Form at St Michael's*, a portrayal that was to command national attention and delighted esteem. With a small troupe of three or four 'boys', including, at varied times, his two nephews and his own son, on stage and on radio, his name became for decades the by-word for the blustering, ineffectual, ill-fated teacher. The husky, querulous voice; the clever use of the sniff and the cough, and the eyeglasses that were the spot-light on his versatile range of expressions, from devious to irritated to complacent to despairing – this was a three-dimensional characterisation of some stature. He was known to refuse to use a line in a script, not because it was unfunny,

GEORGE FORMBY 1904-61

The banjo-strumming innocent abroad, George Formby, the slightly unexpected and devastating success as a film star

but because Dr Muffin would not have said it, and he would wax eloquently for some time about the frustrated life and embittering experience of his fictional other, an interesting example of something akin to 'method' acting on the variety stage.

Where George Formby was barely literate, Will Hay was a Fellow of the Royal Astronomical Society, who discovered a white spot on Saturn's surface in 1933 and published *Through My Telescope* in 1935. Having entertained the troops with Fred Karno in the 1914-1918 War, he was to be found occasionally lecturing them on astronomy in the

1939-1945 War. For his courageous part, George Formby – last out, it is said, before Dunkirk and first in after D-Day – sung to something like 3m service men and women during World War II, often in precarious situations. Where Will Hay was privately an austere and caustic, if much respected figure, George Formby was regarded with great affection, and one should never forget that, on post-war tours of South Africa, both George and the bravely outspoken Beryl Formby were unyielding in their uncomplicated opposition to Apartheid.

Yet, for all these contrasts, these were the two comedians who mastered the cinematic art more profitably than any of their colleagues. Will Hay was able to transfer his mastery of expression to the screen, which, indeed, enhanced it, while his slowest of double takes, not unlike those of the American comedian and film actor, Jack Benny, were also very valuable on film. Another aid was the adaptability of his caricature of the schoolmaster. This was basically an exercise in reduced and inadequate authority, and so, for the cinema, he was able to depict the evasions and dreads of the failing sea captain, fire chief, prison governor, civil servant, police sergeant and disbarred solicitor. He made eighteen films between 1934 and 1944, most notably accompanied by Graham 'Albert' Moffatt (1919-1965) and Moore 'Harbottle' Marriott (1885-1949), as insolent paunchy boy and wizened, irascible old-timer. Their best work together has been favourably compared with that of the Marx Brothers.

The eighteen titles include *Good Morning, Boys, Ask a Policeman, The Ghost of St Michael's, The Goose Steps Out* and *My Learned Friend*. Most critics give the accolade to *Oh, Mr Porter!* (1937), with Will Hay as the anxious stationmaster of Buggleskelly in a film that some regard as the best British comedy of all time.

Through precisely the same period, George Formby was proving a huge success in films, so much so that, by the late 1930s and into the 1940s, he was the top male star, the highest paid British entertainer and, in a peculiar political quirk, the most well-known person in the USSR after Joseph Stalin. After a couple of films with Mancunian Films, Basil Dean signed him on for the Ealing studios and later he made, under the logo of his own company, pictures for Columbia Films. In all, he made twenty movies. The formula was less intellectually exacting than that of Will Hay, but there was one sameness. George Formby was able to clothe his gauche northern innocent abroad in the costume of a variety of tradesmen, such as the gramophone engineer or the photographer. *It's in the Air, Trouble Brewing* and *Spare a Copper* are usually regarded as the jolliest of the series. With scuttling feet and cries of 'ooh mother', this childlike innocent would negotiate a set of distressing accidents and traps to emerge triumphant in his role, be it airman, jockey or motor cyclist, and with his girl, the ever sane, sisterly, rather brusque object of his diffident attentions. 'It's turned out nice again', he would gaily smile. Tricked out with the inclusion of three or four ukulele numbers, they were universally enjoyed, with his working class audiences vicariously pleased that one of their own had won through against awful adversity – just as he always appeared dinner-jacketed in his Blackpool summer shows, evidence that he had 'got on.' It has been recorded that an anti-Hitler sequence in *Let George Do It* (1940) was one of the biggest morale-boosters in the early years of the war.

Slowly, legend and fact merged in the Formby household. Then, on Christmas Day, 1960,

George Formby was released from his dominatrice, when the formidable Beryl Formby died, the simple-minded Roman Catholic freed from the Gauleiter bondage of the militant atheist. To much astonishment, he became engaged six weeks later to Pat Howson, a young school teacher. However, he had suffered a heart attack during the run of the West End musical, *Zip Goes a Million*, which opened in 1951 and his health had been very shaky. This embodiment of good nature was denied his own final reward of some domestic contentment. He died in 1961, just before his planned nuptials, leaving a trail of family litigation over his wealth, with his mother and siblings (two of whom – brother Frank and sister Lou – had not very distinguished stage careers) in dispute with the disappointed fiancée, and lurid tales about suitcases full of banknotes being spirited out of the Formby Blackpool residence, 'Beryldene'. Few comedians have been so widely mourned – and, for his part and whatever the emotional downside, George Formby never failed to recognise that, without his resolute partner, he would have been nothing.

Will Hay, the epitome of the floundering but stealthy incompetent, based his school, Narkover, on the Beachcomber column in the *Daily Express*, but there was a profounder cultural resonance. With crumpled gown and scruffy mortar board, he presented the image of the minor private boarding school to millions who had left school at twelve or thirteen and who had no direct experience of such niceties as 'prep' and 'dorms' and the like. Nonetheless, such had been the long indoctrination of the young by the school tales of, most importantly, the Magnet and Gem comics, with Billy Bunter and Harry Wharton and his pals forever lodged inside Greyfriars School, that everyone perfectly understood every last nuance of the Will Hay canon. Will Hay himself fell ill in 1946 and died in Chelsea in 1949, still honoured as the supreme caricaturist of the schoolmaster.

A final sociological observation and a final contrast might be to point out that they each represented a separate strand of human existence in the Britain of the 1930s. George Formby was the artless working class hero, at a time of woeful depression, who somehow, professionally and personally, managed to transcend the oppressive confines of proletarian life. Will Hay was a figure, Falstaffian in that he engaged some sympathy as well as much hilarious scoffing, of the suburbs, a lower middle class aspirer after professional respectability. As J B Priestley perceptively asserted, the rise of suburban England, with its prim estates and lengthy lanes of semis, was just as significant an aspect of Britain in the inter-wars years as the furtherance of the tough if warm-hearted and compact industrial communities. George Formby and Will Hay produced characters and pictures that drew affectionately and amusingly from both sides of that society.

There were others who contributed to the filmic genre, but no other British comedian, qua comedian, quite made so great an impact in transition from theatre to cinema, so much so that we are now apt to recall, with the assistance of television repeats, these two stars as cinematic rather than their theatrical personages, even recognising how potent their stage presence was.

The screen-plays of George Formby and Will Hay carry us forward chronologically to the latter days of World War II, for thereafter the British fashion changed to a combine of costume dramas, like *The Wicked Lady*, with Margaret Lockwood, and gently satiric Ealing comedies, such as *Passport to Pimlico*. During the rest of the text, we shall encounter more comics with cinematic pretensions, although, in the wake of Will Hay, one finds that in the more successful instances the borderline between comedian and comic actor (the old meaning of 'comedian') blurs: Peter Sellars is probably the supreme example of that blurring. Terry-Thomas is another. Thomas Terry Hoar-Stevens (1911—1990) was the gapped-toothed silly ass, with the Wooster accent, who became the American ideal of the upper class English dolt. He was in over 30 movies between 1956 and 1978, among them *Carleton Browne of the FO* (1958) and *Those Magnificent Men in their Flying Machines* (1965).

The cinema remained, then, for the comic, mainly an opportunity to test his stage-craft against the cameras, not a chance, as a rule, to discover new skills. On the other hand, radio continued to provide just such a chance. In the next chapter we shall make a fairly rapid return to the studios of the BBC to scrutinise its novel comic output in the immediate post-war years and to glean what lessons comedians were learning about their trade.

7 · RADIO REVISITED

It is chronologically advisable to pay another fairly quick return visit to the world of the 'wireless' before embarking on a tour of comic styles, such as stand-up or crosstalk comedians. This is because there was a rich flow of mirthsome lava from the active volcano of the BBC in the immediate post-war years. The 1939-1945 War was and will remain the only major war in which radio was the dominant means of communication. It was a challenge that the BBC met with vigorous application. With 10m wireless licenses purchased in 1939, it meant that the BBC was in communion with the entire nation. During the war the BBC stepped up production radically. It was soon broadcasting in 47 rather than in eight languages; its staff grew from 4000 to 12,000; its transmitters increased from 23 to 138; its hours of broadcasting trebled from 50 to 150 hours a day, with the Home Programme and the Forces Programme at the hub. It was a magnificent response to the call to arms and it served the country well then and thereafter.

The disappearance of John Reith and the loosening, a consequence of warfare, of the censorious bonds produced a wider range of broadcasting, amid which comedy was an important element. Radio was, for a significant period, the main cultural fare of the nation. With the BBC more or less the monopoly supplier, there was an extraordi-nary sense of national togetherness, as, at one and the same time, a huge majority of the population listened to the same programme. That degree of immediacy and incidence was dramatic.

It should be re-emphasised that the radio continued to have an influence on the evolution of British comedy and comedians that the cinema never quite managed. Comedians, like Frank Randle or Tommy Trinder, from north and south respectively, made inexpensive films of passing popularity, but they did not much add to their existing comic persona. Indeed, many of these comics, all of whom will appear under later headings, seem to have made one or two films, almost as if it were part of their professional obligation. Few could have felt they did their talent justice or, at least, that they had surpassed what they had accomplished in the theatre.

It is true that American cinema comedy was largely invested in comedians as such, although it might be argued that, as in the United Kingdom, the higher and more substantial degrees of comic excellence were achieved by actors, after the manner of Cary Grant, a film star who, oddly enough (until you think about it) was something of a hero of Ken Dodd's. Nonetheless, the American comedians made sharper, funnier movies than their English prototypes. After Laurel and Hardy, there were the Marx Brothers, capitalising on their vaudeville skills, honed in pre-film theatrical extravaganzas, and, migrating from their distinctive success on American radio, the likes of the serenely composed Jack Benny or the ebulliently cocky Bob Hope. Jack Benny feasted off his stage meanness: when the highway man, shouted 'stand and deliver; your money or your life', he was forced to repeat the alternatives; 'I'm thinking', muttered Jack Benny. Bob Hope, territorially a Briton, born in 1903 in Eltham, not far from where Frankie Howerd lived, was, armed by a squad of gag-writers, the master of the one-liner, pushing his cowardice as noisily as Jack Benny quietly played the miser's card: 'would you hit a man wearing glasses' – 'you're not wearing glasses' – 'I could have my eyes tested.' Especially in the 'Road' films with Bing Crosby, where he invariably failed to win the girl, in the saronged figure of Dorothy Lamour, he was very popular on both sides of the Atlantic.

This certainly had an effect on British stage and perhaps radio comedy, but it had little or no effect on cinematic comedy in the UK, where brilliant actors – Alec Guinness; Alastair Sim – now starred in more sophisticated English comedies for the cinema, understated, wry and poignant. Conversely, radio continued, for some years, to be a driving engine of comedy, the crucial difference being its self-evident lack of the visual similarity of stage and screen. In brief, the concentration on vocalism, with the pictures being self-painted in the listeners' imagination, made for a critical change of attack with a glittering, pyrotechnical display of linguistics.

The sheer construct of radio programming was also significant. One might see a comedian once a year in a film, whereas radio was a weekly encounter. Unknowns were rarely risked in comic films; comedians had to have earned some degree of fame on stage and radio before it might be anticipated that the public would acknowledge them as film stars. The voracious appetite of radio meant that many young comedians were able to find something of a foothold thereon. Radio offered, therefore, opportunities both to ideas and to people, where the cinema – from the comedians' standpoint – remained conventional. Put pragmatically, radio was where you made your name; cinema was where you might luckily make a little money and reinforce the modicum of fame you had acquired on stage and through broadcasting.

Routeways – the Comedy Series

There were, by and large, two main roads to radio success for comedians in those first post-war years, as there had been during the war itself. One was a regular booking in a showcase variety series, where, if good fortune and good talent prevailed, the regularity might reach the largesse of a weekly or fortnightly spot. The other was a close involvement in a weekly comedy series of a more 'magazine' sort of character.

In an age of brains trusts, both general and – gardening; cookery – particular, and parlour games, there were one or two comedy shows to match. *Ignorance is Bliss*, with the Canadian boxing commentator, Stewart MacPherson, and then the Irish presenter Eamonn Andrews, of *This Is Your Life* fame, as question-master, set unexacting posers – 'who wrote Winston Churchill's autobiography?' – for the plump Gladys Hay (Will Hay's daughter), the mock-upper crusted Michael Moore, and Hal Berens (1902-1995), a Glaswegian Jew of enormous stamina as light comic and character player, with his contemptuous cry of 'wot a geezer'. Later there was *Does the Team Think?*, an excuse for comedians, with Ted Ray in the van and the likes of Tommy Trinder, Cyril Fletcher and Jimmy Edwards in valiant support, to launch a thousand quips.

However, the excellent immediate post-war successor – and it was a worthy one – to *ITMA* was *Take It From Here*, even if the acronym *TIFH* never quite had the magic of its distinguished predecessor. The fruit of the hybrid genius of Frank Muir and Denis Norden, themselves emerging from service life and making their genial way in the world, *Take It From Here* had languished at first, having been first launched in 1948, but, as it greased its own wheels and rid itself of unwieldy bits, it began to shine. It benefited hugely from the demise of *ITMA*, and its three repeats per week, and, with a young and relatively inexperienced team, it was mustered to fill the gap. It survived until 1959.

The *TIFH* trio had met one another on the wartime show, *Navy Mixture*, produced by Charles Maxwell and it was he who recruited the writers and artists for the new, sophisticated series. Along with Jimmy Edwards, Joy Nichols, a young singer, and her fellow-Australian, the more experienced Richard Bentley were the originals, with the female role later being taken by June Whitfield, the beginnings of a grand career in all branches of the comic art. In an expressly determined lifting of cultural sights, *TIFH* was fast-paced and satirical, never talking down to the listening audience, almost as if asserting that, having had the gumption to win a war together, we had the intelligence to laugh at clever, pertinent jokes. At the risk of an extravagant comparison, where *ITMA* shone fiercely like Charles Dickens, *TIFH* gleamed spicily like Jane Austen.

Yet there was a casual, what would now be called 'laid-back' aspect to the format, signified by the catchy signature tune, *It was*

Just one of those Things, 'a trip to the moon on gossamer wings', a sense of release, as with the war well-won, one could relax and, simply, take it from here. There was a conversation piece about one of the threesome's activities, a skit on a topical news item and, memorably, a colourful burlesque of a cinematic genre, such as the western, the costume drama or the Roman epic ('Roman soldiers from the right number', with the response coming in spoken Roman numerals – 'eye; eye-eye; eye-eye-eye; eye-vee' and so on.)

In later years, and probably even more memorably, the salient sketch was the Glum family. Jimmy Edwards was the raunchy dad, with his hesitant son, Ron, played by Richard Bentley and the patient Eth by June Whitfield. Pa Glum's lewd misconstructions and Eth's vain attempts to awaken the feeblest spark – 'Oh Ron' ... 'Yes, Eth?' – in her tepid boy-friend's libido, was, for some commentators, a switch of direction in public taste. The show had its fair ration of catchphrases – Wallas Eaton's despairing wail of 'Come 'ome, Jim Edwards' or Jimmy Edwards' own 'Gently, Bentley' – but was much more reliant on smart word-play, items of which, as in the best days of *ITMA*, were circulating all the public areas the following morning.

If *TIFH* did not quite light the fuse of Jimmy Edwards' comic vocation, it certainly sent it into orbit. James Keith O'Neill Edwards was born in 1920, among the white-picketed fences of Barnes, Surrey, the son of R W K Edwards, professor of mathematics. St Paul's Cathedral School and King's College, Wimbledon, where he began his lifelong affair with the trombone, were his schools and St John's, Cambridge, where he adorned the Cambridge Footlights, his college. His war record with the RAF was exemplary; he won the Distinguished Flying Cross in 1945 on a hazardous mission dropping supplies to paratroops stranded at Arnhem. The raffish moustache that decorated his rascally countenance was useful as a comic prop but it also helped to hide the burns he suffered during that incident.

He developed, almost in paternal parody, his professorial act at Cambridge and in forces shows, before taking it to the Windmill Theatre, where he stayed for some eighteen months, until he had a contractual tiff with the owner, Vivian Van Damm. The bullish, overbearing personage he embodied took root on stage as well as on radio – his roar of 'wake up at the back there' was as much an admonition of purported pupils as, at the Windmill, an exhortation to the dirty mac brigade awaiting the return of the nudes. He had other entertainments on radio and in the theatre, for instance, with Eric Sykes' *Big Bad Mouse* in the early 1980s.

His chief stage act was as the irascible and boorish schoolmaster. Obviously, it owed much to Will Hay in broad terms. Like Narkover, his school was Chiselbury, with a Hay-like bow to the dreary connection of school, especially boarding school, and prison. Like Will Hay, he wore the mortar board and gown. Unlike Will Hay, with his agonisingly claustrophobic class of three or four boys, Jimmy Edwards treated the audience as his form, shouting threats and questions in all directions – 'why did the Australian go in the bush? – that boy, go and wash your mouth out'. There was no need for the audiences' sneaking sympathy, as with the beleaguered Will Hay; Jimmy Edwards, bucolic and assured, brooked no mischief. Plainly, it was more superficial and less well observed than the painstaking care of the Will Hay characterisation, for it was played for guffawing belly-laughs by the boisterous pedagogue. He was a more cheery Mr Squeers, where Will Hay was a less learned

Mr Chips. The formula was transferred to television as *Whack-o!* in 1957/61 and 1971/72. There were occasional re-workings of the basic character, as when he stood as an assertive Jimmunist candidate for parliament, the audience now a political meeting – 'the housing shortage is merely a rumour spread about by those who have nowhere to live'; 'everything is going up; even eggs are going up – the hens have lost all sense of direction.'

He carried some of this rumbustiousness into his everyday life. He spent his money on a farm, polo ponies and a plane. He became a latter-day squire in Sussex, a Yorrocks figure, the Master of the Old Surrey and Burstow Hunt and the failed, not Jimmunist, but Conservative candidate for Paddington North in the 1964 general election. There was a more uneasy side to this portrayal of the roguish schoolmaster and the yeoman gentleman. In 1958 he married Valerie Seymour, only to shock her on honeymoon with the news that he was a homosexual, anxious to reform, while the later announcement by Ramon Douglas, an Australian female impersonator, that Jimmy Edwards and he had shared a lengthy covert relationship revealed even further how strained the comedian's life must have been behind the façade of disruptive, boisterous confidence. Jimmy Edwards was, it seems, the last of the schoolmaster comedians. Did the end of the century long provision of schoolboy fiction about boys in boarding schools – with the *Hotspur's Red Circle* perhaps the last of those secluded establishments – cut off the information flow about fags and about midnight feasts in the dorm that made the Hay/Edwards formula comprehensible to ordinary folk who had never been near such a place? Jimmy Edwards died in London in 1988, aged 68.

Routeways – the Showcase Programme

The other radio roadway was to find recurring employment on one of the BBC's popular variety programmes. Frankie Howerd came to national prominence as the 'resident' comedian on *Variety Bandbox*, a show that, with its mid-Sunday evening spotlight, commanded large audiences and attracted stars on their day off from stage-work. The BBC had always demonstrated a liking for 'resident' acts and ensembles, such as the BBC Dance Orchestra, led first by Jack Payne and then Henry Hall. The 'residence' of Arthur Askey and Dickie Murdoch at the top of Broadcasting House was a mild lampoon of that convention. Frankie Howerd operated weeks about with Derek Roy, a fast-talking gagster, known as 'The Fun Doctor'. He had been a singer (he recorded *With these Hands*) and light comedian with the Geraldo orchestra and, while never hitting the heights that Frankie Howerd attained, he never shrank down to the lows either. He had a steady career and he died in 1981. Borrowing from the Crosby/Hope convention of mutually affectionate insults, they jibbed at one another on those alternative Sundays of post-Reithian merriment.

Like Jimmy Edwards, Francis Alick Howard survived World War II to seek stardom, but his provenance was different. Born in 1917 in York, the son of a regular soldier, he soon moved to Eltham at the dictates of the military, when his father was transferred to Woolwich. He died when Frankie Howerd was a teenager and his mother, Edith Howard (the 'a' was changed to an 'e' for stage purposes) became his chief prop and comforter, as he essayed a vocation that was at once a terror and a lure to him. The author once saw him as a guest of the British Rail chairman, Sir Peter Parker, at the opening of a refurbished London Bridge Station. Asked to do a brief turn, he fussed obsessively about where he would stand in a hotel dining room, what effect the windows and curtains behind him would have – and then, for five minutes, was a comedy treat. That ceaseless search for and worry about perfection was both strength and weakness, giving him something of the introverted self-absorption of a master cricketer, such as Geoffrey Boycott.

From one viewpoint, his apprenticeship was normal enough; the church drama group; the plays at his school, Shooters Hill grammar school; the army concert parties, particularly with the Royal Artillery at Shoeburyness, Essex (his early stage act was often performed in rather untidy soldier's kit); the Co-odments concert party at Southend-on-sea, where he met both his purportedly deaf and mock-maligned accompanists, Vera Roper and Blanche Moore. From another viewpoint, it was an oddly disjointed start, one that epitomised his life's work. He failed disastrously in an attempt to enter RADA and he constantly found that his presentation of self-denigration and embittered banter engaged with no middle ground of opinion. He appeared to be either hailed as an original or mutely dismissed as an incompetent. As opposed to, say, the workmanlike smartness of the more prototypical Derek Roy, his shambling gait, his interpolations of sighs and groans, his reluctance actually to relate a joke, his dependence at best on a rambling shaggiest of dog stories and on his constant critique of his employers, his colleagues, his watchers, his conditions and himself was unusual.

After a spell in 1946 at the Stage Door Canteen, the forces' social club in London, he was booked for *Variety Bandbox* and, for him, this had the same effect as *Take It From Here* for Jimmy Edwards. His prissy disparage-

Tony Hancock, the creative genius who made both radio and television the servants of his essentially button-holing comedy

ment of self and others, discussed in tones of exceptional range and with a spread of usages – 'Ladies and Gentle-men'; 'Hearken, hearken to Francis'; 'I was amazed'; 'Titter ye not at the Afflicted' – was ideally suited to the radio and to the times. Jack Payne and then Stanley Dale managed him, controversially and sometimes unfairly, but he did find solace in business and creative engagement with Eric Sykes, a name that turns up in several comedic biographies; Johnny Speight, the Frankenstein of Alf Garnett, the TV monster; the 'Steptoe' writers, Ray Galton and Alan Simpson; Spike Milligan and Tony Hancock.

His credits included more radio, in, for instance, his own *Frankie's Bandbox*; films, such as *The Runaway Bus* (1954); a Roman holiday of theatrical achievement with *A Funny Thing Happened on the Way to the Forum* (1956) and its televisual spin-off, *Up Pompeii* (1962), scripted by Talbot Bothwell, of 'Carry On' fame; in fact, Frankie Howerd appeared on the *Carry On Doctor* tile of that pruriently bawdy cinematic mosaic. He also made a comeback in 1960s, following a downturn in his fortunes, as a mildly blistering satirist at Peter Cook's Establishment Club and on the soft-centred BBC *That Was The Week That Was*, hosted by the then nose-thumbing David Frost.

His was always a snakes and ladders sort of career. Frankie Howerd contrived to combine self-belief in his comic mission with self-loathing about his vocational chances. It made of him a not always cosy companion, for his temperament was mercurial, bordering, at times, on the neurotic. Like Jimmy Edwards, he suffered from sexual demons, a homosexual before such actions were socially or legally acceptable, and given, whatever the explanations, to uncomfortably misappropriate behaviour. First the actor, Lee Young and

then, with loyalty and discretion in difficult circumstances, the waiter and later Frankie Howerd's personal manager and attendant, Dennis Heymer, were his mainstay partners. The extremes of his personal perhaps reflected those of his professional existence. He died in Somerset in 1999, aged 71.

Frankie Howerd's material has been described as 'conversational inuendo'. He exhibited a slightly camp mien, with a gamut of body and spoken language that shifted from outrage to fear to dismay to offence. Essentially, he was a gossip, always believing, as gossips do, the worst of everybody and everything, with his objects of tittle-tattle and scandal updated to suit the needs of the post-war decades. One way of describing his caricature would be to suggest that he was an old-style 'dame' in rather slovenly masculine dress. There was something of Norman Evans in his shocked revelations about those who employed him and his dismissive contempt of those around him. At its best, it was a full and comprehensive piece of characterisation, bitingly observed and, with every 'ooh' and 'ahh' perfectly rehearsed and intoned, a masterly demonstration of the comic art. His artful control of his audiences was not unlike that of George Robey in his annoyance with their unseemly response. It is a pity he did not find a little more contentment in his genius.

On to the Goons

There were other examples, some of which – Peter Brough, the ventriloquist; Jimmy Clitheroe, the boy-man comedian; the nonpareil Tony Hancock – are to be covered in chapters relating to their specialism, even if their success did have a decided broadcasting bent. A more straightforward instance than either these specialists or, indeed, Jimmy Edwards and Frankie Howerd, is Ted Ray.

Charles Olden was born in 1909 in Wigan, the son of a jobbing comic singer, Charlie Alden. Having flirted with professional football, he became, in turn, one of the double act Wardle and Olden; Hugh Neek (Unique) and Nedlo (Olden reversed) the Gypsy Fiddler, before, in 1930, he finally settled on Ted Ray, the name of a winning golfer of the time. 'Fiddling and Fooling' was his bill-matter, for he played the violin and cracked jokes. He was not alone in that respect. Apart from Vic Oliver, there was, for example, Jimmy Wheeler, Harry Bailey and Stanelli. The brusque Jimmy Wheeler (1910-1971) graduated from a double act with his father, 'the Sailor and the Porter', as Wheeler and Wilson, to a single turn, interrupting his violin playing with rudimentary gags, like 'my father said beer never hurt anyone and then a barrel fell on his head'. Harry Bailey was an Irish version, pausing in his fiddle-playing to relate how Mrs O'Brien's 28 children had left her in good order but the stork was dying. Stanelli (Edward Stanley de Groot, died 1971) was an accomplished musician and quite a suave comic. His musical bedstead-cum-wind instrument was a clever piece of apparatus and he told, alongside the fiddling, some good tales, although his inclusion of stutterers and other unfortunates among the subjects might leave him open to moral attack in the present day. On a less controversial note, he told of a little Lancastrian girl who declared, after a night in the air raid shelter, 'ee bai gum, mum, me bum's numb'.

Ted Ray was unusual in that, rather than adopting the outlandish working class garb of Jimmy Wheeler or the sleek evening wear of Stanelli, he eschewed either of the two mainstream comedic costumes and opted for ordinariness. He was one of the first comedians to wear a lounge suit and utilise a classless accent, with just a hint of mid-Atlantic twang. He tried to convey the notion, in his own words, that 'he had walked in from the street', or, as *The Times* described, him, he was 'the pub humorist relaxing with his friends'. Armed with a fiercesome memory, potent capacity for fast recall and unbeatable assurance, he was perhaps the nearest English equivalent to Bob Hope, seeking 'a big laugh every seven seconds'.

After a long but worthwhile schooling, inclusive of Palladium dates, Ted Ray earned meritorious reward with the radio series, *Ray's A Laugh*, a programme that ran for twelve years from 1949 and made his name. Curiously, contractual difficulties had prevented Ted Ray doing much broadcasting hitherto. It was a belated BBC essay in a Burns and Allen, wife-and-husband relationship, such has had been planned for Tommy Handley a decade earlier. The Australian singer and actress, Kitty Bluett, was enlisted as the intelligent, resigned wife in a programme that combined bits of sit-com with bits of comedy magazine. Fred Yule, an *ITMA* survivor, the comic actors Kenneth Connor and Graham Stark, the musical duo, who also added to the gaiety as players, Bob and Alf Pearson, and a tyro Peter Sellers were all drafted. There were the by now traditional catchphrases – 'he's looovely, Mrs Hoskin'; 'if you've never been to Manchester, you haven't lived'; 'it was agony, Ivy' – and ITMA-style names – the criminal, Al K Traz or the Russian, Serge Suit. Patricia Hayes made her mark as Crystal Jollybottom – 'stop it, you saucebox'.

Ted Ray, as befitted his fashioning and the mood of the era, inhabited a rather featureless suburban plateau, the whole culture one of middle class predictability. In a fascinating departure from the comic norms, there was Ted Ray's portrayal of 'George, the Man with a Conscience', the conscience in question being played by Leslie Perrins. This was a

The People's Jesters

quietly amusing but thoughtful feature with something of an ethical dimension.

Ted Ray had a wholesome career, on radio, where he starred on shows like *Jokers Wild*, *Does the Team Think* and *Spot the Tune*, on stage and on television, where he appeared on the children's programme, *Jackanory*, and joined Kay Walsh in a brisk presentation of Noel Coward's *The Red Peppers*, a one-act tale of a music hall act. With his wife, the dancer, Dorothy Stevens, he led a conventionally affluent home counties lifestyle and his offspring sustained the 'fiddling and fooling', with Robin the musician and Andrew the actor. He died in hospital in Enfield in 1977.

The vocally gifted Peter Sellers went on, of course, to star in *The Goon Show* and move on to cinematic glories. *The Goon Show*, originating as *Crazy People* and first broadcast in 1951, was, like *ITMA* and *Take It From Here* before it, clouded in initial obscurity, but it won through to command and merit the loyalty of a brand new bright generation of listeners. Building on the surreal possibilities of radio, already mined by *ITMA*, an anarchic wartime series, *Danger; Men at Work*, and other shows, it perfected the concept of performing within the imaginations of the listeners. The 'Goon' itself was an idiotic Yeti-like figure, created by the American cartoonist, Elzie Segar, formulator of the Popeye model, and several commentators have noted how the show was, in fact, close to a sound cartoon. It was sound animation, with weird noises, strange accents and violent clashes all part of the mix. The pace was manic and the humour overtly enjoyed by its celebrants. With *ITMA* and *TIFH*, it rightly may be counted as one of radio's best three comedy series, as each responded ideally to the cultural call of a tight generational slice, one for the early 1940s, one for the late 1940s

and early 1950s, one for the late 1950s, the trio of programmes fitting snugly into radio's 'golden age'.

Analysts have pointed out the derivation of the characters, several of them stock comedy fare, such as rustic yokel of Eccles, the incoherent babbler of Bluebottle, the suave, plausible toff of Gryptype-Thynne, the doddering ancients of Minnie and Henry Crun, the melodrama villain of Moriarty and the Blimpian soldier of Major Bloodnock. However, the Goon performers gave them such bizarre and energetic life, partly because of the insane circumstances – the removal, for instance, of a completely occupied Dartmoor prison to the sunnier climes of the South of France, but mainly because of the inventive delights of the voices. There were identifying catchphrases and familiar linguistic devices, as in all radio series or, for that matter in all serialised novels à la Dickens, but, with the Goons, the joy lay chiefly in the flamboyant, lunatic range of intonations. It was the tone, rather than the words, ('how many sexes are there? – two - it's not enough, I say; go out and order some more') which adherents of the cult relished and tried to imitate, as they drank their coffee next morning on the university campuses and elsewhere.

There is little argument about the stature of *The Goon Show* as a pinnacle of radio comedy. It probably more nearly approached, as a broadcast comic equivalent, the best of atonal music, abstract sculpture and painting, modern verse and free association fiction. The question here is to what degree it furthered the careers of its talented performers as comedians.

The four founding protagonists were all ex-servicemen with a toehold in show-business via forces concert parties, dates at the Windmill Theatre and the like or on minor radio programmes. Michael Bentine (originally,

Michael James Bentin; 1922-1966), in a sample of nature imitating art, was an Etonian born in Watford, the son of a scientist from Peru, and he had some variety experience, billed as 'the Happy Imbecile', with his broken wooden chair and sink-plunger as props. Like some abstruse religious or political sect, he soon broke away from the quartet on ideological grounds and carried on in solitude, his *It's a Square World* on television in later years being a personal celebration of his take on absurdity. Later still, he seemed to dabble in deep thoughts and flirtations with the supernatural and wrote his memoirs, entitled *The Long Banana Skin.*

Harry Secombe, born in Swansea in 1921, was a more straightforward comic, who, with his variegated shaving routine and 'cod' duet of Nelson Eddy and Jeannette MacDonald on stage, had been recruited for radio shows like *Welsh Rarebit* and *Educating Archie.* Among the Goons, he was the jolly and optimistic Neddy Seagoon, the picaresque hero, as brave as Tom Jones or Nicholas Nickleby, taking to the crazy-paved road of those lunatic journeys. He would travel on, his rich singing voice an essential element in his performances, doing everything from panto to musicals, like Pickwick (*If I Ruled the World*), to be knighted, the decent personification of uncomplicated patriotism and homely religion. If, as a Goon, he threatened, like Samson, to pull down the columns of the temple, it was not long before, without menace and always of good cheer, he became a veritable pillar of the establishment.

Terence 'Spike' Milligan was the devisor of much of the material, with occasional assistance from Larry Stephens and, a name that flits in and out of these tales of post-war comedy, Eric Sykes. He was born in India in 1918 and forewent the joys of jazz trumpeting to become something of an icon for the surreal and alternative humorists of the next two generations. A deeply caring man, it is difficult to discern the borders between his public and private worlds, both of them beset with frantic and disruptive strains of perception. It certainly meant that, from a creative viewpoint, there was an unceasing torrent of sub-Carrollian fantasy and antilogic. The downside was that, perhaps, he could be indulgent, repetitive and ill-disciplined. Some of his copyists have occasionally reversed the precept, believing that to be formless is to be brilliant, whereas some would argue that true art requires shape and principle. Be that as it may, his influence on British comedy was to be quite telling.

Peter Sellers – Richard Henry Sellers, to grant him his full title – was born in Portsmouth in 1925, a mixture of Catholicism and Jewishness, as well as the entertainment business, in his environmental make-up. A dance band drummer and Ralph Reader RAF 'Gang Show' alumnus, he had an exceptional gift for mimicry that made him a certainty for broadcasting fame, as witness his nine year stint of glittering display of vocal technique with the Goons. He then demonstrated that his capacity for impersonation was physical as well as oral, as he began his career as a film actor, his first real success coming in *I'm All Right, Jack* (1959) with his compelling study of the hidebound trade union leader. Among the many splendid films he made, most would select his portrayal of the incompetent French detective, Inspector Clouseau, first seen in *Pink Panther* (1963) and then six more times thereafter – Peter Ustinov having turned down the role.... Incidentally, it is interesting yet again to observe how policing has attracted English comics, from James Fawn's music hall ditty, *Ask a Policeman*, via Charles Austen's P C Parker, Sandy Powell's bewildered constable, Charlie Penrose's *The Laughing Policeman* and Robb

Wilton's dithering desk sergeant, to Rowan Atkinson's television inspector in *The Blue Line*, not forgetting the cowardly constables of *The Pirates of Penzance*.

Peter Sellers admitted sadly that, if asked to play himself, he would not know what to do, for he did not know who he was. Four shallow failed marriages paid testimony to the truth of this. Here was an actor who only found himself when locked in the complete absorption of another, a fictional, personality; this was the key to his outstanding film career and the key to his less than contented private life. With the last fifteen years of his life dogged by ill-health, he died in London in 1980.

It was almost as though this quartet came as incipient comedians to *The Goon Show* and, on departure from it, each found a separate career path that, for all they never set aside their delicious talent for making people laugh, somehow concluded with none of them continuing to become an established comedian in any regular usage of this descriptor.

The Gold Mine Exhausted

This was the end of radio's golden age, with the precious metals abundant in quantity as well as quality. There would be qualitative radio comedy in the future; Kenneth Horne in *Round the Horne* would attract a cult following, not least because of Kenneth Williams' highly ambiguous folksongs of Freudian patois and his spicy gay lib duologue with Hugh Paddick, as Sandy and Julian. It was the quantity, in respect of listenership, that would dwindle, for, by the 1960s, television was the pre-eminent medium.

The last decades of BBC supremacy were, fortunately, distinguished by the work of a comedian with some claim to be the greatest

of the puristic radio comics. Alfred 'Al' Read was born in Salford in 1909 and became salesman and then director of the family business, E & H Read Ltd, meat processors, whose 'Frax Fratters' were a comedians' butt in World War II. He married Joyce Entwistle, served in the Prestwich Home Guard and pursued his profitable business career. In the 1960s he sold the business and divorced, marrying the model, Elizabeth Ann Reed in 1970. In between whiles he became a perceptive observer of and communicator about what he termed 'the small embarrassments and frustrations of daily life'. Aptly enough, it is said his professional career began when a BBC producer eavesdropped on him entertaining his work-force at a staff function in a Manchester hotel, while the Read vans carried the inscription 'right, monkey', a catchphrase Al Read overheard in a queue for the turnstiles at Old Trafford football ground.

His 'pictures from life' were first revealed on *Variety Fanfare* in 1950, whereafter he commanded a massive following for 20 years with his own show *Such is Life*. The voice, the voices, were everything. Seeing him live in revue or pantomime, one was tempted to close one's eyes, so quintessential was the voice as the fuse for imagination's explosive. With the help of Ronnie Taylor's scriptings, he insightfully conveyed the authentic accent of grey Mancunian realism – the bus conductor, the car park attendant ('you stay where you are; I'll move all the others') and a whole bunch of know-all tradesmen; the flustered man, with his 'just...just...just...just a minute; the over-inquisitive boy, an embarrassment to his father, with his 'dad...dad...dad...dad; and, of course, 'the wife in the kitchen', that ever-present bogeywoman of so many comedians – 'are you going to cut that lawn, or shall we put sheep down'; or 'when are you going to get a latch on that gate...when you roped it up nobody could get in or out. All that fuss we had when the men came to empty the dust-bins. I won't forget it, I won't. I'll give 'em 'we're bin-men, not mountaineers'.'

A friend of the author was sitting in Ancoats Hospital, Manchester, apprehensively awaiting a surgical consultation. The gruff-voiced man next to him struck up the ensuing conversation piece: 'how d'you do' – 'h-h-ello' – 'is this your first time here?' – 'y-y-yess' – 'it won't be your last, I say, it won't be your last' – that linguistic habit of forceful repetition being used in the 21st century by Fred Elliott (John Savident), the Coronation Street butcher. That hospital exchange had all the genuine intonation of Al Read's gloomy prognosticator and anxious respondent; all that was lacking was that damning concluding judgement of 'you'll be lucky, I say, you'll be lucky.'

Al Read died in Northallerton in 1987. He offers a fitting end to an opening set of chapters on entertainment vehicles or 'band waggons' that have influenced the comedians of the hour. Radio was, at base, Al Read's sole medium; it created him absolutely and he responded nobly by gracing the BBC's final years of 'wireless' prominence with exceptional comedy, appreciated, like the best of humour, for its truth as well as its funniness. Nothing could be more authentically profound or more mystically perplexing than the sober judgement of Al Read's 'wife': 'there was enough said at our Edie's wedding.'

8. 'OUR GANGS': COMIC GROUPS

Apart from a later chapter on the effects on comedy of television and a sideways glance at the influence of satirical revue thereon, the examination of comic settings has now been completed. It is time to turn the analytical spotlight on comic styles, always recalling that the cross-references are legion and the same names will invariably reoccur to exemplify differing aspects. The next two or three chapters will illustrate, in a profession where the singleton is the preferred option, the alternative formats of the team-handed approach, like Harry Tate and his motor car cameo; the 'sketch' comics, such as Jimmy James, where there were one or two supporters, and the lengthy string of double or crosstalk acts, of which Murray and Mooney are an example. Then there will be an examination of the interesting input of women comedians, in a vocation where, like so many others, male dominion was the bigoted assumption, and then a scrutiny of speciality comedians, such as humorous magicians and ventriloquists. This will be followed by a couple of chapters on the regional and metropolitan sway on the development of comic styles and techniques.

Beginning first with the ensemble companies, a well-known one from the old days of music hall was Casey's Court, managed by Will Murray. It was one of the first troupes of boys, a forerunner of the cinema's Dead End Kids, a representation of a bunch of cockney children playing in an alley in a slum district. Will Murray was the first Mrs Casey and the company ran, off and on and with vacillating profits, from before World War I until after World War II. The slant was crude and crazy and, at any one time, there might have been 30 or so youngsters in the troupe. One of its useful by-products was to act as a school for clowns. Some already mentioned and others yet to take a bow were Casey 'courtiers', among them Charlie Chaplin (he started with Will Murray in 1906, doing among other things an impersonation of the stage Mesmerist, 'Doctor' Walford Bodie), Stan Laurel, Dave Morris, Robbie 'Enoch' Vincent, Tommy Trinder, George Doonan and Tom Gamble.

Fred Karno's Army

But much more famous and fruitful was Fred Karno's army. Frederick John Westcott was a cabinet-maker's son from Exeter, born in 1866. He was a circus acrobat with the Karno Trio, from whom he took his stage name in the 1880s. He married Edith Cuthbert, a Stockport box-office girl, who ran away from home to marry him in 1889, to lead a married existence of unremitting misery. She lost six of her eight children, while Fred Karno was a physically brutal and sexually abusive husband who eventually married, in 1927, his long-term mistress, Marie Moore, daughter of Thomas Moore of the Moore and Burgess Minstrels. In 1913 he launched the fun palace and hotel, the 'Karsino', at a huge expenditure of £70,000 (about £4m at today's prices), on Tagg's Island, an inlet on the Thames between Hampton and East Molesey. The first world war intervened and the venture proved a financial fiasco, with Fred Karno declared a bankrupt in 1926. A year later he became co-proprietor of the Lilliput Wine Stores in the village of Lilliput, near Poole, Dorset, where he worked and lived until his death in 1941.

Thus it was chiefly in the Edwardian period that Fred Karno worked his clever theatrical wiles, so much so that his name still remains a metaphor for a shambles and the 1914-1918 soldiery sang, in funereal hymnal mode, 'We are Fred Karno's Army; Fred Karno's infantry;/ We cannot fight, we cannot shoot; what bloody good are we?/ But when we get to Berlin, the Kaiser he will say, 'Hoch, hoch, mein Gott, what a bloody fine lot?/ Fred Karno's infantry'. The 'bloodys' have optional alternatives – the 1914-1918 War was the time when the dreaded f-word became common. Few music hall performers have been so celebrated.

In 1895 Fred Karno, with Rick Klaie and Bob Sewell, premiered his first sketch, *Hilarity*, at the Gaiety Music Hall, Birmingham. So satisfactory were the results from this and his succeeding sketches that, in 1901, he opened his 'Fun Factory' in Camberwell, London, a depot for his squads of slapstick comics, with space for the manufacture of scenery, costumes and props, whilst he later hired the nearby Montpelier Theatre, Walworth, for rehearsals. Fred Karno was a showman in the Barnum circus and fairground tradition of hyperbole, using extravagant language and gestures – a giant balloon; a Black Maria – to advertise his 'Speechless Comedians'. Nonetheless, he was a shrewd theatrical producer, as his percipient advice, 'leave 'em wanting' denotes.

His principal products were *Jail Birds, The Bailiff* (in which Fred Kitchen (1872-1950), the Karno chief comedian, as Simpkins, originated the famous catchphrase, 'Meredith, we're in!', with assistant bailiff Meredith played by Jack Melville); and *The Football Match* (giving Harry Weldon (1881-1930), complete with dejected sibilant cries of 's'no use', his best-ever role as Stiffy the Goalkeeper, with Charlie Chaplin as the Villain). In the saucy *Yap Yaps* promenade sketch, Fred Karno sent delicious paroxysms of shock through audiences, with, shades of Marilyn Monroe in the 1955 movie *The Seven Year Itch*, powerful fans blowing the girls' skirts over their heads.

Nonetheless, and for all that, his most famous sketch was *Mumming Birds*, a burlesque of the music hall, first performed at the Star Theatre, Bermondsey in 1904, and finding much success in the United States as *A Night in an English Music Hall*, opening in New York in 1910. It was while playing the role of 'the Drunk' or 'Inebriated Swell' in that sketch, with its stage within a stage formula, that Charlie Chaplin was spotted by Mack Sennett, and he was not the only one of Karno's players so to be recruited. What should be remarked is that, in compliance with the theatre licensing of the epoch, the Karno skits were mostly mimed; his first spoken sketch was *Her Majesty's Guests*, another prison spoof, which opened at the Palace Theatre, Manchester in 1901. It comes as no surprise to learn that Fred Karno's well-trained mimes were tailor-made for silent films. Many other comedians, apart from Chaplin and Stan Laurel, had an early schooling with Karno, among them Billy Bennett, Robb Wilton, Syd Walker, Will Hay, Sandy Powell, Max Miller and Wee Georgie Wood, although one or two of those connections are marginal.

These were rough and ready days for many 'pros'. Fred Karno, like many he would enlist for his army, had in his early days hung around 'Poverty Corner', as the Stamford Street area near Waterloo Station was known, hoping for a booking. Pay ranged for non-stars from £1.50 to £3 a week, out of which 10% went to the agent, a drink had to be bought for the theatre manager and a cigar for the conductor. Digs, often with four in a room, would have taken another 7s (35p) and many lived on a cup of tea and a 'doorstep' of bread and margarine. It was from such circumstances that great stars such as Dan Leno and Marie Lloyd arose.

Charlie Chaplin also spent some time with the Eight Lancashire Lads troupe. They had been originally formed by John Willie Jackson, of Golborne, Newton-le-Willows and included five of his own children, one of them a girl. They first appeared at the Central Pier, Blackpool, in 1896 – in 1897 Charlie Chaplin joined them, no doubt grateful for the pound a week that brought. They were a hit at the Folies Bergère in Paris in 1909 and J W Jackson, a one-time white lead worker, found himself running five troupes of boys and girls. Tommy Handley was another comedian to have youthful experience of what was chiefly a clog dancing and 'cake walk' act. Although it leaned away from direct comedy, it illustrates the then vogue for juvenile troupes, from which sprang several great comics – Jimmy James, for example, was, as a boy, a member of both Phil Rees' Stable Boys and Will Netta's Singing Jockeys, while a youthful Wee Georgie Wood starred in a juvenile music hall sketch, *The Black Hand Gang*. There were also Joe Boganny's Lunatics and Charles Baldwin's Bank Clerks.

In the United States The Seven Little Foys, the offspring of the vaudeville entertainer, Eddie Foy (Edward Fitzgerald; 1854-1928) are a prime transatlantic example, made even more famous when reconstructed on film by Bob Hope in 1954. Once more cinema was the imitator. The Dead End Kids, after a Broadway stage success, began their film career in 1937, with a series of films like *The Dead End Kids, Little Tough Guys* and *Angels with Dirty Faces*. Initially six strong, they transmuted into the East Side Kids and the Bowery Boys, bending from straight crime into a more comic style. It is hard to credit, but the Bowery Boys made no less than 48 films.

Our Gang was more straightforwardly a slapstick presentation. With changing personnel, the 'gang' made short films from the mid 1920s to the mid 1940s. Many of these scores of films were later released for television and video under the title *The Little Rascals*, while, earlier, the gang were celebrated in strip-cartoon form in the *Dandy* comic. Thus two or three generations of young English audiences became habituated to the adventures of Spanky McFarlane, Alfalfa Switzer, Buckwheat Thomas, Porky Lee and the rest. *The Beano* comic ran, for even longer, Lord Snooty and His Pals, an anglicised version of Our Gang. It is not without relevant interest that English children's literature has a constant thread of gangs, from the exploits of Robin Hood and his Merry Men to the japes of sundry fictional school groups, like Harry Wharton and his 'Famous Five' at Frank Richards' Greyfriars, or the *Coot Club* and *Swallows and Amazons* of Arthur Ransome and Enid Blyton's even more youthful grouping.

On stage, on radio and on film, Will Hay worked with small groups, such as his obstreperous schoolboys, to highly effective comic advantage

Naturally enough, one had to be team-oriented in a concert party, such as those that adorned the seaside resorts. Magicians, soubrettes and instrumentalists would be drafted in to augment the casts of the blackout sketches that were a consistent part of such shows. All in all, there was a pleased acceptance of the value of the 'band' approach and there were one or two variety acts that met this requirement.

Harry Tate and Company

One that, through longevity, demonstrated an enduring popularity at all levels of society from George V upwards or downwards, according to political perspective, was Harry Tate and his 'boys'. Ronald McDonald Hutchinson was born in Kennington, London, in 1872, the son of a mercantile clerk; he married Julia Kerslake Baker in 1918, and he took his stage-name – in 1898 and, according to one legend, at Marie Lloyd's suggestion – from the sugar refiners for whom he first worked before the lure of the theatre proved overpowering. He began as an impressionist, with an ingenious array of paper costumes that enabled him to make 40 or more changes in his brief act. However, from the early 1900s right through to the late 1930s, he built and sustained a team-handed set of sketches, normally being assisted by six others. He is often cited as the kind of comic who was able both to work on and keep fresh his act by circulating the British Isles, appearing perhaps only once every three or four years at any one venue. The British variety circuit certainly gave its performers the opportunity to hone their skills and its audiences the time to begin to yearn for a return visit from their favourites.

Harry Tate was, in his art, the child of his nature. He played someone like his own father, a late Victorian/Edwardian lower middle to middle class gent, with a clerkly occupation and a sneaking social ambition. In his loud and garish clothing, with his impossible moustache twirling like a hirsute windmill and with his extravagant wink, he was, as he forever claimed 'master of the situation'. It was an age of newfangled apparatus and techniques, with the concept of holidays and hobbies released by increased leisure and increased income for many in suburbia. Harry Tate's equivalent today would be the DIY enthusiast and IT know-all; Harry Tate would have had a field-day with the present-day manias for home improvement and the computer.

In all, he was responsible for some sixteen cameos, many of them devised by Wal Pink, among them Gardening, Fishing, Going Round the World, Wireless, Billiards and Golfing, in the last two of which he was the antecedent of Sid Field. Each one was an ordinary situation in which those around him undermined Harry Tate's authority. By a long way, however, his most favoured sketch was *Motoring*. As the inexorable fan of every craze and unceasingly intrigued by gadgetry, he waxed genially then waned testily, confident in his knowledge and ability and rarely guilty of honest self-appraisal. It was said of Mussolini that he was an autodidact with a poor teacher – Harry Tate was il Duce of the halls. His motoring was subject, inter alia, to the failings and interruptions of his chauffeur, an interfering policeman and a passing drunk, with his stage son, played by Tommy Tweedly, piping Eton-collared protests from the back of the car.

The act was launched at the exact moment when the motor car was becoming something of a bourgeois status symbol, the 'horseless carriage' being a replacement for the horsed version. It should be remembered that, at first, the car was constructed and marketed for the rising middle classes, as a substitute for the private coach, the transport for a decided minority. W S Gilbert was one who took up the fashion; he said of his Rolls Royce, 'it rolls but it doesn't royce'. The genius of Henry Ford was not just, as is sometimes suggested, the utilisation of mass production for car manufacture (one or two industries had already adopted that process in the USA) but his prescient view that the car could offer populist transportation to all classes.

It was against this social and cultural canvas that Harry Tate's *Motoring* became one of variety's most famous presentations, featuring a stage car that had, he claimed, three speeds – faith, hope and charity – and paraded the number plate 'T8'. His booming tones echoed around the halls, with something of Jimmy Edwards about his boisterous assurance. His repeated long drawn farewells as the car almost moved – 'Good-bye-ee' – became the title of a poignant First World War song, while two other phrases also became popular: the assertion of doubt and disbelief, 'I don't think', and, as the standard conversation changer but later sexual euphemism, 'How's yer father?' His son, Ronnie Tate, joined the gang and continued to appear with him, as Harry Tate Junior, until his father's last show in 1939. Harry Tate died in Sutton, Surrey in 1940.

The sham motor car, exploding and collapsing, was, of course, a standard of the circus arena from soon after its appearance on British streets and Harry Tate was not the only comic motorist on the variety circuit. Another was Duggie Wakefield (1900-1951), his tilted nose, centre parting, buck-teeth and Formby-like accents indicating that motoring as a pastime really was descending the social ladder. His motoring sketch was pacier than Harry Tate's and more reliant on physical interplay. It was good fun, with Duggie Wakefield joined by Jack Butler, Billy Nelson and Chuck O'Neill. As well as the car scene, they did a number of other sketches, including a baffling handcuff vignette. The gang was recruited by Archie Pitt, Gracie Fields' first husband, for his revue *Boys will be Boys*, and then became an independent act, popular at Blackpool and other seaside resorts, well into the war-years. Duggie Wakefield hailed from Sheffield and served with the Duke of Wellington's Regiment in World War I. He married Edie Fields, Gracie's sister, and appeared in one or two of the Rochdale songstress' films. He was a strenuous worker and it is said that this contributed to his premature death in 1951.

Duggie Wakefield had also worked with Albert Burdon, another comedian who performed team-handed. Albert Burdon (1900-1981) was Duggie Wakefield's precise contemporary, although thankfully he enjoyed a much longer life. He was born in South Shields and became a tiny bundle of comic energy, who contrived to find himself in films, in West End shows and as dame in panto. As a kind of precursor of Tommy Cooper, he was billed, in his early show-business guise, as 'The World's Worst Wizard', a bounteous turban surmounting his minute frame as he struggled with his magical cabinet. His penchant was more for the 'gang' format and he toured in revues, especially in the north of England, well after the Second World War, performing in such sketches, latterly with his son, Bryan Burdon. His mainstay was *The Means Test*. This included the acerbic exchange of the dole officer asking Albert Burdon how much money he had in the bank: '£50,000' – '£50,000; you must be joking' – 'well, you started it.'

The man who made his name purely on the basis of show-biz gangs was Ralph Reader, who was born in Somerset in 1902 and died in 1982, and who, for all his London and New York success as a producer of musicals, devoted his life to the boy scout movement. He did so to the despair of several, such as Ivor Novello, who valued his assistance in their ventures. Launched with his breezy number, *We're Riding Along on the Crest of a Wave*, the Ralph Reader *Gang Shows* lasted from 1936 to 1974. They were naturally laundered to the sentimental, ultra-patriotic, excruciatingly jolly mood of scouting, with its emphasis on the Boer War uniform and, indeed, Boer War values, espoused by its oddball founder, Robert Baden-Powell, that strange assortment of atavistic credo and propagandist wiles.

If that betrays something of a revulsion for the concept of scouting and its offshoots, nothing can gainsay the triumph of its spread – there were 8.5m worldwide in mid-20th century – still less the cheerful, noisy output of its gang shows, the formula of which was taken up locally by neighbourhood scout troops. During the 1939-1945 War the bustling Ralph Reader organised the RAF *Gang Shows*, choreographing large cast numbers with the same mix of dexterity and élan. He is also responsible for the tear-jerking precipitation of poppies at the Albert Hall annual Festival of Remembrance.

The Crazy Gang

Ralph Reader contributed songs, including the relaxing *Strollin'*, and sketches for Crazy Gang consumption. For metropolitan audiences in search of buoyantly anarchic but unmenacing humour in the decades on either side of World War II, the Crazy Gang supplied a consistent flow and thereby provides a major example of team comedy. The Crazy Gang was a composition of double acts, plus the single act of Eddie Gray, but these performers gained, with the possible exception of Flanagan and Allen, their chief claim to fame because of their allegiance to the team ethic.

Apart from Flanagan and Allen and Eddie Gray, there were two main duos, Nervo and Knox and Naughton and Gold. However, at the outset, in 1931, two other double acts were briefly involved. These were Dehaven and Page – Billy De Haven and Dandy Page – who went on to act as principals in the touring companies of 'the Crazy Gang' shows, and Billy Caryll and Hilda Mundy, not the first and not the last to offer a 'drunk' cameo. Flanagan and Allen did not join the team until 1932.

Jimmy Nervo and Teddy Knox were the chief protagonists of the Crazy Gang formulae. James Henry Holloway (1897-1975) and Albert Edward Cromwell Knox (1896-1974) both had circus-oriented backgrounds that stood them in good stead in their 'Crazy Gang' years. Combining first in 1919, they mastered the pantomimic act of the two ballet dancers with the outsize balloon and they did a wholesale variety of burlesques of bull fighters, apache dancers and the like, with top favourites being their slow motion wrestling and silent film representations. It was this inventiveness and performing skill around which much of the Crazy Gang material was built.

Their associates were Charles John Naughton (1881-1976) and James McGonigal (1886-1974), the Glaswegian double act, Charlie Naughton and Jimmy Gold, who joined forces in the far-off days of 1908. Billed somewhat sonorously under the heading of 'The Comedy of the British Working Man', their main offering was a slapstick decorating act, entitled *Turn it the Other Way Round'*. It was the sort of 'slosh' turn deployed by the old music hall comic, Will Evans and beloved of pantomime addicts. It was later processed with similar mess and muddle by Laurie Lupino Lane (born in 1922, the only son of Lupino Lane) and George Truzzi, who, coming from a circus background, added the juggling of the paintbrushes and other props to the melée. Typical of the Naughton and Gold dialogue was: 'I wrote three columns in the paper about milk' – 'did they publish all three columns?' – 'no, they condensed it'.

Edward Earl Gray was a shopkeeper's son, born in Pimlico in 1898. The member of a juggling group at the age of nine and associated with Nervo and Knox as early as 1919, he was an idiosyncratic comedian in his own right, although a substantial amount of his fame came from his involvement with the Crazy Gang, for whom he adopted the 'Monsewer' title. With his startlingly big glasses and a moustache that out reached those of either Harry Tate or Jimmy Edwards, he indulged in comic juggling and some conjuring, the explanatory commentary uttered in cockney franglais – 'now I shall put la glasses in la skyrocket.' Claiming to descend from 'a long line of bachelors', he was primus inter pares in that bunch of obsessive practical jokers. He later joined Frankie Howerd in his mock-Roman extravaganzas and he died in Shoreham-on-Sea in 1969. David Goldie perceptively sees him as the 'semi-detached' Crazy Gangster, for he had the unique quality of the sublime clown.

The comic mayhem of Crazy Gang activities, with the interruption of other acts and the assaults on the audience, had been pioneered by Nervo and Knox in *Young Bloods of Variety* in 1925 and, after trying out a couple of 'Crazy Weeks' and a 'Crazy Month', George Black embarked on the first long-running

show in 1931 at the London Palladium. Jack Hylton revived the idea at the Victoria Palace in the post-war years. All in all, the Crazy Gang operated, with the wartime break, from 1931 to 1962, with 826 performances of *Young in Heart*. Other affectionately recalled show titles are *These Foolish Things* (1938) and *The Little Dog Laughed* (1939).

Scatological and vulgar, the broad-veined humour of the Crazy Gang exerted a strong appeal, lightening the darkness for many people with its combine of slapstick knockabout and the pricking of the inflated bladders of dignity. The Crazy Gang were jesters in the very genuine sense of making fun of the formalism of established authority. They indulged in a considerable amount of drag, among their best remembered lampoons being those of fashion models, Ascot duchesses and – 'Six Little Broken Blossoms' – flower sellers. Charlie Naughton's baldness, smallness and lisping voice made him the ideal baby, once christened by Bud Flanagan as vicar. Bud Flanagan and Chesney Allen were once Ancient British bookmakers, on the lookout for counterfeit stone money – 'there's a lot of cement about'.

The practical jokes were played on other performers and the audience might expect imminent invasion. Misrule was the disorder of the day. For the most part, both performers and audiences relaxed and accepted the near-anarchy and there was a classless welcome for the Crazy Gang, much beloved by the Royal Family. Bud Flanagan was a royal as well as a people's jester, notching up some fifteen royal performances and congratulating royalty, when visiting Buckingham Palace for his OBE in 1959, on the size of their audience for a matinee.

There can be no doubt of the enormous affection and regard felt for the Crazy Gang.

Their banquet of bawdiness and pranks was thoroughly enjoyed. For 30 years generations of theatre-goers basked in their puncturing of human pomposities and it is not too ostentatious to grant them that often over-vaunted label of being a national institution. They also showed a sentimental side, mainly in the Flanagan and Allen type ballads they sometimes featured, that was part of the attraction. Was there a darker side? It seems like lèse-majesté even to hint at a flaw in the makeup of the court jesters, but occasionally one has the sense of an insensitive self-indulgence. Other performers were supposed to smile bravely and sportingly when the comic duos interfered with their speciality acts, but the border between amusing by-play and harassment is a thin one and there are one or two tales of performers who suffered as a consequence.

The japes were offstage as well as on. Here again the frontiers are easily crossed. Two stories frequently cited as classic practical jokes illustrate the point. First, Eddie Gray, out in the street, would assume someone had been trapped inside a pillar box and hold an anxious conversation with the unhappy victim, to the consternation of a growing crowd of passers-by. Second, a dog trainer, supplying dogs for one of the show, was persuaded by the theatre fireman, on the Gang's prompting, that her dogs had to be fire-proofed and she spent hours hurrying about London, searching for appropriate canine gels. The first is diverting and harmless but, at the risk of a degree of solemnity, the second is less so. It was not as though an audience was being enthralled, so that it was just a backstage joke at the expense of a fellow-professional, for whom it was a tiresome nuisance to boot, no quick April Fool's prank but an elongated annoyance. Deflation of the high and mighty is the task of jesters,

not sniggering at the misfortunes of the little man or woman. Professional indiscipline is a perilous recipe.

For all that sermonising, one cannot argue with the 30 years of unsullied and open-hearted welcome offered to the Crazy Gang by a delighted British public. Some commentators have gone so far as to suggest they predated the Goons and the 'Monty Python' team and that they could be compared with the American Marx Brothers or Ole Olsen and Chic Johnson in movies such as *Hellzapoppin* (1942), a riotous, zany mix of burlesque routines. However, it is probably more helpful to glance laterally at the circus ring for proper comparison. It was in the circus ring that the clowns assailed one another and authority, in the figure of the florid and smartly attired ringmaster, with occasional forays into the ranks of the circus-goers themselves, in a series of visually overt and none too refined tricks. The Crazy Gang would never have pleaded guilty to subtlety. What they did was to convey onto the stage the gusto, the earthiness and the disrespect of the circus clown; and they did so with consummate dispatch and mastery.

While Bud Flanagan was lord of the revels, the less boisterous Chesney Allen never re-entered the lists of madness after World War II, for all he made occasional appearances elsewhere with his long-time partner. Born in 1894 in Brighton of respectable lineage, William Ernest Chesney Allen, retired because of ill-health – and then, perhaps predictably, outlived his busier comrades, dying in 1982. Chaim Reuben Weintrop was a Londoner, born in Whitechapel in 1896, the son of a barber-cum-tobacconist. A theatre callboy aged ten, his apprenticeship was as colourful as most of his contemporaries, ranging from being 'Fargo the Boy Conjuror' and Chick Harlem, a blackface comic, to a tiny role in a Broadway show and trying out a couple of partners in crosstalk harness.

During the 1914-1918 War, in which he suffered gassing, Bud met Ches, and, in 1924, they reconnected. Chesney Allen had been bitten by the theatrical bug and eschewed the chance of staid bourgeois employ. He tried the straight theatre and then he, too, had a couple of double act exploits. Now he was managing the Florrie Ford touring company, Flo and Co, and Bud Flanagan was summoned to join the troupe as Ches Allen's partner. The somewhat counterfactual surname of 'Flanagan', incidentally, derived from a beastly anti-Semitic sergeant major who had tormented his Jewish underling, so much so that the comedian vowed to have him laughed at, if only notionally, for years to come. It was about this time that Bud Flanagan married Annie Quinn and he remained active in the entertainment business almost until his death in Kingston in 1968.

They became known as the 'Oi' Comedians, because that was the shout Bud Flanagan would emit at the end of one of their pieces of rather obvious nonsense, with the pit orchestra responding likewise; as in, of a dockyard scene: 'see all the Salvadors' – 'the what?' – 'the Labradors' – 'the stevedores, you fool' – 'Oi!' Similarly they would, in medical mode, confuse 'stiff ticket' and 'certificate' or 'crispictions' and 'prescriptions'. Basically, they were a straightforward double act, with the well-groomed taller Allen the foil for and sorely-tried Mentor of the scruffy, smaller Flanagan, with his emblematic moulting fur coat and battered hat. Nonetheless, there was a quiet charm about the one and an infectious geniality about the other that appealed, while they espoused, beyond that and now their most precious inheritance, an entrancing and harmonious musical duet.

Bud Flanagan modelled his warm, husky warbling on that of 'the Coster Comedian', Alec Hurley, already encountered in his domestic role as Marie Lloyd's second husband, albeit Bud Flanagan added a soaring note or two of Cantor-like proportions. Ches Allen, confidential, pacific, mellow, blended in perfectly with his almost spoken recitative, the two voices making for a tunefulness that was very easy on the ear. As Chesney Allen was wont to remark, 'lovely melody, Bud'. These were sentimental songs, registering the banal ordinariness of the existences of their listeners, and speaking to their fears, hopes and dreams. The titles are, in this regard, self-explanatory: *Yesterday's Dreams; Home Town; Let's Be Buddies; On the Outside Looking In; Nice People; Are You Havin' Any Fun?;* and *Down Forget-me-not Lane* ('you'll find a table well-laid and you're welcome to a chair'). There were also gently romantic airs of unrequited love like *Why Don't You Fall in Love with Me?,* whilst in *The Umbrella Man,* with its cross-reference to Neville Chamberlain, whose cartoon identity tag was his rolled brolly, or in *Run, Rabbit, Run,* there were attempts to keep up people's peckers in harsh times. Their close-harmony singing had the virtue of being closer in mood to the British psyche during the late 1920s, 1930s and early 1940s than any bright, booming martial choruses.

Underneath the Arches was and remains their greatest number. Feeling a trifle glum himself, Bud Flanagan wrote this song in his dressing room at the Hippodrome, Derby in 1926. The twosome performed it for the first time at the Pier Pavilion, Southport, the following week. It became the unofficial signature tune of the British depression, with its plaintive description of the all-weathers life of the unemployed, homeless and hungry. It was the equivalent of *Buddy, Can You Spare a Dime,* that forceful theme song of

The People's Jesters

the American slump, although the strident acerbity of the latter contrasted strongly and perhaps accurately with the patient resignation of the former.

It is fair to assert that Flanagan and Allen, one of the best-loved of English double acts, deserve that affection more because of their balladry than their jokes.

One might end on a further musical note with a brief roundup of the comedy bands that fall into this category of team-based entertainments. They reflected the success of the 1940s American model of Spike Jones and His City Slickers, with his lunatic variations on well-known tunes, such as *You Always Hurt the One You Love* and *Chloe*. Lindley Armstrong Jones (1911-1965), a minute figure of a bandleader, became known in the United Kingdom through his records and his film appearances, for example, in *Thank Your Lucky Stars* (1943). Sid Millward and His Nitwits aped his emphasis on the din and variation that percussion and woodwind could produce in Britain, although the City Slickers' forte lay in the destruction of well-known classical pieces.

Sid Millward (1909-1972; born in London) was himself classically trained, and, with his long hair, Chaplinesque moustache and lengthy tail-suit, he would conduct these versions of musical assassination. His chief accomplice was the comic, Wally Stewart, while another, Cyril Lagey, kept up the bad work with a group called Nuts and Bolts. They had tried out similar tactics both before and during the war, with, for instance, *Stars in Battledress*, but it was when the Nitwits tendered appropriate backing to the radio programme, *w*, that they became popular. Dr Crock and his Crackpots was a similar outfit, which succeeded the Nitwits on *Ignorance is Bliss*. Their founder, Harry Hines (1903-1971), was a dance band clarinettist, who,

in clown make-up, arranged crazy musical adaptations for his colleagues.

During the dance band era most of the orchestras pursued a stage as well as a palais career, taking on half or more of a variety bill. This meant that they had to leaven the dance music with comedy, something they were already habituated to because of the demands of radio. Harry Roy, Henry Hall, with Meth Smith doing the vocals, even Geraldo – they all included some comic interludes. However, the king of the band-show was Billy Cotton, whose Sunday lunchtime radio programme, with his stirring call of 'Wakey, Wakey!', was a lively adjunct to what used to be called PSA, that is, Pleasant Sunday Afternoons. William Cotton was born in Westminster in 1899 and was a chorister at St Margaret's Church Westminster, where he was buried in 1969. After a flamboyant career that embraced army bugling and survival of the Gallipoli campaign, flying, motor car racing, bus driving and drumming, he emerged as the man who, with the quiet assistance of the brass player, Clem Bernard, created what was a show-band rather than a dance-band. Balancing the sentimental quicksteps and slow fox trots of the day with uproarious comic numbers, with the versatile Alan Breeze ever ready with the vocals, there was gusto in abundance. The roofs of old variety theatres were menaced when the Billy Cotton band cut loose with *Oh, Oh, Oh, Oh, What a Referee* or *I've Got a Loverley Bunch of Coconuts*. The rotund girth and chubby, bespectacled, smiling face of Billy Cotton, latterly on television, made him one of the favoured sons of entertainment in the two decades after the Second World War.

In the next chapter we will shift the sights slightly to examine the lives and works of some of the great 'sketch' comedians.

9. SKETCHINESS: COMEDY PLAYLETS

Variety was totally varied, as we must continue to note. Analysis is dogged, not only by the different vehicles in which comedians have starred – stage, radio, film or television – but by their metamorphosis from one style to another and also by the very blurred boundaries between styles. The 'sketch' comedians amply illustrate the difficulty. Will Hay, eminent on stage and radio but exceptionally well recollected for his cinematic work, was definitely a 'sketch' comedian, usually operating with two or three others in set cameos – although, when his class of boys was enlarged to something like a genuine school form, he might have been tagged a 'gang' comedian. The Happidrome trio of Mr Korris, Enoch and Ramsbottom is another example, already encountered, of the 'sketch' genre, while several double acts – Old Mother Riley and her daughter, Kitty, among those already met in these pages – basically performed established and familiar sketches. On the other hand, there is the instance of Hylda Baker, whose career will be examined in the chapter on women comedians. Hylda Baker did a sketch-like routine that incorporated her silent friend, Cynthia, but she always regarded herself as a stand-up comic, with her many 'Cynthia' assistants destined to anonymity, not even acknowledged as the minor part of a double act.

In essence, the 'sketch' comic worked with one, two or sometimes three others, something close, in many examples, to the double act, with the extras acting as foils or straight men for the mainline comedian. Perhaps the principal determinant was the evolution, in these cases, of a carefully prepared piece of characterisation, almost amounting to a brief drama or playlet, with the two or three participants engaged in definitive roles, succinctly crafted with beginning, middle and end. In this, if in anything, it differed from the traditional double act, where the two indulged in an exchange of repartee, normally on a question and answer basis. Although the two protagonists might have adopted sustained characters, such as the irritated straight man and the 'wise fool' comic, the actual dialogue was frequently subject to constant alteration and rarely had the same shape and purpose of the 'sketch' situation.

It is the intention to examine the significant contributions made to British comedy by three self-confessed 'sketch' comedians of supreme stature, namely, Jimmy James, Sid Field and Robb Wilton, although the last named had an equally important persona as a single turn, and, in passing, to note the activities of one or two others of some note.

Robb Wilton . . . 'The Day War Broke Out . . . '

Robb Wilton, christened Robert Smith, was born in Liverpool in 1881 and died in that city in 1957, a year after his wife, Florence Palmer, whom he married in Stalybridge in 1904. Their only son, Robert, was born in 1907; an actor, he fell to his death in a blackout accident in 1943 during the Second World War. The couple remained extraordinarily close, travelling together whenever the comedian's commitments permitted. But Florence Palmer, herself an actress, was initially much more than a travelling companion; she was an integral part of the Robb Wilton sketches.

Originally intending to take up engineering as a job, Robb Wilton made his theatrical debut in 1899 at the Theatre Royal, Garston, in his native Liverpool, where he relieved the image of his being cast as the villain in melodrama with interval fill-ins as Pie-face, a comic commentator. Spotted by the impresario, Sir William de Frece, the comedic element soon burgeoned and he made his London debut, at the Holborn Empire, in 1909. He enjoyed both domestic and overseas tours and earned a royal command appearance in 1926. It was on this occasion that 'the Confidential Comedian' introduced 'the Magistrate' sketch, with its jibes at the lethargy and confusion of the legal system. It became the base of his portrayal of Mr Muddlecombe JP, presiding over the *Court of Not So Common Pleas*, the caricature that won him his first major radio success in 1937.

Before and around this time, he became renowned for his two sketches, mercifully preserved on film, of the fireman and the policeman. These were very similar in situation to his judicial skit, in that he was the fire or police officer behind the desk, dealing with the laity. Florence Palmer's house was on fire in the one and she had murdered her husband in the other. In both cases her reception was dilatory and pernickety. 'I see Chelsea made a draw on Saturday', he observed placidly to the woman whose house was ablaze, while, when she remonstrated that the route he described for the fire engine was unduly convoluted, he calmly explained, 'ay, but it's a prettier run.' Unable to find the requisite form among the untidy mess of papers on his desk, he wondered whether the confessed murderess could come back the next day.

Robb Wilton described himself as a 'comedy character actor' rather than a comedian, a precise and thoughtful distinction. He adopted his roles as carefully as Will Hay did his and they were alike in their choice of characters. The magistrate, the fire chief and the police sergeant, like the schoolmaster, were all figures of minor bureaucratic authority, sucked into a bog of fussy and delaying inaction. Robb Wilton understood how laypersons sometimes found themselves locked in irritated contest with these professional officers and how their rules and regulations, lovingly adhered to, coupled with a compulsive lack of urgency, often made for heated frustration. It is a constant theme of modern literature and drama. Shakespeare's fumbling, inept constable, Dogberry, in *Much Ado About Nothing,* is an Elizabethan example, while Charles Dickens was an inveterate assailant of incompetent and insensitive officialdom, of which his remorseless satire of the Circumlocution Office in *Little Dorrit* is a prime instance. Robb Wilton was a Mr Bumble for the mid 20th century.

It is, of course, one thing to spot grounds for such wry humour and another to raise the parody to high levels of achievement. Robb Wilton was a burly but very still figure on stage. His white face (he rarely used makeup)

The People's Jesters

was the focus for his characterisation. His large eyes changed expression with flawless regard for the passing emotions; his rapidly mobile tongue darted in and out and then was thrust hard into his cheek; the one fascinating motion was his right hand, flirting nervously the while with his cheek and ear, the little finger popped for a moment in his mouth, before resuming that uneasy facial ballet.

The voice was gruff and measured and the sentences were beset by hesitations and left unfinished in little fits of exasperation. The timing was ideal. It was once reported in *The Times* that the enunciation of his script was 'a tug of war between performer and audience'. Like Jack Benny, the fine American comedian, not only did he understand the value of silence, he had, more importantly, the supreme confidence to sustain the silence. Robb Wilton was never emulated, but he was frequently imitated, but not one of his mimics has ever had the courage to pause for as long as the master before delivering the killer blow.

His lugubrious temperament was maintained offstage, along with a genuine taste for the withering comment, delivered in kindly tones. Unlike many comedians, he seems to have carried much of his own nature into his performance. Standing in the wings, watching a Japanese family acrobatic act exhaust themselves in a perspiring frenzy of hoops, pyramids, somersaults and the like, he muttered, 'all because the buggers are too lazy to learn a comic song'. Once at the Palladium, commiserating with the top-of-the-bill American vocal group, the Deep River Boys, when their act had been halved by Val Parnell, he murmured sympathetically, 'it's hardly worth blacking up for, is it?'

Such tales are legion, and yet it was the 1939-1945 War that brought Robb Wilton ultimate and enduring fame and adoration. After Tommy Handley, he was the most loved of wartime comedians, and his opening gambit, 'the day war broke out ...' still rests memorably in popular usage. Even his post-war introduction, 'the day peace broke out ...' was affectionately received, the laughter and applause an accolade to a great comedian.

Wartime Britain, with its pother of controls and bureaucratic rigmarole, provided Robb Wilton with an exact niche for his percipient jabbing at the follies of Bumbledom. The Civil Service doubled to 700,000 and the Food Offices, which controlled rationing, employed as many as 50,000 clerks. Although he occasionally varied the routine to become, for instance, a special wartime policeman, it was for his home guardsman that Robb Wilton would always be admired and remembered. He moved away from the sketch format but intrinsic to the monologue was his steely wife, Rita, named with a sidelong glance at the glamorous 1940s pin-up, Rita Hayworth. He peevishly reported, in fact, their conversation, and, as she was the dominant partner, forever scoffing – 'what good are yer? – at his feeble attempts to help the war effort, the effect was as close to a duologue as one might find.

Spluttering, breathing heavily, sighing audibly, Robb Wilton tried vainly to cope with the wifely onslaught. 'You'll have to go back to work', he reports Rita as angrily demanding; there is an audaciously long pause before the drawn-out rejoinder, 'ohhh, she's a cru-ell ton-guer, that woman'. Unimpressed with his strategy for guarding the coastline against Adolf Hitler, his wife wants to know how they would know Hitler if he did land; 'doesn't she know', is his impatient thought, ' I've got a tongue in me head'.

Robb Wilton caught the sensibilities of the British wartime public to a tee. The British people realised that authority and control was necessary; after all, rationing was introduced in answer more to popular demand than to political initiative. Nonetheless, they found it tiresome and they were fighting for the freedom to grumble about such petty restrictions. Robb Wilton, much more than any other comedian, comprehended this ambiguity and earned a place in domestic history as the man who, by making fun of such travails, cheered up and encouraged the British public to stand firm. It was an important responsibility and Robb Wilton had the comic genius to fulfil it with remarkable aplomb.

Jimmy James . . . 'Are You Putting it around that I'm Barmy?'

Jimmy James and Robb Wilton indulged in a rare and unselfish competition in which they each accused the other of being the best 'waiter' – that is, exponent of contemplative repose – in the 'business'. Good judges find it hard to decide who was right, whilst most accept that there are no other rivals in the list. In both case it arose from an inner assurance and the benefit of a stable temper, neither of them virtues profusely visited on entertainers.

James Casey was born in 1892 in Stockton-on-Tees. His father, Jeremiah, was a clog dancing steel worker, an antithesis that his son perhaps relished, for he would later make such announcements in his act as, 'I've got a letter here from a singing lighthouse keeper in Bootle.' He started show-business life, as previously remarked, in sundry 'boy' troupes, before, in 1925, he adopted the single whimsical character that would serve him well. He was noticed in variety in Sunderland in 1929 and was whisked off to London and national fame. He appeared at the Palladium in 1943 and again in 1948, when he salvaged the show in the face of Mickey Rooney flopping disastrously. Restless with the restraints of a script or a studio, he was not by any means as regular on radio as Robb Wilton and there is not much film or televisual footage of him.

Moreover, he did not kow-tow to imperious management and certainly did not gain the centrality of presentation that he merited. It must be said that this was not helped, especially in the latter half of his career, by his penchant for the racetrack, as he liked to juggle his performing dates to coincide with horse racing. He was an inveterate gambler, as a consequence of which he was made bankrupt three times, in 1936, 1955 and 1963, asking, on that third occasion whether he had won the official receiver outright. He married Isabelle Darby in 1921 and, along with his brother, Peter Casey, she often accompanied him on his professional and leisure jaunts.

Jimmy James also told of a one-legged relation who acted as his assistant. He claimed that this cousin knew a man in Northampton who had lost the other leg. Periodically, they would contact one another for the economical purchase of a pair of shoes. Jimmy and Isabelle Casey's son, James Casey, was born in 1922 and, as well as being a splendid stooge for his father, he was to become a very much respected and very amiable senior light entertainment producer with the BBC. Amid much rejoicing among the aficionados, he resurrected his father's main act toward the end of the 20th century – and it earned another royal command performance. Jimmy James died in Blackpool in 1965.

Jimmy James was 'the comedian's comedian'. Comics completely unlike him in style regarded him as their tutor. Tales redound of comedians rushing to watch him time and again or of comedians on the same bill, from Peter Sellers to Tony Hancock, standing, night after night, in the wings to observe and admire. It was Jimmy James who summed up the whole philosophy of his craft with the wise statement that 'a comedian is someone who says things funnily, not a man who says funny things.'

Jimmy James had the consummate skills to put into action that homespun ideology. His rough-hewn countenance was rubbery in expression. His throaty voice – aided by the unsought effect of gassing whilst serving with the Northumberland Fusiliers in World War I – was like that of a man speaking through gravel. Like Robb Wilton, he had the ultimate gift of tranquillity, whatever the occasional alarums and excursions of his fellows. Dressed like an on-course bookmaker of the kind he probably knew only too well, his chief prop was the cigarette, which he whirled about him in strange circular movements, puffing out the smoke in eerie rings, like a demented Thomas the Tank Engine.

Like many comedians – Les Dawson and Ken Dodd are other examples – he loved and caressed language and doted on words. His sketches were beautifully compiled but never rigorously so; they were, as he criss-crossed from one to the next of the nation's variety theatres, delicately amended and adjusted, like a great painter returning again and again to his masterpiece and adding to or subtracting from the already sublime canvas. This brought immense freshness to his cameos – and then there was his timing. James Casey told the author of his first brush with his father when, in an exchange about some linguistic mix-up, he was supposed to whisper to the senior partner the right interpretation. Leaving the stage at the end of the sketch, his father upbraided him for muttering 'rhubarb, rhubarb' instead of the actual words. 'How the bloody hell do you think I know what to say unless you tell me properly?' It was a curt, definitive lesson in timing. Jimmy James was able to suspend belief in a much-used routine to the extent that his reaction was always new and unsullied.

There were three major sketches. One was 'the Drunk', wherein Jimmy James, in this part costumed in bedraggled evening wear, wandered unsteadily on to the stage to the strains of his signature tune, *Three O'clock in the Morning*, already finding it an arduous task to convey his erratic cigarette in the general direction of his waiting lips. The lamppost and the policeman – 'what time are you due back on board ship, sailor?' – alike attracted his bemused attention, as this exercise in intoxication continued. There were two other 'drunk' sketches, both with more domestic milieux. Jimmy James was, take comics or straight actors, the best stage drunk there has ever been. A total abstainer for much of his life, he grasped a significant truth about the inebriated. The drunk does not realise his drunkenness. Most actors act exaggeratedly, lurching and befuddled. Jimmy James essayed a dignity unconsciously undermined by alcohol and it became a classic cameo.

For the 1953 royal command performance he developed 'the Chipster', destined to become one of two or three legendary set pieces with so regal a baptism, in a setting where comedy has often been restrained or hackneyed. He was, indeed, the champion chipster ('beat Joe Davis three times. Of course, he's a fair snooker player, but he's rubbish at the chipping'). It was a vocation beset by industrial injuries. There were lost digits, and Jimmy James would hold up his two outside fingers and order 'four pints, please'. There was 'batterer's elbow', the cocked arm resultant on long plunging of sieves and baskets in the sizzling vats, and the 'chipster's wink', consequent on flying splashes of hot fat. In tandem, these two afflictions created a decidedly camp appearance.

The third and most famous sketch is 'the Shoebox', in which the balance of the insane and the normal is carefully and delectably, if precariously, maintained. Jimmy James' companions are the bellicose, overcoated Hutton Conyers (named after a Yorkshire village) and, in shrunken suit and wearing a deerstalker hat, the docile Bretton Woods (named after the American site of the post-war fiscal agreement). Hutton Conyers carried the shoebox, which contained, it gradually transpired, two man-eating lions ('I thought I heard a rustling', murmured Jimmy James) and a giraffe, although there was insufficient accommodation for the ele-phant, even if, as Bretton Woods diffidently proposed, the giraffe might 'move over a bit'. Hutton Conyers would also ask aggressively, 'are you putting it around that I'm barmy' – 'why', replied the ever-conciliatory Jimmy James, 'are you trying to keep it a secret?'. The sketch ended with the trio finding refuge, after faltering warblings of 'fah, fah, fah' as they tried to find the pitch, in songs, such as *Oh, What a Night it was.*

As an exercise in a triangular dialogue, expressive of a close but complex relation-ship, it was a small masterpiece. As a brief example of the Theatre of the Absurd, it matched much of Ionesco, Samuel Beck-ett, Genet and Harold Pinter, offering a ready gloss on Beckett's salient question, 'what has one thing to do with another?' In motive, language, structure and execution, it must be regarded as the finest of all variety sketches.

Jack Darby, Jimmy James' brother-in-law, and Dick Charlton, as well as Cass James aka James Casey, were involved at one time or another, while the regular Bretton Woods was another relative, Jimmy James' cousin, Jack 'Eli' Casey, who kept going as a stage vacant idiot for some years. In an emphatic reinforcement of Jimmy James' powers of tutelage, Roy Castle broke into his own career to serve with Jimmy James from 1956 to 1959, taking the Hutton Conyers portfolio. Roy Castle was born in Holmfirth in 1932 and brought up in Scholes, Yorkshire, where his mother encouraged him musically. He married Fiona Dickson in 1963 and they had four children, but cancer cut short the life of this engaging personality in 1994. He died in Gerrards Cross, Buckinghamshire, and, of committed religious beliefs, he had undertaken a vigorous campaign on behalf of cancer research in his last years and was appointed OBE.

He sang, danced, played scores of instru-ments, and told stories, all with a bright and intelligent keenness, so much so that he had a successful career on both side of the Atlantic. He fronted the BBC children's show, *Record Breakers*, for an astounding 22 years, and, among other achievements, starred with Tommy Steele in a Palladium version of the mould-breaking film musical, *Singing in the Rain*. A most versatile and likeable performer, such was the range of his talents that it would be wrong to describe him as a comedian. He more snugly fits the category of all-round entertainer. Another who might be so described is Max Bygraves (Walter William Bygraves, of London's dockland, born in 1922.) By the conjunction of friendly stories and unpretentious songs, all delivered with verve and affability, he has contrived to attain esteem and affluence in the world of entertainment. In the 1950s, in particular, his line of tunes, such as *Tulips from Amsterdam* or *You Need Hands*, captivated the millions, as he came to be recognised as the complete family entertainer.

Des O'Connor has enjoyed something of the same reputation; neither a singer who tells occasional jokes nor a comic who occasionally sings, but a smiling face offering light-hearted chat and sentimental music. They just seem to be good company and the sort of person to make a party go with a swing. Sometimes with this sort of entertainer, however good they may be, there is a feeling that they are neither fish nor fowl, whereas, with the genuine comedian, such as Jimmy James, the specificity was paramount.

A further cigarette-waving stage drunkard was Freddie Frinton. He was born in Grimsby in 1909 and, partially as a result of being fostered, he was both Frederick Bittiner and Frederick Hargate. He swiftly moved from being a fish packer to entertaining in pubs and on beaches, before being signed up in 1931 by Tom Moss at the Theatre Royal, Sheffield. He did concert party stints with Ernest Binn's Northern Concert Party, Jimmy Slater's Supper Follies and his own road show and then the war found him, after a spell with a searchlight unit, joining George Black's revue, *Stars in Battledress*. He played in a Sid Field revue, as dame in panto, alongside Arthur Haynes on television in the 1960s, and, after some ventures into summertime farce at the resorts, five series of *Meet the Wife*, with Thora Hird. Thora Hird was the uppity wife with social pretensions; Freddie Frinton was the downcast husband without social ambition.

He had long developed the drunk act, with his slurred 'good evenin', ossifer' to the severe policeman, and his drooping, fractured cigarette, but, like some unheralded artist whose pictures only become valuable after his demise, it was as the butler in the *Dinner for One* sketch that he was to attain post-mortal renown. His employer, Miss Sophie, played by the actress, May Warden, is celebrating her 90th birthday, with places laid for guests who have already shuffled off the mortal coil. Freddie Frinton grows ever drunker, as the

wine has to be imbibed and the toasts are called, with the seminal phrase 'the same procedure as last year' the repeated text. It was written by Laurie Wylie for Bobbie Howes and Binnie Hale in the 1920s, but bought by Freddie Frinton for his own use. Harry Rowson and he added to the material and from 1945 Freddie Frinton included it in his act. The pair televised it in Hamburg in 1963, and this black and white eighteen minutes of antiquated social manners has earned iconic status in Germany and Scandinavia, where Christmas and New Year repeats are regular and well-received. Poor Freddie Frinton died in Middlesex in 1968 and never knew how famous he would become.

Back to Jimmy James for one last illustration of his unruffled disposition. The practice in theatres and cinemas during the German blitzes of the 1939-1945 was to warn the audience, should they wish to seek shelter, but, where possible, to keep the show going. During one air raid, while appearing at the Crown Theatre, Eccles, a bomb blew out every door of the building and broke several windows. 'It's that wedding party at the back again' quipped Jimmy James, 'will someone tell them either to shut up or get out.'

Sid Field . . . 'What a Performance!'

The third of the three superb 'sketch' comedians of mid-20th century, Sidney Arthur Field, was born in Birmingham in 1904, the son of a whip-making father and a whip-cracking mother, Bertha Workman, who, with the encouragement of a music teacher, Mrs Kent, steered her self-conscious lad towards the stage. After conventional experience with 'child' groups, like the Kino Royal Juveniles and the Harry Orchard Toyland Troupe, and even as an unused understudy for Wee

Georgie Wood, he gradually hauled himself into the limelight and, along the way, married a fellow-artiste, Constance Dawkins. He worked on a Tate-like golf sketch and as an angrily complaining cockney, auditioning but never quite getting round to doing his turn. The first sketch formed the base for one of his most adored vignettes, *Following Through*, where he finds a golf lesson distracting and bemusing – 'address the ball'; 'Dear Ball'. The second metamorphosed into Slasher Green, the prototype 'spiv', shoulders padded, shadow-boxing and street-wise.

That curse of the waxing star, contractual restraints, had kept him from the central London theatrical scene, but rid of these in 1942, he teamed up with Jerry Desmonde – and George Black saw them in a Nottingham pantomime. James Robert Sadler, to give him his real name, was born in Middlesex in 1908, and is regarded on all sides as the prince of foils. Urbane, unctuous, suave in theatrical manner, he later became the help-meet of Norman Wisdom, but his later years were arduous ones, as his type of assistance fell from favour. He died in 1967. A sensitive and flexible feed, he aided Sid Field in his London triumphs, in the old, old story of the sudden success of the star that, for years, has twinkled dimly in the far-off darkness.

In George Black's revues, *Strike a New Note* (1943, at the Prince of Wales Theatre), *Strike It Again* (1944) and *Piccadilly Hayride* (1946; it ran for 777 performances), Sid Field scored notably with his usually two-handed sketches. As well as the golfing and the spivvery, there was the snooker player, the cinema organist, the landscape artist, the tubular bell ringer, and, a major achievement, *Portrait Study*, with Sid Field the fruity photographer and Jerry Desmonde the self-important mayoral model – 'let's have some books on the table; that gives the impression you can read'.

With his lodestone song, *You Can't Keep a Good Dreamer Down*, and his exclamation, through pursed lips, of 'What a performance!', Sid Field seized his opportunity and, for just a few desperately short years, was king of the comic castle,

'What a Performance!' - Along with Jimmy James and Robb Wilton, Sid Field was the greatest of British 'sketch' comedians, especially in tandem with Jerry Desmonde

The People's Jesters

especially in the West End, where he was courted by the critics and commentators of the upmarket newspapers and journals. Like Jimmy James and Robb Wilton, he was quite a sturdy figure, but he was more mobile, stepping out with an elephantine graciousness, eyes glistening with impish mischief. Gossipy and camp in several of his sketches, he was the sly, rather artful activist. Where Harry Tate was the unconscious butt of those around him, Robb Wilton the stolid minion of overweighty clericalism, Will Hay the victim of his own insufficient authority and Jimmy James, like Bismarck, the 'honest broker', negotiating between two madcaps, Sid Field, arch and wily, was, as one obituarist put it, the 'merry child', taking some positive delight in his trouble-stirring antics. In all his outrageous presentations, his range of intonation and movement was astonishing, on a par with the finest of 'straight' or classic comic acting. As with Jimmy James and Robb Wilton, as with the purported caricatures of Charles Dickens, there was always the feeling that, for all the harebrained traits, these were people one had met.

In 1949 he took to the legitimate stage with enormous panache, playing Elwood P Dowd in the Mary Chase comedy, *Harvey*, made famous on screen by James Stewart in 1950. Harvey is the drunken Dowd's imaginary white rabbit. Alas, art and nature were in tandem. Unlike Jimmy James and Robb Wilton, who were comfortable with their stage persona and both of regally calm temperaments, Sid Field was inveterately nervous and anxious. On the hazardous advice, apparently, of his ambitious mother, he ever employed alcohol to stiffen the sinews of resolve and his health suffered lamentably. He died in Wimbledon, a relatively young man, in 1950. Luckily, that extravagant flop of a British musical film, *London Town* (1946)

preserves several of his best sketches, with Jerry Desmonde on hand, for a fortunate posterity. Sid Field was 40 before, after 30 years of provincial campaigning, he became a star, a star that illumined the principal West End theatres for no more than six years. It is difficult to know whether to grieve the brevity of that incandescent comic light or to be thankful that it shone so glitteringly at all.

The sketch construct was suited to Sid Field's multiple identities. They were wider ranging, if perhaps not so profound, as the identity presented by Jimmy James, Will Hay and Robb Wilton, all of whom, even if they did change the title and the costume, retained the same essence of comic personality. Nonetheless, and in spite of the impact of Slasher Green, Sid Field is most fondly recollected for his slightly effeminate, slightly fey, slightly waspish – snapping, 'don't be so foolhardy' – character. There are premonitions here of Frankie Howerd, swinging in mood from exasperation to astonishment, with vocal scales to match, and replete with shrewish gossip. There are forward glimpses of Larry Grayson, another who, as the 'pros' say, 'knocked it out' in all-male revue, provincial clubs and the like, before hitting the high spots with television exposure in the 1970s, including the hosting of BBC's *Generation Game* programme.

Larry Grayson (1924-1995) was born in Banbury and in real life was William White. Fastidious, limp, hypochondriac, he was the antithesis of the fast-talking, raunchy stand-up comic, and, like Sid Field and Frankie Howerd, he came closer to being a traditional 'dame' in male dress than most other comedians. His health and relationship worries were many, as his despairing asides suggested – 'shut that door'; 'there's a draught in here'; 'have you seen the muck in here?'; 'I wish I could lie down.' The gallery of friends he commented on showed an inventiveness worthy of a more roguish Gillie Potter or a more knowing *ITMA*. His local pub was 'the Friend in Hand', from whence he would bring news of Slack Alice, 'my friend' Everard, Pop it in Pete the Postman and Apricot Lil. Such was his companionable and welcoming nature that audiences found nothing offensive or distasteful in his discourse. It is fair to say he was laughed with and at in a spirit of amiable fondness.

The 'sketch' comics, widened in number to embrace the likes of Harry Tate and Will Hay, include several who must be regarded as among the premiership of British comedians. Moving down the arithmetical sequence to two, there will next be a chance to decide whether any double acts might be promoted to that top league of champions.

10. 'KINDLY LEAVE THE STAGE'
THE DOUBLE ACT STORY

Some theatre historians are inclined to trace the double comedy act back into the mists of time, recruiting for their interpretive bidding the Italianate origins of Punch and Judy, Mr and Mrs Noah in the medieval 'mystery' play, the master/servant relationship in ancient classical or renaissance drama, and even the two malefactors crucified either side of Jesus. If, however, one cuts in sprightly fashion to the mustard and examines the double act familiar to the post-1918 generations, the derivation is of a distinctly modern and, indeed, transatlantic source.

Seaside Beginnings

In the fourth chapter there was some analysis of the phenomenon of the urban seaside holiday, part of the aftermath of the Industrial Revolution, and some description of how entertainment was initially brought to the piers and beaches by the black-up minstrel shows, very much an American craze. When the minstrels set up on beach or pier, it was their custom to erect or form a wooden enclosure, its focus, to the despair of the modern liberal, a 'nigger ring', a semi-circle of seated performers, sometimes only six or eight in number, ready to sing their plaintive spirituals and jollier Stephen Foster and Leslie Stuart favourites. At either end

of the ring were the two funny men, almost always the backing instrumentalists, often called, after the tools of their trade, 'Bones' and 'Tambo' (not Sambo; but a diminutive of tambourine). Between the melodies, they would converse with and across the minstrel leader, 'Massa Interlocutor', sitting centrally, frequently asking riddles of the 'why did the chicken cross the road' variety – 'for some 'fowl' reason, as Max Miller would later suggest. It was because the twosome interrupted the interlocutor and called across him that the terms 'crosstalk' and thus 'crosstalk comedians' arose.

Older readers may remember the last vestige of these origins in Scott and Whaley, who were Cuthbert and Pussyfoot with the Kentucky Minstrels, a popular group both on BBC radio and Radio Luxembourg, as well as appearing independently on the halls. It was earlier noted that after their reign of 30 or so years, the minstrels were displaced by the pierrots and the concert parties, but the vogue for crosstalk was maintained, with the result that the double act became a standard turn on the variety stage.

There was one possibly sound reason why double acts had not flourished in the days of music hall before World War I. Until the joint managements' agreement of 1907, with its allowance of up to 30 minutes dialogue on the music hall stage, a lengthy crosstalk act would have been more or less illegal. The rights of the legitimate theatre were jealously guarded, for the music halls created plenty of competition for the straight theatre without adding the spoken word. There were several cases of music hall managers, even the great Charles Morton, being fined for infringement of their purely music licenses. In 1912, when the Lord Chamberlain took control of the licensing of all stage productions, the process was formalised much further. Strictly speaking, the 'crosstalk' of double acts should have been presented for licensing to his august office, simply because it was a piece of continuous dialogue, and some examples of this exist in the archives.

The minstrels, assembling informally on the sands, may have been free of that legal incubus and thus got away with more dialogue. It follows that, where there were double acts in the days of the music hall, they tended to be song and mime based. Examples include Bella and Bijou – Bella Fothergill and Tommy Cannon – who performed a 'lawyer and client' turn and Joe Tennyson and Joe O'Gorman, who did joint numbers like *The Wild Man of Poplar*. Interestingly enough, the latter's sons, Dave and Joe O'Gorman inherited the dual disposition and, as the O'Gorman Brothers played the halls in the inter-wars years, mixing comedy and music. Dave O'Gorman died in 1964, aged 68 and his brother died in 1974, aged 85. A third illustration might be Clarice Mayne and 'That'. Again, this was musically founded, with 'That', aka J W Tate at the piano, with his wife, the attractive Clarice Mayne, being rather condescending of him – with just a hint of Frankie Howerd's patronising attitude to his pianists. J W Tate composed the songs they featured and these included *Put on Your Ta-Ta, Little Girlie; Joshua*, and *I was a Good Little Girl*, all winners in their time.

This legal restriction helps explain why entirely 'verbal' double acts, although by no means unknown, were not so often in use before the First World War No show seemed complete without a crosstalk act, often beginning each of the two halves of the bill and remaining popular in the seaside shows. A much more prominent niche was developed for them in pantomime. As well the robbers in *Babes in the Woods*, there was a proliferation of Chinese policemen in *Aladdin*, brokers' men in *Cinderella*, captain and mate in *Dick Whittington* and so forth.

Double Acts: All the Rage

In pondering the outbreak of this rash of double acts, one must not underestimate the sheer pressure of fashion. Just as there would be a wave of so-called 'alternative comedy' at the turn of the 20th century, then there was a craze for double acts. It was an idea that caught on; the public came to expect double acts and comics hurried to team up and supply the demand.

Cultural fashions often reflect the social and political climate. The 1920s and 1930s were decades of economic depression and foreign turmoil, with the British people in a general mood of nervous and inward looking inertia. This was an era that has been characterised as one of 'immobilism'. There was a tendency to turn to avuncular or strait-laced politicians, like, respectively, Stanley Baldwin and Neville Chamberlain, away from the more flamboyant style of David Lloyd-George or, until the call for expedient action was urgent, Winston Churchill. There was dependability and solidity about partnerships. Who would then have visited a doctor (think of the TV representation of Dr Finlay and Dr Cameron up in Tannochbrae) or, even more so, a solicitor practising alone?

Partnerships were the rage. One might have shopped at Marks and Spencer, Marshall and Snellgrove or Timothy White and Taylor, possibly buying a tin of Crosse and Blackwell soup, a tin of Huntley and Palmer's biscuits, a packet of Tate and Lyle sugar and some Proctor and Gamble's soap powder, before going to the cinema to watch an American film, starring Jeannette Macdonald and Nelson Eddy, Fred Astaire and Ginger Rogers, Olsen and Johnson or Dean Martin and Jerry Lewis. If threesomes were required, one might have visited the theatre to see the North American trio, Forsythe, Seamon and Farrell, having just purchased a pair of shoes in the high street at Freeman, Hardy and Willis. The Canadian, Charlie Forsythe, a baritone; his wife, beaming Addie Seamon, from New Jersey, a dancer, and the chubby pianist, Elinore Farrell from Rhode Island, joined together in 1931 and the three of them mixed in plenty of comic pleasantries along with the song and dance.

There seemed to be more of a stress on dualisms in the world of sport. Cricket had well-established pairs of opening batsmen, such as Hobbs and Sutcliffe and Hutton and Washbrook, or bowling couples, such as Larwood and Voce, Lindwall and Miller, Laker and Lock, and Trueman and Statham. There were even well-known pairings of football's full-backs, like Arsenal's Male and Hapgood, England's Scott and Hardwick or Manchester City's Sproston and Barkis.

Should it be thought that this analysis is tinged with slight hyperbole, consider the modern scene. The fashion now is for single, brusque, well nigh brutalist titles, with rampant capital letters, both in show-business and elsewhere in the popular culture and in social affairs: MADONNA, CHER, STING, ARGOS, TESCO, TRANSCO, ENRON, ORANGE, MENCAP, RELATE... Take a stroll down your local high street and glance at the shop and company fronts – the majority have one word titles. Or take a train ride: as a logo, ARRIVA is a far cry from the London and North Eastern Railway.

A Litany of Double Acts

Such is the profusion of crosstalk acts crowding the stages and airways of this epoch that the simplest manner of dealing with this flourishing outcrop may be to list many examples briefly, for it is the abundance of rather than the differences between them that are most meaningful. Almost all of them opted for the straight man, sharp, irritated, better dressed (even Cuthbert was more expensively garbed than Pussyfoot with Scott and Whaley), and the comic, friendly, put upon but rarely outwitted. Almost all of them chose some form of banter and riposte wherein the comic had the last laugh. As if in deference to the past dominance of melody in the old music hall, they almost all ended and sometimes began with a song.

Several of them have been encountered previously. No less than seven double acts were connected to the Crazy Gang at one time or another and the Crazy Gang was an institution of that age, which yearned for security. Some others, like Wheeler and Wolsey and Old Mother Riley and her daughter, Kitty, have also been described, while two or three all-female duos must await the later chapter on women comedians and a couple of others in the chapter on regional humour. The doyen of straight men, Jerry Desmonde, has, too, been mentioned. This still leaves a legion of examples culled roughly from the mid-1920s to the late 1950s, the age of variety. They will be described in an approximate order of their chronological peaking, beginning with a range of all-male partnerships.

Old Mother Riley and her daughter, Kitty – the man and wife team of Arthur Lucan and Kitty McShane; not only a famous double act, but an example of cinema comedy and of 'sketch' comedy

1. Bennett and Williams – they were two for the price of one Vic Oliver or Ted Ray, the fiddling comics. Bennett and Williams sat and sawed at phonofiddles, stopping periodically to exchange sallies.

2. Clapham and Dwyer – Charlie Clapham (1894-1959) was a Birmingham born comedian, who carried on alone when his partner, Billy Dwyer, fell ill in 1940 and died in 1943. They stood rather aloof one from the other, Billy Dwyer, biggish, assured, bespectacled, as the straight man; Charlie Clapham, thinner, vacillating, wearing slightly shabby evening wear, as the comic. Partnered together from 1925, they made a hit with their adventures, *In a Spot of Bother*, which necessarily involved the inconsequential intervention of Cissie the Cow.

3. Morris and Cowley – in reality the brothers Harry and Frank Birkenhead from Staffordshire, they began with the Birkenhead Family quintet, before starting out as a double act, first of all as the Vesta Brothers, and then adopting their vehicular names in 1923. Dressed as antiquated Chelsea Pensioners, they mumbled about past glories, never forgetting the bromide purportedly added to their Boer War tea to weaken their libidinous longings – 'I think it's beginning to work', was the doleful realisation. They would end with a long drawn out rendition of *The Boys of the Old Brigade*.

4. Lowe and Webster – they were a very straightforward question-and-answer team, but they do have a singular claim to fame, and that is that they are reputed to have been the first to utilise the 'I say, I say, I say' formula, when the comic arrived on stage to interrupt the feed.

5. Murray and Mooney – they have gone down in show-business lore as the classic double act. Harry Murray (1891-1972, real name, Church) worked for 25 years with Harry Mooney (born in Richmond in 1869, real name, Goodchild) and then did a further stint with Victor King. Harry Murray would begin a monologue, commencing, 'It's a Funny Old World we Live in, but the world's not entirely to blame" or 'Jack was a Coward, a Great Big Coward with a Turned-up Nose'. The monologue, as we shall later note in the chapter on speciality acts, was a standard variety spot, so the provenance was well comprehended by the audience. Harry Mooney would venture on with a set of unconnected interruptions, along the lines of 'it's put-up job' – 'what's a put-up job?' – 'paper-hanging', at which Murray would sternly order, 'I don't wish to know that; kindly leave the stage', the classic rebuttal and dismissal that they made customary, if did they not invent it. They were well organised and clear-cut and they have a strong right to be regarded as the model of the conventional double act.

6. Gordon and Colville – Gordon Horsewell, born 1911, and Peter Colville, born 1918, were southerners, who, when they became partners in 1948, concentrated on the smart exchanges of the usual kind, Vic Gordon being the comic and Peter Colville the foil. They were especially successful in seaside holiday shows.

7. Holt and Morice – they were another pleasing example of this fine old tradition of the one annoying the other with awkward and groundless enquiries; their bill matter – 'shredded wit' – has the authentic ring.

8. Eno and Lane – a Channel Islander, Leon Enot, as the little comic with the wispy moustache, and George Max Korelin, from Surrey, as the feed, formed another solid, standard variety act.

9. Desmond and Marks – they were a visually oriented act, concentrating on pratfalls and other violent measures. Frederick George Dawson and John Henry Marks were both born in 1915 and, after pre-war stage apprenticeships and war service, they formulated their act.

10. Bartlett and Shaw – this was a very dressy double 'drag' act, of which there were several quite popular in the immediate post-1945 years. Terry Bartlett was the

comic and Colin Ross the feed. They were a gift to *Cinderella* as the Ugly Sisters, but they did other routines, such as the ever popular mock-ballet.

11. Collinson and Breen – Bill Collinson, the tall foil, worked first with Alfie Dean, soon to be one of Sid Field's accomplices, before partnering the diminutive Breen. Their most notable routine, which immediately roots them chronologically, was the strict sergeant and the bemused private. It revolved around a cookhouse fracas. 'Someone's pinched me puddin', cried Breen, unhappily and perhaps phallically, 'the sergeant shouted 'all put yer puddins out for treacle' – and when I put mine out, someone pinched me puddin".

12. The Two Pirates – tiny Reg Mankin, a Londoner, and giant Jock Cochrane, a Glaswegian, dressed as skirted buccaneers, perfected the mock balancing act, courtesy of a thin wire attached to the smaller partner's shoulders, indulged in odd moments of banter and involved audiences in much 'oh, no there isn't'/'oh, yes there is' altercation.

13. Baker and Douglas – Joe Baker was the son of a double act: Joe Baker and Olga, their crosstalk based on the home and on marital dispute. Jack Douglas, the straight man, later developed something of a niche as a comic with a pronounced nervous tic, not seen since Jimmy James and his cronies had attempted to peer at and around each other in neurotic swivels. Like several of the late 1930s and 1940s breed of comics, they had sound experience in the redcoats of Butlin's holiday camps. Joe Baker, a very funny man, opted for life in the United States and some bit parts in films, while Jack Douglas pursued a long career at home, including being the helpmate of Des O'Connor.

14. Kirby and Hayes – Sid Kirby (Sidney Joseph, born in Bristol in 1926) and Mickey Hayes (Michael Hochrad, born London 1927) were another act of similar vintage, emerging from wartime ENSA-type appearances to find lots of work together in pantomimes and at Butlin's holiday centres. Smartly dressed and versatile, they danced, sang and played guitars along with the comic patter.

15. Len and Bill Lowe – from 1935 to 1950, these two brothers, with plenty of other and varied entertainment experience before and after, developed a strong act, being among the first duos where both men were well-groomed and suited. Len Lowe later developed a double act with his brother, Don, another with army and summer season work to his credit under various names. They were known as Lowe and Ladd, but, such are the processes of show-biz evolution, that Don Lowe, aka Don Smoothey, after some time as a singleton comic, teamed up with Tommy Layton – and Smoothey and Layton were born.

16. Max and Harry Nesbitt – they were another act that sang – they composed, among other tunes, *I Kiss Your Little Hand, Madame* – and played, in their case, banjos. They were born in Cape Town, Max in 1903 and Harry in 1905, and they came to Britain in 1927. They were a plump, jolly pair, full of madcap wheezes.

17. Connor and Drake – They were, in some respects, an updated version of Clapham and Dwyer. They adopted the costume of two tramps, the one, Vernon Drake, as the gentleman hobo, known as the Duke, and acting as straight man for Eddie Drake, the proletarian down-and-out.

18. Earle and Vaughan – Kenny Earle was born in Liverpool in 1930 and Malcolm Thomas in South Wales in 1929, so their career were demonstrably post-war. Kenny Earle, having been half of Macey and Macey, joined Malcolm Vaughan, then with the Street Singers, and, boosted by the latter's tuneful singing voice, they won a decent share of fame and fortune in the late 1940s and early 1950s.

19. Mike and Bernie Winters – Mike and Bernie Weinstein, born respectively in 1927 and 1930, came from the East End of London to lead a chequered career of fits and starts, sometimes banded together, sometimes not. They then enjoyed the distinct achievement of being about the first of the double acts to score heavily on television. As the rock'n'roll era dawned, with Tommy Steele riding high, it was realised that they were liked by the new youthful audiences that revelled in the novel music. They became resident comedians on *6-5 Special*, the first pre-*Top of the Pops* modern songs show, broadcast in the Saturday early evening peak time. It was a little like Frankie Howerd finding his feet on radio's *Variety Bandbox*. Bernie Winters, with his goosey features and goofy smile, his beaming face surmounted by a large hat, the brim bent back, fenced verbally with Mike Winters, the irked respondent to his brother's simple-minded enquiries. After a further break, they had later TV successes, although the rather juvenile exchanges that pleased the first generation of 'pop' youth did not always answer well with the last generation of hardy variety watchers. The anecdote is told, as the author heard it, of the Hulme Hippodrome, Manchester, but, as there are other sightings of the tale, it is either apocryphal or it happened to them more than once. Mike Winters entered to begin the routine, to a muted and cool reception; when Bernie Winters joined him, there was a strangled cry from the gallery, 'Jesus Christ, there's two of them...'.

20. Jewel and Warriss – James Marsh (1906-1995) and Ben Warriss (1909-1993) were cousins from Sheffield, with a formidable background in variety. They joined forces in 1934 and evolved an act that endured for 32 years to 1966, bringing them Blackpool summer seasons and royal command performances in some abundance. *Up the Pole*, their delightful radio series, which ran for five years from 1947 to 1952, cemented their national standing and, indeed, paid them handsomely. They were indubitably the leading double act of the period before Morecambe and Wise. At first sight, they were a conventional comic duo, but, in fact, they were more rounded than that. Jimmy Jewel, lugubrious of face and demeanour and easily puzzled, and Ben Warriss, astute, positive, bright eyes gleaming, had a rapport that was genuinely based on the alternating currents of their comic personalities. Somehow the concept of one funny man and one straight man was modified into the sense of an authentically humorous pairing.

With their deep roots in such matters, their playing of the Robbers in *Babes in the Woods*, with its haunted house scene and with their throat-cutting exit threat, 'and when we find those babes, we're gonna murrrrrrder them', tricked out with a mock-menacing humming of *The Harry Lime Theme* from the prestigious film, *The Third Man*, was a joy. Good as Morecambe and Wise could be, for instance as the King and the Jester in *Sleeping Beauty*, one would, if permitted to cast the ethereal panto for eternity, choose Jewel and Warriss for the double act role. Ben Jewel soldiered on as an entertainer after their severance, while Jimmy Jewel had extraordinary success as a straight actor, not least in Trevor Griffiths' 1970s play, *Comedians*. They apparently were of differing temperaments.

Theatre lore has it that Jimmy Jewel, forever worrying and lonely, died rich and miserable, whilst Ben Warriss, companionable and fun-loving, died poor and happy.

The male/female double acts

21. Eddie Gordon and Nancy – the American Eddie Gordon, a sad, bald, shabby clown, offered the ultimate contrast to Nancy, his glamorously Junoesque assistant. This was a silent act that could, licitly, have played the pre-1914 music halls. His fascinated delight when the curtains opened to reveal an empty stage was really amusing.

22. Ken Barnes and Jeanne – Ken Barnes, whose father was Barnes of Barnes and Elliot, met his future wife and stage partner while both were working for ENSA in the Second World War. Ken Barnes was also well known as a highly competent panto dame.

23. Adrienne and Leslie – Jean Adrienne was born in India in 1905 and, although she had some status as a singer and dancer in her own right, she worked intermittently in a double act with Eddie Leslie, a noted feed on stage and in films, with the two of them finding joint niches in revue and pantomime.

24. Whitaker and Law – Billy Whitaker was the son of the ventriloquist, Coram, whom we shall meet in a coming chapter. He was born in London in 1913 and, like Ken Barnes, he was an entertaining panto dame, with something of Norman Evans in features and manner. In wartime days, he formed a double act with Mimi Law, also from a show-business background, and they displayed a warm-hearted enthusiasm in a variety of comic sketches.

25. Gay and Barry – Cliff Gay (born in Truro in 1903) and Ivy Barry (born in Leicester in 1915) were another husband and wife team, who, as concert party stalwarts, teamed up in 1934 and, with a varied hand of comedy chat, magic and acrobatics, offered ENSA valued service as a supporting act.

27. Scott and Foster – another illustration of marital dualism, Arthur Simpson (1901-1968, born Leamington Spa) and Betty Fielding, from Great Yarmouth, had concert party and repertory experience and, from 1935 until after the second war, they peddled their amusing line in historical cameos.

28. Winters and Fielding – Joan Winters was the daughter of Charles Shadwell, the famed radio musical director, and she was, as previously explained, Jack Warner's 'little gel' in the *Garrison Theatre* programme her father originated. She married Guy Fielding, her partner in a light comedy and music turn, before they moved to the United States in 1961, not, it seems, with enormous success either personally or professionally.

29. Ken Morris and Joan Savage – Ken Morris (1922-1968) from South Wales, emerged from service with Charlie Chester's *Stand Easy* to join with Joan Savage, from Blackpool, in music and mirth of a brand that enabled them to have some early picking on television in shows like *Hi Summer* and *The Black and White Minstrel Show*.

30. Miki and Griff – they were a Celtic mix, with the Scot, Barbara Macdonald, born in 1920, and the Welshman, Emyr Morus Griffith, born in 1923, forming another married act that did well at Butlins, but which later tended to abandon the comedy in favour of the singing element.

31. Ernest Arnley and Gloria – Brighton's Ernest Arnley was, amid other valuable experience, in a double act with his brother, before, keeping the familial flame burning, he invited his wife, the soubrette, Gloria Day, to partner him on stage as well as by the hearth. With some eccentric dance steps and extravagant gesticulation, Ernest Arnley, with his wife's assistance, sustained this turn from 1944 over a score of years. He died in 1988 and Gloria Day died in 1993.

32. Hatton and Manners – 'The Cockney Chap and the Lancashire Lass' thrived in the war years, as Ethel Manners' emphatic catchphrase, 'don't you know there's a warrrrr on' betokened. Interestingly, it was a rarity: a catchphrase borrowed from the people's discourse and played back to them. With Will Hatton she formed a solid enough turn, with her argumentative nature parried by his circumspect cast of mind. They were the sort of act that turned up on *Workers' Playtime*, at the seaside or playing Idle Jack and Sarah the Cook in *Dick Whttington*.

33. Nat Mills and Bobbie – probably the funniest of the man/woman double acts, in part because both were really funny, clown-like prototypes. Nathan Miller was born in London in 1900 and, with Bobbie McCauley, he enjoyed a highly successful connubial and stage relationship, until Bobbie's sadly premature death in 1955. Nat Mills himself lived on until 1993 and he composed the pleasing song, much crooned by Flanagan and Allen, *Nice People*. They both stood awkwardly and bandy-legged on stage, she in a skimpy frock and frumpish black hat, he in long jacket, bow tie and boater, their faces dead-pan expressions of blank idiocy. High-pitched and squeaky voices emitted sundry messages, often a syllable short of simultaneously, which led to the complaint from Nat Mills that 'we both can't talk together, can we?', 'they won't understand us, will they?', and similar querulous enquiries, all answered by Bobbie with a bleating 'noooooooooooh'. Thus to Nat Mills' rejoinder, much copied in normal life in the 1940s and early 1950s, 'then let's get on with it.' Theirs was so fine a compound of visual and verbal humour that their act worked equally well on radio as on the stage.

34. Claude Dampier and Billie Carlyle – a final example of the married couple operating happily together on and off stage. Claude Connelly Cowan (1879-1955) was born in Clapham but founded his career during a long spell abroad, where he met and wooed Doris Davy, who was an Australian, born in 1902. They perfected an act and came to the UK in 1927, when Claude Dampier was nearly 50 years old. They did variety and film, where her pleasant manner and his bumbling mien won many friends. His slightly bent figure, his protruding teeth, his bulbous glasses and his upper crust accents played well, in a fashion that Claude Hulbert did so ably in English comedy films. Like a secretive infant, Claude Dampier had a phantom friend, a certain 'Mrs Gibson', a lady to whom he made consistent reference. It was the stuttering, genteel tones and Mrs Gibson that made Claude Dampier, 'the Professional Idiot', a radio star and his startled 'well, if it isn't Mrs Gibson' was yet another catchphrase to pass into everyday parlance. Some of his lines – 'I promised to squeeze Mrs Gibson's oranges' are certainly non-Reithian.

Radio and the Double Acts

Claude Dampier and Billie Carlyle are convenient signers-off of that lengthy roll call of double acts, in that they found much of their fame on radio, for radio was destined to play a major part in the furtherance of comic dualism. Two elements have been already identified by way of explication of the sudden explosion of such duality. Apart from the 34 acts rostered above, others have been and will be mentioned, to a total of may be 50 or 60 – and all but a handful fall in the period from about 1920 to 1955. The negative impact of possible illegality and the sheer compulsion of fashion have been paraded as explanations. The radio, obviously in intimate alliance with the weight of fashion, offers the third factor by way of clarification.

It has been previously noted in the 'radio' chapters five and seven that radio was generous to comedians and that there were many shows, of both showcase and magazine type, to accommodate them. Moreover, the radio welcomes two voices. One voice may grow monotonous and more than two may become confusing. There was a quite conscious decision on the part of radio producers to deal two-handedly. Few BBC 'wireless' light entertainment shows lacked a double act, very frequently one of the ones described above. But it went much further than that. The BBC invented double acts, beginning with John Henry and Blossom and scoring magically with Arthur Askey and Dickie Murdoch. It will be remembered that the original production idea for *ITMA* was a Tommy Handley/Celia Eddy pairing, a notion later made good by Ted Ray and Kitty Bluett, but that the trio of Tommy Handley, Francis Worsley and Ted Kavanagh had more imaginative thoughts.

However, on analysis, what they did was to create a string of double acts, with the fast-talking Tommy Handley, with his ordinary, slightly northern accent, the foil to a set of bizarre creatures, each armed with a funny voice and some form of vocal mannerism.

Apart from the odd occasion, as when the broker's men, Horace Percival's Claude and Jack Train's Cecil, were demonstrating the ultimate in courtesy, with their 'after you, Claude'/'no, after you, Cecil', it was all couples enwrapped in weird converse. That aspect of *ITMA* has been insufficiently weighed in the discussion of its overriding success.

The reliance on partnerships, like Eric Barker and Pearl Hackney or Richard Murdoch and Kenneth Horne, is self-evident, while sometimes there was a reverse effect. Nan Kenway and Douglas Young, as we earlier found, were thrown together to meet radio requirements. Existing comics were harnessed together purely for radio purposes. Tommy Handley and Ronald Frankau joined together, with breathless pace and clever verbiage, as Murgatroyd (Frankau) and Winterbottom (Handley), the Old Etonian toff and the amiable provincial, but with equal shares of the sallies. Ronald Frankau, who died in 1951, had brought the sophisticated charm and impishness of pre-war cabaret to the airways, as well as the concert parties. With his massive brow and egg-shaped dome, he was the ideal partner for the quick-firing Handley, as they sang gaily or delivered rapid commentaries on mythic Boat Races, Grand Nationals, Derbies and Cup Finals or the League of Nations: 'he was a Czechoslovakian' – 'Serbia right' – 'I don't understand foreigners, neither Swedes nor Wegians' – 'Argentine to pull my leg?'

Billy Bennett, another who must await longer appraisal, teamed up first with the actor, James Carew, and then with Albert Whelan. Albert Whelan was an Australian singer, renowned for his jaunty rendition of songs like *The Preacher and the Bear, I'll be out of the Calaboose*. A gentlemanly figure, he had his song, his gloves and his smile – plus, so it was said, the first entertainer to have his own signature tune, *The Jolly Brothers* waltz, which he whistled as he removed his gloves and his top hat in a lengthy prelude to his singing. He died, aged 86, in 1961. What is interesting is that, in a throwback to the old minstrel shows (or a casting forward to TV's 1960s *Black and White Minstrel Show*) they reverted to the blackface style and were billed as Alexander and Mose. They broadcast this often excruciating – 'you baboon-faced inkstain' – crosstalk in lazy drawls on radio from 1930, but soon their secret was revealed and they played it on the halls along with their own single acts.

As the BBC's affection for George Burns and Gracie Allen ('when I was born I was so surprised, I didn't speak for a year and a half') testifies, the American style was sought after by the broadcasters. There had been plenty of American double acts, like Sweeney and Ryland, some of them, like George Moores and Charles E Mack, blacked up for the purpose. It was probably, however, the model of Amos 'n' Andy on American radio that persuaded the BBC authorities to go ahead. Freeman F Gosden (1899-1982) and Charles Correll (1890-1972) were Amos and Andy.

In any event, the twosome syndrome affected all parts of broadcasting. The 'aunties' in *Children's Hour* often hunted in pairs, for instance, on the nature trail of Romany, who had his dog – 'woof, woof'; 'down, Rack' – as his mate. All fictional detective yarns, from Holmes and Watson to Morse and Lewis, combine deep thinker and unpretentious pragmatist, and BBC radio came up with the sleuth Paul Temple and his wife Steve, while their wartime 'pop' classical music lecturettes were given by Dobson and Young.

The combined forces of fashion and broadcasting produced a thousand examples in other branches of entertainment other than comedy. Music was especially vulnerable to this effect, for, again, two voices or instruments made for a pleasant contrasting sound on the 'wireless'. Anne Ziegler and Webster Booth, (Turner) Layton and (Clarence) Johnstone, Flotsam and Jetsam (B C Hilliam and Malcolm McEachern), the Two Leslies (Holmes and Sarony), Cave and Morgan ('the Singing Dresdens'). Albert and Les Ward, Les Allen and Kitty Masters, Rupert Hazell and Elsie Day, Bob and Alf Pearson, Pearl Carr and Teddy Johnson and Ted and Barbara Andrews are forceful examples of singing acts in this style, sometimes made up – as with the Two Leslies – of two singers active as single turns.

On a personal note, the writer, as a boy in the 1940s, attended monthly variety weeks held at the Longford Cinema, Stretford, not far from Manchester United's football ground, and there saw the likes of Albert Burdon, Jimmy Clitheroe, Frank Randle, Robb Wilton and Billy Cotton. Ted and Barbara Andrews were on one such bill. After performing their melodious duets, with Barbara at the piano, they took a bow. A prettily dressed small girl joined them: they were blooding Barbara's daughter, Julie, for life on the stage. It proved a good investment.

Some singing pairs, including the Two Leslies but also Flotsam and Jetsam in ditties like Little Miss Bouncer ('...loved an announcer, down at the BBC'), were close to being categorised as light comedians. That verdict very much applies to the Western Brothers, whose topical, ironical take on the news preceded Michael Flanders and Donald Swann and some of the supposed satirical songs of the 1960s. They were cousins, George at the piano and Kenneth leaning nonchalantly against it, both debonair in tails and monocles, the old school tie metaphorically to the fore. 'Sing a song of Britain that will make

your bosom swell', they would languidly drawl, 'of Britain and the Empire – and the Hippodrome as well. Play the game, you cads, play the game'. Radio added considerably to their range and fame. They joined together in 1925, with some concert party experience behind them, and, on their own admission and with an expensive car apiece, believed it would never end. Kenneth ended up running a kiosk at Weybridge Station. He died in 1963 and George Western in 1969.

On the instrumental front, there were Rawitz and Landauer or Reub Silver and Marion Day. or Desmond and Landseer at two pianos; Jules Adrian and Grace Spero, another married couple, achieving a classy effect with violin and accordion; the multi-instrumental Cox Twins, Frank and Fred...and a great assemblage of paired musicians, dancers and acrobats of all and varied description. There was even a brace of impressionists in the figures of the Bristolians, Tony Fayne and David Evans. They would actually impersonate singing double acts, like Bob and Alf Pearson, or copycat sports commentators, an echoing John Arlott being a particular standard. Although they did appear on stage, they were more strictly the creatures of the airways – 'imagine two radios side by side' – in further evidence of broadcasting's affection for pairings of voices.

Chatting with Charles Shadwell in his lovely Trumpington pub about this very subject of double acts (including his daughter's 'little gel' flirtations with Private Jack Warner in *Garrison Theatre*) we were musing over the many such turns that opened the bill for Saturday night's *Music Hall*, which ran until 1952 and was introduced by the compere and actor, Norman Wooland (1905-1989; he made his film debut in Laurence Olivier's *Hamlet* in 1948). When reminding him of how Norman Wooland used to announce, 'but let us begin as always with the BBC Variety Orchestra, conducted by Charles Shadwell, in our signature tune, *The Spice of Life...*' adding a few tootled bars for effect, Charles Shadwell reached an arm across the pub counter, tiny tears in his eyes, 'I wrote that', he said softly. Its lively strains caught the essential bonhomie of variety and served as a veritable national anthem for such entertainment.

Morecambe and Wise

The case that the double act phenomenon was crowded into a particular era is hard to contend. But why did it end as abruptly as it had flourished? Apart from Morecambe and Wise, who were, in any event, part of the variety scene well into the earlier period, there were precious few double acts of note after about 1955 or 1960. Hope and Keen were one of these. Born in 1935, Mike Hope and Albie Keen were cousins, the sons of a previous double act, Syd and Max Harrison, who brought a mix of music and fun to the stages of the 1930s and 1940s. Hope and Keen, who turned professional in 1956, were an enthusiastic and youthful act, comprising comedy, musicianship and some acrobatics. Two other acts, Cannon and Ball, and Little and Large, soared and fell in the post-Morecambe and Wise phase, when there was a vain belief that there might be a substitute for the brilliance of the older pairing. Both turns, Cannon and Ball and Little and Large, with a background of northern clubland and summer shows, worked hard in an old-fashioned knockabout fashion. Both acts enjoyed moments of high attainment on peak time television, while Tommy Cannon and Bobby Ball made a forgettable re-hash of Will Hay's police masterpiece in their film, *The Boys in Blue* (1983). Neither team had the sparkle or

wit to endure for more than a year or so in the harsh spotlight of the TV cameras.

The collapse of the double act vogue has, of course, much to do with the termination of its contributory growth factors, to wit, a switch in fashion and the replacement of radio by television as the salient home-based medium. The role of television as a vehicle for comics must await a later chapter for fuller exegesis. Suffice it for now to argue that, where radio was kind to comedians, especially perhaps crosstalk comedians, television was severe with them, especially perhaps crosstalk comedians. And yet, against the tough grain of this tendency, Eric Morecambe and Ernie Wise emerged, from a long and never wholly successful apprenticeship in the mainstream period for double acts, to become the best all-British double act there has been. How did this happen?

John Eric Bartholomew was born in 1926 in Morecambe, thus making it the third shore-hugging site, after (George) Formby and (Freddie) Frinton, to be utilised by a comic for his stage name. Ernest Wiseman was born a year earlier across the Pennines in Leeds. Apart from that geographic contrast (and the two never quite forewent the theatrical personae of the Lancashire droll and the cocksure Yorkshireman) their impetus came from different sides of the family. Whereas it was Ernie's father, Harry Wiseman, a spare time entertainer, who involved his son from an infantile age in his localised activities, it was Eric's mother, Sadie Bartholomew, who, first, encouraged her son to take up the stage and, second, persuaded the two to join forces. They had met in Brian Michie's *Youth Takes a Bow*, a famous stage and sometime radio showcase for juvenile talent, backed by the impresario, Jack Hylton, who had given young Ernie Wise his West End debut in the stage version of *Band Waggon*, yet more testimony to the influence of radio on stage productions.

They first performed as a duo at the Liverpool Empire in 1941, although soon World War II intervened, with Ernie Wise serving in the merchant navy and Eric Morecambe as a 'Bevin Boy' (a controversial scheme of 'optants' and 'ballotees' within the conscription process) down the mines for eleven months, until ill-health ruled him, and many others, out of a life in the collieries. They resumed peacetime comedy service in 1947 and both married dancers at much the same time – Eric Morecambe to Joan Bartlett in 1952 and Ernie Wise to Doreen Blyth in 1953. It was about this time that the author first saw them. It was at the Manchester Hippodrome and, singing and fooling, 'the boys' opened each half with their somewhat brash crosstalk.

In a mark of serendipity, G H Elliott topped the bill. With his anti-PC bill matter of 'the Chocolate Coloured Coon', he was the last of that long line of black-faced minstrels, reaching back to the sandy beaches upon which the modern crosstalk comics first ventured. He was born George Henry Elliott in 1883 and in appearing at the Manchester Hippodrome, he was close to his homestead, which was not Alabama but Rochdale. In the lineage of his model, Eugene Stratton, he had a lengthy career, dying in 1962. *Lily of Laguna, Hello Susie Green* and *The Silvery Moon* were among the melodies he sang and danced to, always superbly clad and with a magic that defies analysis.

For their part, the young comics, spry and eager, dealt in dialogue reminiscent of their models – Abbott and Costello, who, from 1939 to 1956, made dozens of films and were the best known new American double act of the 1940s. William 'Bud' Abbott (1895-1976), the thin, irritable, sly straight man, and

Louis 'Lou' Cristillo (1890-1959), the dumpy, dumb-witted, frightened comic, epitomised the genre. Just as British comedians had essayed to transfer their routines into the cinema, so did Abbott and Costello depend basically on a whole set of past vaudeville cameos. Their dialogue is well illustrated by their most imitated piece, wherein a baseball team have 'Who's' at first base, 'What's' on second base and 'I don't know's' on third base, an ambivalence of names that caused predictable confusion. Lou Costello had his well-tried phrases, such as his troubled 'chi-chi-chi-chi' and his penitent 'I've been a baa-aad boy'. Morecambe and Wise copied them fairly ruthlessly.

After no more than average success with a 1953 radio series, *You're Only Young Once*, they flopped badly in their first television show, the BBC's *Running Wild* in 1954. Their attempt to be televisually adept with a battery of mannered comedy exchanges went crudely awry and it would be seven long years on a learning curve, including some time overseas, before they had evolved something like an organically satisfying relationship, as opposed to a mimicry of the American duo. Slowly, they crept back into the reckoning and found favour on television. In 1961 they were offered their own programme, *The Morecambe and Wise Show*. For twenty years, an incredibly long time given the voracity of the medium, they would be the pre-eminent TV comedians.

There were three arcs to the curve. The first, from 1961 to 1968, when Eric Morecambe suffered a heart attack, was with commercial television and with Sid Green and Dick Hills as their able writers. The third, from 1978 almost until Eric Morecambe's death in Cheltenham in 1984, was also under the colours of commercial television. The central sector was from 1968 to 1977 at the BBC and with Eddie

Braben as the inventive script-writer. Overall, the standard of humour and presentation was high, but it was in that middle period that Morecambe and Wise achieved their own greatest effects and rightfully earned the affection of an entire nation. Like so many of their predecessors, they made films – there were three in the mid 1960s, hopeful of cashing in on their popularity. These were *The Intelligence Men, That Riviera Touch* and *The Magnificent Two*. Like those of many of their predecessors, these movies, if competent enough, failed to capture the essence of their comedy.

As for Ernie Wise, self-styled as a 'cheerer upper', he battled gamely to reinvent his career after the death of his partner in 1984, but it was a struggle. He died in Buckinghamshire in 1999. A double act that endures, given some wartime gaps, from 1941 to 1984, is something to celebrate for its sheer longevity. Professionally, they never lost, once it was discovered, their supreme rapport, even if, socially, they distanced themselves a little by residence in Harpenden (Morecambe) and Peterborough (Wise). What, then, was the secret for this amazing 'rags to riches' story, that rarity in terms of variety, an act that attracted both popular and critical adulation and also earned pots of money?

Firstly, it must be asserted with the utmost conviction that they were very talented and that they worked with rigour to hone the talents they had. A necessary element in this experimentation was the focus on Ernie Wise and the creation of a secondary character, rather than just an ordinary straight man. Ernie Wise, enthusiastic but gullible, brimming with ideas ruined by underlying ignorance, upwardly ambitious but prone to disaster and everlastingly at the mercy of the native cunning of his fellow, became a three-dimensional figure. This was paralleled by the assumption by Eric Morecambe, something of a worrier and anxious about their reception by audiences, of a more authoritative presence. He, too, developed a three-dimensional personality, complex in the fashion of dramatic comedy. They came the closest of any British duo to emulating the ideal of the Transatlantic pairing of Laurel and Hardy, indubitably the finest comic double act known to the civilised world. With Laurel and Hardy, it was, fundamentally, impossible to decide which was the comic one of the two, such was their joint artistry and character formulation. Morecambe and Wise ventured close to that perfection; perhaps only Jewel and Warriss, maybe Nat Mills and Bobbie, among British examples, have even approached near to them in this basic and telling respect.

Second, Morecambe and Wise made a conscious decision that, rather than adapt to television, television must adapt to them. They took a deep breath and determined that they would chance their arm at re-presenting on TV an old-time variety act, albeit now screened through the confident lenses of the characterisations they had slavishly built up. There is a definitive moment in one of the sketches where Ernie Wise, ashamed at the thought of acting on some suggestion, cries, 'but we would seem like a cheap variety act.' 'Ernie', Eric Morecambe soberly replies, 'we are a cheap variety act.'

Especially when Eddie Braben did the scripts, the whole kit and caboodle was geared to the assertion that they were an old-fashioned turn from the 1930s or 1940s. It was an exercise in nostalgia. It was unthreatening and traded relentlessly on familiarity. The great television playwright, Denis Potter, one of their many admirers from the cultural high life, reckoned that they trawled through yellowing copies of the *Dandy* comic for

The People's Jesters

material. A spoof item spotted in *The Stage* trade paper – 'Sylvia and Herbert Hargreaves – still at it on the grand piano' – illustrates the tone.

Like the radio shows of the immediate past, they inaugurated a series of mannerisms and linguistic tics, something like 30 or 40 of them, that turned up in every show and were as keenly anticipated as the litany of *ITMA* sayings. The slapped face; the invisible stone dropping in the empty bag; 'this play what I wrote'; 'you can't see the join'; 'short fat hairy legs'; 'get out of that', with the hand thrust, karate-style under the throat; 'be honest'; 'good evening, young sir', to a glamorous actress; the stock responses, such as, 'my mother's got a Whistler'; 'now there's a novelty' – all were consistently and persistently utilised.

They cribbed off Jimmy James, as in the 'pardon?' querying of a suspected double entendre. Eric Morecambe told Jimmy James' son, James Casey, that they used his father's materials for two reasons; first as a mark of respect and second because it was funnier than anything they could think of. They lay in bed together like Laurel and Hardy, placing themselves an age away from Gay Lib, with Eric Morecambe clinging to his pipe for manhood's sake. It was from that bedroom that he heard the police car tear past, sirens screaming: 'they'll never sell any ice cream travelling at that speed', was the comment. The humour was often a cleverer version of George Formby's giggling voyeurism or the 'rude' Donald M'Gill picture postcard: jeweller Ernie Wise, selling a diamond ring, 'would you like me to take it out so you can have a good look at it' – Eric Morecambe, 'well, there's not many people in the shop, so how do you feel about it.'

They did the normal bickering of crosstalk acts. Ernie, opening a Christmas show, 'it doesn't seem a year since last time'; Eric, 'don't bring your personal problems to me, Ern'. In a spoken biography of Ernie Wise, Eric Morecambe announced: 'then came war – when your country sent out a plea for all able-bodied men to take up arms, you didn't hesitate – you put on your mother's frock and pleaded insanity'. It was the joshing that watchers recognised from seeing Bob Hope and Bing Crosby arguing in the 'Road' films or listening to Derek Roy and Frankie Howerd trading insults on *Variety Bandbox*.

The offensive was turned on the celebrities who queued up to win the accolade of being their guests, itself, a throw-back to the radio days of Henry Hall's *Guest Night* or *Hi Gang!*, to which celebrities were invited and routinely involved in the comic action. This reduction to size of famous people was jestership in the fullest sense of the concept. Taking the high and mighty down a peg or two, without really damaging them, for the comic release of the masses, was exactly what jesters had been employed to do. Morecambe and Wise were master jesters: 'terrible news; Des O'Connor has made an unbreakable LP'; 'in our lifetime, will a man ever land on Julie Andrews?'

They persuaded their guests to join them in the sort of costume sketches beloved of the old-style concert parties with scripts akin to the Muir and Norden cinematic skits on radio's *Take It From Here*. They mimicked old-time variety acts, like their royal command conjuror, Marvo, with the beautiful Dolores, played by Ernie Wise, as assistant: 'send the budgie up' was Eric Morecambe's urgent command down his sleeve, as feathers fluttered out of his evening dress tails. The ventriloquial acts were guyed, with Eric Morecambe's gigantic dummy – 'you know that clearing in Epping Forest? That's him.' Ernie Wise enquired, 'have you ever drunk a glass of water while doing it?' 'No', replied Eric Morecambe, 'but I've often drunk a glass of water instead of doing it.'

They insisted it was a theatre. This explains the constant by-play with the curtains, swishing and twitching to find the opening, the belated entrance, or the portrayal of the mad throttler. They had a stage built 18 inches above the studio floor, so that the angle at which they were seen by the studio audience and viewed by the public at home was the same as it would have been at Rhyl or Clacton those long summers ago. Moreover, it was a wooden floor, so that, however subconsciously, when they danced or when Eric Morecambe stamped his foot, the sound you heard was an ancient variety stage and not a new-fangled, hard-core studio floor. All was carefully thought through; nothing was left to chance, even to ending, as all the best double acts had done, with a song, like *Bring Me Sunshine*, the lyric of which was spoken as a poem by Ernie Wise at his partner's funeral in Harpenden, Hertfordshire, at which Dickie Henderson and Roy Castle also gave eulogies.

Some of it was arcane. When the plump lady, Janet Webb, burst on at the end and scattered the twosome as they took a bow,

it was very amusing, but there was a hidden agenda. George Formby and his wife, Beryl, had themselves formed a double act but soon, of course, he was completely a solo turn, even if under her stringent control. When, in later years, he was, say, playing the Central Pier, Blackpool, and taking a curtain, Beryl Formby, now of podgy proportions, would bustle on to share the applause of the surprised holiday-makers. Morecambe and Wise were paying their own esoteric tribute to show-biz lore.

It was a gargantuan, unthreatening and beautifully organised exercise in reminiscence. The pinnacle on Christmas Day 1977, when, with the Sandringham yuletide dinner delayed, a record 28,835,000 people tuned in to the Morecambe and Wise show for what Ernie Wise described as 'an office party for all the nation'. It was a defining moment, which, for an amalgam of technological and cultural reasons, will never be rivalled.

Certainly the Morecambe and Wise 'nostalgia' gamble had paid off and it could only have paid off once. They were the last and they were the greatest of British double acts and their shows were a last 'hoorah' for the variety stage that had schooled them.

11. FUNNY TURNS: SPECIALITY COMEDY

Each variety bill was a conscious effort to provide a multiplicity of acts. The normal night out at the variety theatre offered a more diverse entertainment than anything on the live stage before or since. It inexorably followed that the specialist turns, borrowed from an array of disciplines, from the circus and the fairground to the ballet and the legitimate stage, were parodied by observant comics. Some comedians rose to definitive prominence, often in excess, as is sometimes the way with literary parody, of their models. It is the intention of this chapter to trace the careers of some of the most popular of these specialist comics.

'Boy-men'

As well as men dressing up as 'dames' and women doing male impersonations, there was the curio of adults cast as children. In the fashion of Ethel Revnell and Gracie West or some of Will Hay's purported pupils or even in the example of the small-statured men still occasionally employed in the theatre, this was straightforward acting, but there was also the case of the authentic 'boy-men'. It is unlikely that, because of either medical progress or cultural dictates, we shall see their like again. They were a little too close for ethical comfort to the anatomical and physiological 'freaks' of the old fairgrounds

and shows, with the Elephant Man perhaps the most notorious example. On the other hand, they did offer an opportunity to some people who would have found difficulty, in unsympathetic days of yore, in finding a place in society. The theatre has often acted as a tolerant hidey-hole for those judged abnormal by a narrow-minded community; hence, the flight of many homosexuals in the past to the comparative safety of backstage life.

As a boy, the author was taken to see Wee Georgie Wood at the Palace Theatre, Manchester. He topped the bill, as he had done for years, engaging his stage mother, Dolly Harmer, in cultivated conversation. Eton collared and short-jacketed, he was the assured schoolboy, clipped in his treble accent, addressing her as 'Mother' in a condescending way. As the curtains fell on his applause, he stepped onto the apron stage and made a little speech. He was taking the opportunity, he announced, of thanking the generous-spirited people of Manchester for the support they had always offered him, as he had struggled with what he called his 'affliction'. The author failed to understand why a youth of about twelve or thirteen should be addressing his watchers in these terms, and, rather like Al Read's persistent child – 'dad; dad; dad; what does he mean, dad?' – sought parental guidance. He was amazed to learn that George Wood was pushing 50.

Wee Georgie Wood was born George Balmer in 1897, and he hailed from Jarrow on Wearside. He was, in the probably politically incorrect terms of his era, a midget, not a dwarf, in that he was small, height 4ft 9ins, rather than stunted, but with an unbroken voice. He first appeared, at the tender age of five, with his mother very much the driving force, at the Jubilee Gardens, Seaham Harbour, and, after work with concert parties, like the Arcadians at Seaham and the Busy Bees at Harrogate, and in music hall as an impressionist, he had much success at home and abroad, including the first of some 50 pantomime engagements, one of them when he was aged ten, with Stan Laurel, in *The Beauty and the Beast*. He settled into the role of the juvenile, assisted for a number of years by Ethel Burns, and with 'the Black Hand Gang', first presented in 1917, with its sort of 'Emil and the Detectives' theme, his most well known sketch. In 1933 he married Ewing Eaton, an American vaudevillian, also of short stature, but the marriage was short-lived.

He was soon billed as 'the Peter Pan of the Music Halls'. In 1916 he first met up and later teamed up with Dolly Harmer and, although there were many variations of their domestic discussions, the template remained the same, almost until their joint retirement in 1953. In the last two or three years they dropped the mother/son routines and George Wood adopted the role of the spiky 'Wee McGregor'. Dolly Harmer died in 1956, aged a remarkable 90. Wee Georgie Wood lived on until 1979, a formidable autodidact, self-opinionated, vociferous, supremely self-assured, writing and commenting not only on showbusiness matters but also on theological and constitutional affairs.

It was about the time of Wee Georgie Wood's retirement that his notional heir, Jimmy Clitheroe, rose to fame and fortune. James Robinson Clitheroe was born in 1921 in Blacko, Nelson, not far from Clitheroe, although, unlike Frinton, Formby and Morecambe, his was not a stage name. His condition of glandular disablement caused him to stop growing when he was eleven, and he never reached puberty. He undertook to plough the hard furrow of entertainment, in the Winstanley Babes, doing female impersonations, roller skating, playing the saxophone and accordion and taking bit-parts in northern films. His work in revue, particularly with Albert Burdon, led to radio commitments, in shows like *The Mayor's Parlour* and *Call Boy*, but soon he was made the focus for his own series.

The Clitheroe Kid ran from 1958 to 1972, a record for a radio comedy programme, and, in *Holiday Hotel*, there was later some television appeal. Over this longish period on stage and on air, the 'Dolly Harmer' maternal role was taken by Renee Houston and Patricia Burke and then, definitively, by Mollie Sugden, later to star in TV's department store sit-com, *Are You Being Served?* There was a distinctive contrast between the two major 'boy-men'. Where Wee Georgie was more the upper class choirboy, who, in topper and morning suit looked like a miniature of the Young Winston, the Clitheroe Kid was quite plebeian. In his way, he was just as knowing as Wee Georgie, but it was street wisdom, not book knowledge. With the scruffy look of his short trousers and jauntily perched school cap, he was the cheeky brat, constantly bemused by the stupidity – 'some mothers do 'ave 'em' – of adults.

In some ways it was a 1950s theme that held up in the swinging sixties. Jimmy Clitheroe was the impudent child of the working class anti-hero, lauded by John Braine's Joe Lampton in *Room at the Top* and Alan Sillitoe's Arthur Seaton in *Saturday Night and Sunday Morning*. They all waved the two fingers of scorn at authority.

Jimmy Clitheroe, only 4ft 2ins tall and 5 stones in weight, never reconciled himself to his disability. Where George Wood's defence was a rampant demonstration of outspokenness, Jimmy Clitheroe forbade discussion of his size and lived as a recluse behind the high walls of his Blackpool residence. There it was that relatives, arriving for his mother's funeral, found him unconscious and close to death, having taken a heavy dose of alcohol and pills. He had had some health problems and the loss of his mother, Emma Pye, his lifelong support and helper, was a dreadful blow. Perhaps a little charitably, the coroner recorded a verdict of accidental death.

Ventriloquists

The small 'boy-man', arguing with his mother, had something in common with the usually shrill accents of the dummy arguing with his mentor. Ventriloquists were not, of course, comedians as such; on the other hand, there were no serious 'vents', like there were serious magicians. All ventriloquists strove for laughs, even as they strove for public adulation through the mastery of their age-old technique, a skill, apparently, once utilised in augmenting the magical aura of some ancient religions.

It was, self-evidently, a gloss on the double act, normally with the 'vent' acting as the straight man for the cheeky dummy. Some of the old-time music hall acts, men like Walter Cole, who introduced the much-imitated sailor doll, or Frank Mordaunt, used – shades of Eric Morecambe – large dummies; it was Fred Russell who was the first to deploy the sort of dummy we would recognise as conventional now, to wit, one

that perched on the operator's knee. Fred Russell's dummy was Coster Joe, who first appeared in 1896. Fred Russell, the father of Val Parnell, died in 1957, at the ripe old age of 95. His son, Frederick Russell Parnell, father of the drummer, Jack Parnell, was also a 'vent', performing as Russ Carr, with his wife, Olive Grey, as his assistant. Two famous names from those olden days were Coram, with Jerry Fisher, and Johnson Clark, with the rustic dolls, Giles and Hodge. Arthur Prince, with Jim, the sailor dummy, was very popular, especially when Jim continued chatting as his minder drank a pint of beer. They first appeared in 1902 and the act continued until Arthur Prince's death in 1948.

The variety stage welcomed such speciality performers. Arthur Worsley, born in Failsworth in 1920, was one such. From an early age he proved to be one of the most technically accomplished ventriloquists, with his feisty little doll, Johnny Green, doing all the talking, while Arthur Worsley stood or sat in monk-like silence. Roger Carne (1912-1997) was another 'vent', with two dummies, Willie Hackle and Canasta the Cat, one of the first 'animal' dummies, while Bobbie Kimber (1918-1993) contrived to baffle many as a 'drag' ventriloquist, with his doll, Augustus Peabody. Senor Wences (Wenceslao Moreno, of Spanish origin) was one of the first to construct his doll on stage, by the expedient of making his thumb and first finger the moving mouth and adding the physical and wardrobe accoutrements. His and his dummy's purported impoverished grasp of English was another trademark. The Parisian, Robert Lamouret, with Dudulle the Duck, was another clever 'vent' of the immediate post-war period. Later there would be Saveen (Albert Saveen, born in Southwark, 1914-1994), with his coy, lisping little girl doll, Daisy May, and another noted for the exactness of his technique, Dennis Spicer, killed in a car crash at the height of his young powers in 1964. Ray Allen and the haughty if slightly inebriated Lord Charles have enjoyed much modern success. Subtle touches, like Lord Charles wearing a lapel mike on TV similar to Ray Allen's, remind one of the tantalisingly human face of the dummy, rather like cartoon characters who threaten to be too believable. Studio engineers asking if the dummy could be moved closer to the microphone is one of the consequences.

One or two well-known comics used ventriloquialism in their acts, especially in their more youthful days. Ken Dodd and Dicky Mint is one example, while there was also Harry Worth (1919-1989), the Yorkshire born comic, who began as a 'vent'. It is difficult to square his professional beginnings in a Barnsley colliery with the bespectacled, bewildered, apologetic, mumbling figure he presented on stage – 'do you remember the war? – it was in all the papers'. There was also Sandy Powell doing his famous spoof act as a ventriloquist, but it was, in fact, a regular 'vent' who made the greatest single impression in the post-war years and who, in so doing, created as a by-product a school for up and coming comics.

This was Peter Brough. It is easy enough to see why television should offer a great fillip to the ventriloquial craft, because the close-up camera offers such an exacting test. Radio did nothing for 'vents'; they were entirely reliant on their patter, should they find themselves booked for *Music Hall* or *Workers' Playtime*. Thus the phenomenal success of Peter Brough was almost counterfactual.

Peter Royce Brough was born in Hammersmith in 1916. His father was Arthur Brough, a part-time ventriloquist, whose dummy, Tim, was used in the Michael Redgrave film, *Dead of Night*, with its scary plot of the 'vent's' doll assuming control. Peter Brough joined his father in his daytime trade in the woollens business and, like Al Read and Kenneth Horne, he long retained his profitable links with commerce. He was married twice, to Peggy Franklin and then to Elizabeth Chantler, and he was invalided out of the forces in World War II. As for his theatrical life, he picked up the skill from his father and, indeed, grandfather, whose hobby 'venting' had been. After an uneasy start, he settled on the Archie Andrews motif.

The doll, with its staring eyes, grinning jaws and striped blazer, was cleverly designed, by Len Insull of Streatham, to convey the notion of the early teenage schoolboy, and the *ITMA* scriptwriter, Ted Kavanagh was responsible for the 'Archie Andrews' christening. After a good stage baptism, Peter Brough and Archie took to the airways, joining the *Navy Mixture* team, with an 'Archie Takes the Helm' item, and then, with the imitator, Peter Cavanagh, in *Two's a Crowd*. Just as George Burns and Gracie Allen had prompted the BBC to think in terms of a husband-and-wife comedy, there was the American ventriloquial example of Edgar Bergen and his dummies Charlie McCarthy and the dull-witted country boy, Mortimer Snerd. Charlie McCarthy might be properly regarded as a USA model for Archie Andrews. The schoolboy had to be schooled and thus, after the usual series of difficulties that attends such gestations, *Educating Archie* was born.

Archie's was a private tutor, initially Robert Moreton, a gently spoken, polite comedian, noted for his 'Bumper Fun Book', and, sadly, his later suicide in 1956, like that of Tony Hancock, in Australia. A native of Teddington, born in 1922, he ambled indecisively through torturous stories, missing the punch lines in his confusion, crying 'get in there, Moreton', when he felt he had attained some pinnacle of the narrative art.

Bob, the odd job man, was played by Max Bygraves, making his first major entry into the homes of the public and, with his catchphrases, 'I've arrived and to prove it I'm here' and 'a good idea, son', doing so attractively. His unhurried cockney charm was very appealing. Robert Moreton was replaced by Tony Hancock, with his jaundiced aside, 'Flippin' Kids', and he, too, saw his career boosted by acquaintance with Archie Andrews. Alfred Marks, at that time the comedian on the BBC show, *Starlight Hour*, Gilbert Harding, the irascible TV personality, Beryl Reid, in fizzing form as the schoolgirl, Monica, Hattie Jacques, who had delighted in the later *ITMA* series, Bernard Miles, Dick Emery, Harry Secombe, James Robertson Justice and a host of other comics and actors were, at one time or another, on the programme, whilst the musical interlude was first proffered by the thirteen year old Julie Andrews.

The show was not as intelligent as its immediate predecessor, *Take it from Here*, but its unpretentious good cheer saw its audience totals rise from 4m to 15m. It kept its shape and allure for almost ten years from its starting point in 1950, making Peter Brough the highest paid broadcaster of his time. The writers were Eric Sykes, a name that deservedly keeps turning up in these annals, and Sid Colin, who had done scripts for *Hi Gang!*, *Ignorance is Bliss* and *Navy Mixture*. It was, in truth, very formulaic, with probably some 30 or 40 phrases, references, responses and so forth packed into the half hour show, with Archie the focus, together with 'Braff', as the impertinent schoolboy always called his governor. Nevertheless, it prospered, perhaps because it was undemanding. Radio comedy then had the fruitful habit of finding audiences who wanted both to be treated as *Educating Archie* children and *Round the Horne* adults.

It certainly prospered for Peter Brough. There were photographs of Archie flirting with beautiful women; Archie was kidnapped to national consternation; his children's fan club was 250,000 strong; there was Archie Andrews Imperial Leather soap and he was employed to urge the value of road safety and the virtues of National Savings; the Meddocream firm launched Archie Andrews lollipops and sold 15m in the opening year. This was one of the first examples of modern commercial exploitation, with a full round of painting, story and cut-out books, jigsaws, key-rings, scarves, slippers and the like, all with the Archie imprimatur, and fetching in the then tidy sum of £5000 a year profit. In spite of occasionally poor health, to do with the chest ailment that had shortened his army career, Peter Brough lived until 1999, dying in Hillingdon, the notable dummy still hanging from a hook near the door of Peter Brough's room.

The strength of this impact means that, for a couple of generations, Archie Andrews remains the most famous ventriloquial dummy there has been, and, incredibly, all done on radio, along side the making of a dozens reputations for other entertainers.

At this juncture, with Peter Brough raking it in on all sides, his fellow-'vents' murmured, maybe a little enviously, that he was technically a moderate exponent of their esoteric vocation. Admittedly, he was no Arthur Prince or Dennis Spicer and there were those who described him rather as a 'child impersonator'. There were, in fact, confessed child impersonators on the theatrical block. The most well-known was Harry Hemsley. His was a family of four. There was the solemn Ethel, the disconsolate Johnny, the incomprehensible Horace and – 'what does Horace say, Winnie? – Winnie, the earnest interpreter of Horace's infantile gibberish.

Harry Hemsley, quietly and affectionately, acted as their father, sitting on the stage with a newspaper, in part to give the impression of the suburban pater familias, in part, to shield his mouth, although, in truth, he made no attempt to be ventriloquial in mode. That was not the point. Indeed, like Al Read, he was possibly more effective heard on radio than seen on stage.

Rod Hull and Emu were a further gloss on this scene, for the rangy antipodean, Rod Hull, did all the talking, as he plainly failed to control his malevolent, anti-social avian companion. His assault on Michael Parkinson during a purported interview is still voted high on lists of best remembered television cameos. During the 1970s this dummy animal was very popular and there were, of course, other humanly animated creatures on the telly, such as the cheerful fox, Basil Brush.

This might be the appropriate moment to insert a reference to Stanley Unwin, the man who did not usurp language like a ventriloquist but, instead, invented his own patois – Unwinese – and made it the centre of his act, one that, obviously enough, was more effective on radio than elsewhere. In fact, he was a radio engineer, born in South Africa in 1911 and it was not until 1960 that he became a full-time broadcaster and entertainer, spreading the 'deep joy' of his alien tongue across the nation. Rather like 'backslang', his was a language that was sufficiently close to the original for one to comprehend the gist of his discourse, although one had to concentrate and, for most people, ten or so minutes were enough. Small, bespectacled, amiable, Stanley Unwin died in 2003.

Impressionists

Harry Hemsley was an impressionist, albeit with a highly specialised focus. Like both ventriloquists and other impressionists, there was a wish to raise laughter, but the real value was in the correctness of the impersonation. Nonetheless, the material was important and, while a Robb Wilton mimic might ride on the back of that star's dialogue, those who aped political or other celebrities often fell down in this respect. One might admire the actual image created but, after a minute or two, without wittily relevant patter, it could pall.

The lineage of impressionists is a long one, with several who became stars in their own individualistic manner, beginning their show-business lives as mimics, Wee Georgie Wood, Jack Warner and Peter Sellers among them. Three or four excellent impersonators set their mark on the variety era. One was Afrique, a South African, Alexander Witkin (1907-1961), who made his name in Britain with a passable take-off of the Prince of Wales, the Duke of Windsor to be. During the war he ended his act with a stirring spotlighted Churchillian flourish. Then there was Victor Seaforth, 'the Man of a Thousand Voices', who was born in 1918. He tended to concentrate on characterisations, some of them of a serious nature. He is a reminder of how the popular image of historical or literary characters is set in stone by filmic studies; Charles Laughton's Henry VIII, Captain Bligh and Quasimodo are, for instance, how we all remember them. What Victor Seaforth did was, in effect, an imitation of Charles Laughton as Quasimodo.

Clifford Stanton, born in Dorset in 1909, designed his clever act, *Personalities on Parade*, directly for cabaret and variety, while Peter Cavanagh (1914-1994) was more of a radio man, as his billing 'the Voice of

Them All' suggests. A South Londoner, his vocal range and control was outstanding, demonstrated by his brilliant finale when, in rapid succession, all the stars he had imitated bid a quick-fire farewell. One of his 1940s specials was a clever run-through of *ITMA*; he managed all the characters with aplomb; if anything, he never quite captured, and nor did anyone else, the distinct accents of Tommy Handley himself.

Several entertainers continue to include impersonations in their acts. Ken Dodd may provide, for example, an uncanny Billy Bennett and Robb Wilton. Roy Hudd has had a lengthy and wide-ranging career as a comedian and comic actor. His *The News Huddlines* was the pick of radio comedy in the last years of the 20th century and his own flair to amuse has, for some 50 years, been consistent and brisk. What has also been notable is his adulation of his peers and forebears, so that he has offered loving portraits of the likes of Dan Leno and George Formby and has written and played Bud Flanagan in the *Underneath the Arches* musical tribute to the old double act. He is knowledgeable and reverential of his profession and he is, in this sense, an admirable model not only to his own colleagues but also to members of other professions.

Television demanded impersonation of a high level of definition, but, on the bonus side, its make-up departments loaned technical assistance of a prosthetic and allied kind, so that the impersonators were heavily camouflaged. From Mike Yarwood to Rory Bremner, they have strutted their stuff, often embracing politicos and celebrities. Mike Yarwood, for example, found impetus in his excellent portrayals of Harold Wilson, Ted Heath and the telly pundit, Malcolm Muggeridge. Time takes its toll of politicians and gurus, and impersonators may sometimes find themselves abandoned by their models.

Monologuists

The impersonators were but the light entertainment angle on the serious stage, cinema and television element of actors playing real people. From Bette Davis' Elizabeth I to Prunella Scales' Elizabeth II, with a score of Churchills, a dozen Hitlers and even a handful of Jesuses for good measure, this was and is commonplace in the dramatic realm.

As the owners of the old-time music halls both tried to court respectability and dodge the attentions of the watchful 'legit' managers, they were keen to present serious acting for their patrons. One method that avoided dialogue as such, and was also less expensive than paying for a troupe of actors, was the inclusion of a monologue often to a necessary musical accompaniment. This might have been presented by someone like Bransby Williams, who died in 1961, at the great age of 91. He first appeared on the music halls in 1896, doing imitations of well-known actors and gradually developing a specialist range of Dickensian characters, complete with quick-change costumes, as well as introducing monologues like *The Street Watchman's Story*. Once again, we should note the fact that the music hall audiences were literally aware enough to pick up the cultural references.

The monologue, defined as a publicly performed piece of narrative verse, emerged as a popular genre during the 19th century, when it was adapted as a campaigning vehicle for political and social themes. The temperance movement utilised the monologue form. The author's maternal grandmother and great–aunt Bertha could, in their dotage, recollect the abstinence verses they had learned as little girls at Band of Hope meetings, although it should be added that, in their cases, the message had not endured as long as the medium. The most famous and frequently misquoted line in English doggerel is 'It is Christmas Day in the Workhouse', composed by the anti-poor law campaigning journalist, George R Sims in 1877. That emotive tale of the elderly married couple, threatened with separation should they resort to the workhouse, was part of the social crusade to alleviate the grimness of the workhouse system. It was often declaimed on the music hall stage.

There was also a taste for yarns of derring-do and imperial splendour. Rudyard Kipling's *The Absent-minded Beggar*, Robert Service's *The Shooting of Dan M'Grew* and, a great favourite, Milton Hayes and Cuthbert Clarke's *The Green Eye of the Little Yellow God*, first recited in 1911, are examples of this rich vintage. Milton Hayes was himself a spirited reciter of such epic tales. In the variety years a well-known serious monologuist was Nosmo King, titled after the notice, who appeared with his son, 'Hubert', in reality, Jack Watson, born in 1925, who became a hard-working straight actor. Nosmo King was the stage sobriquet of Vernon Watson (1886-1949). His monologues were of more domestic flavour, like *The Touch of a Master's Hand, My England* ('yes, I mean to keep it just like that') or *Civilians* ('...Fall on our knees and thank our God that we are British born'), the sort of sentiments that were very acceptable to audiences as World War II raged.

There was a contrasting lineage of humorous monologues. We have already visited those of the Western Brothers and Jack Warner and should mention the similar contributions in revue and cabaret of, most famously, Noel Coward and Joyce Grenfell. Gracie Fields awaits our pleasure in the following chapter. We have noted how the arrival of records and the 'wireless' accentuated the value of the spoken word. In the later years of the 20th century there was the harmonious combine of Michael Flanders and Donald Swann, for much of their output was of the nature of the musically backed monologue.

Another exponent was Cyril Fletcher (1913-2005), a native of Watford, who rose from being an insurance clerk, via the Fol de Rols concert party, to a long career, culminating in a spot on Esther Rantzen's *That's Life* on TV. With his wife – he married Betty Astell in 1942 and their daughter, Jill Fletcher, sustained the family theatrical tradition – he diversified cleverly and in business-like vein, shifting from pantomime, where he was normally dame, to the formation of his Associated Speakers agency. If his slight pomposity and old-fashioned views were as much part of his real as of his artistic person, he still contrived to enjoy an affluent career, no more so than through his reciting of *Odd Odes*. These stemmed from the success of his comic interpretation of *Dreaming of Thee*, a sentimental poem of a Boer War soldier missing his girlfriend, and, indeed, *Dreaming of Thee* became Cyril Fletcher's own identity tag. His *Odd Odes*, delivered in a nasal accent that descended from plumy to plebeian, then ascended again, recounted the humdrum misadventures of, inter alia, the stout Bertram Bees who 'couldn't not never see his knees' or the serving girl Norah Gutt, upon whose 'nut' the serving hatch fell. On Cyril Fletcher's own admission, it was gentle amusement, no more, without any hint of bitter satire or social purpose. It was a fashion more suited perhaps to the radio and concert party than the variety stage.

The premier humorous monologuist of that age was Stanley Holloway (1890-1982). He was born of decently prosperous parents in London's Manor Park and trained formally as a singer, before war service with the Connaught Rangers. He then transferred to the concert party arena, where he became the baritone and utility man with the famed Co-optimists. Later he would, not unlike Gracie Fields, succeed in an array of fields, from the legitimate theatre, as, for instance, Bottom in *A Midsummer Night's Dream*, to a distinguished film career, with delightful comedy playing in movies like *Brief Encounter* (1945) and *The Lavender Hill Mob* (1951). He ultimately crowned this satisfying and versatile career with his Alfred Doolittle, the sage-like dustman in the musical *My Fair Lady*, appearing in the Broadway, Drury Lane and cinematic productions. Hollywood moguls were disconcerted when, having paid him a six months contract, he only required, such was his professional competence, six weeks for his portion of the film making. His bluff and relaxed personality was the key to his bravura conquest of all the entertainment vehicles. He was married twice, first to Queenie Foran and then the actress, Violet Marion Lane. He died in Sussex, at the close of a busy and broad-ranging life.

However, he will be most recalled by radio and variety addicts for his recitations. He introduced these into his variety act in 1928 at the shrewd behest of Leslie Henson and Gracie Fields, interspersing the hearty ballads, such as *The Company Sergeant Major* or *Old Father Thames*, sung in his rich baritone voice, with these newly minted poetic coins. There were 34 monologues in sum, the majority of them written by Marriott 'George' Edgar, himself a stage monologuist, and the half-brother of the thriller writer, Edgar Wallace, who, curiouser and curiouser, composed *Dreaming of Thee* of Cyril Fletcher notoriety. Marriott Edgar (1880-1951) deserves a further mention in despatches, having been the screen play writer of many of the great Will Hay movies. There were, in chief, three brands of monologue: the ones that involved Sam Small, a Peninsular War soldier who famously dropped his musket; those relating to the Ramsbottom family, in particular Albert of that clan, and his difficulties with Wallace the lion; and the historical ones, dilating on the Battle of Hastings or the signing of the Magna Carta.

Unlike Cyril Fletcher's *Odd Odes*, there was more to them than superficial amusement. These droll accounts, relayed in flat, unemotional tones, the context the industrial belt of the Mersey Valley, conveyed much of the patience, prudence and resignation of working class Lancashire in the depression period. They have not been forgotten. If one begins, 'there's a famous seaside place called Blackpool...' in any crowded room, it is rarely one does not find one or two joining in with 'that's noted for fresh and fun.' From that reverently penned and loved canon, Stanley Holloway's own favourite stanza must be deployed as the sole example:

'And it's through that there Magna Carta, that was signed by the barons of old,

That in England today we can do what we like, so long as we do what we're told.'

One of Stanley Holloway's revue items, first tried out at the Savage Club, London, prior to inclusion in *Up and Doing* at the Saville Theatre, was his recitation of *The Green Eye of the Little Yellow God*, with pukka sahib intrusions from Leslie Henson and Cyril Richard, correcting and amending from a box. It is a reminder that the monologue was a regular part of variety and concert party work and that the notion of the monologuist being interrupted, Murray and Mooney style, was founded in that fact.

Equally, it was the uniform frequency of such recitations that enabled Billy Bennett to tender such nuggets as *The Green Tie on the Little Yellow Dog*. This was the purest form of 'monologue' comedy. Billy Bennett, in his raucous parodies of the authentic form, did, in overall effect, for Bransby Williams what Sandy Powell would do for Arthur Prince. The engaging conjuror, John Wade, has told of how Sandy Powell would prefer him to perform his magic first, ere he proceeded to unveil his Powellite burlesque of the stage magician. Similarly, especially in his early days, Billy Bennett would often follow an earlier 'straight' version of, say, *The Charge of the Light Brigade* with his own 'cod' *The Charge of the Tight Brigade*. As with these and with, another instance, *It is Christmas Day in the Cookhouse*, he followed the plot-line of the original with religious care, so that the audience could trace the neatness of the skit. There were other themes, too, like the hilarious *My Mother Doesn't Know I'm on the Stage* or faintly political gibes like *No Power on Earth Can Pull it Down* or *The League of Nations*, which met, somewhat unpredictably, at Berwick Market.

Billy Bennett was born in 1887 in Glasgow of Scottish descent, but he was mainly bred in the family home in Liverpool and retained just a trace of Scouse in his accent. His father, John Bennett, had been half of a slapstick partnership with Robert Martell in the 1890s, so that his son was soon plunged into show-business, doing a stint with Fred Karno, but really coming to the fore in the aftermath of the First World War. He fought valiantly in that conflict as a cavalryman with the 16th Lancers, being awarded both the Distinguished Conduct medal and the Belgian Croix de Guerre. Recovering from wounds, he joined the Shellfire Concert Party, in which Mark Lupino, one of the famous family of Lupinos, was starring. It was as a 'canteen' or 'trench' comic, performing in fields and barns, that Billy Bennett evolved his strident, combative, forceful tone.

In his ill-fitting masher togs of shrunken jacket and dickey trying to reach his floppy trousers, with army boots to complete this disarrayed garb, his was a burly figure, with bulging features and an Old Bill moustache, bellowing out the verse in accusatory style. Many years before Basil Brush appropriated the idea, he had the pit drummer beat out 'boom boom' to mark the triumphant conclusion to couplet, as he slammed in the bolt of the clinching rhyme. All the traditions of low comedy, back to Shakespearean clowns, were met in his delivery – and yet the material itself ('the little sardines had gone into their tins and pulled down the lid for the night') often had a surreal, sub-Carrolian quality. Consider:

'He said, 'where has the kidney bean? What made the woodbine wild?

Is red cab-barge greengrocery? And tell me, friends,' he smiled,

'Can a bandy-legged gherkin be a straight cucumber's child?'

So, although there was a remarkable visual emphasis, the words mattered considerably. This made Billy Bennett's recitations not only a natural for radio and records, but, as with the Holloway monologues, for publishing. In this he was assisted by his chief collaborator, W H Connor. A bachelor, Billy Bennett was, off-stage, cheerful and companionable, a man who uncomplicatedly enjoyed the company of ladies. Come World War II, and he threw himself into the task of entertaining troops and war-workers. In 1942, while appearing in Blackpool, at that time a main RAF base as well as the spot where hard-pressed munitions workers might grab a day

The People's Jesters

or two of respite, he suffered a heart attack and died. James Agate said of him that 'he raised every night of the week to the level of Saturday night.'

Space for a final extract from the great tradition with reference to his mother:

> 'She can think that I'm a murderer before she'll know the truth;
>
> I have to have respect for her old age.
>
> She knows that I'm a bigamist, a blackguard and a crook –
>
> But thank heaven she don't know I'm on the stage.'

Magicians

Tommy Cooper was the Billy Bennett of magic, the supreme parodist of an established convention.

Stage magic tends to veer towards two extremes. There is the rather serious, silent mystery man, often with the glamorous assistant, as guyed by Morecambe and Wise. There is the chatty conjuror, the insouciant talk all part of the adept 'misdirection' of a mystified audience, as burlesqued by Sandy Powell. Tommy Cooper certainly had a host of targets. The ranks of monologue makers, ventriloquists and mimics were thin compared with the serried procession of illusionists and magicians that paraded across the variety stage. It was predictable enough, for the music halls had earlier welcomed, among several others, the flamboyant magic of Horace Goldin, who sawed a woman in half; Chung Ling Soo, in reality, the more humdrum William Robinson, who died in 1913 attempting to catch a fired bullet; the great and legendary Maskelyne, and the superb illusionist, David Devant.

Thus the variety stage was awash with magical acts, often with arcane oriental titles, such as Shek Ben Ali, Cingalee, Ali Bey, Rameses and Sirdani. Others had less exotic bill matter but equally imposing routines, Billy McComb, David Berglas, Benson Dulay, Jack Kodell, Channing Pollack, Harold Taylor, Mark Raffles the pickpocket and Howard de Courcy among them. Television led to an augmented interest in magic, for, as with ventriloquialism, the close-up stuff, such as card manipulation, was that much more fascinating. At the same time, the scope for trickery was obviously greater than on the bare boards of the variety stage. Several names came to the fore, including Chan Canasta, David Nixon, Robert Harbin, Uri Geller and the chirpy Paul Daniels. Radio may have seemed something of a setback for magicians, but John Wade did a 'Peter Brough' from the late 1960s onwards, with his fast-talking radio magicianship, as well as having his hands immortalised on screen with the fluorescent card displays that formed the credits for the renowned *The Avengers* series.

Although Tommy Cooper had had one or two predecessors in the field of 'cod' wizardry, such as Tommy Dee and Donald B Stuart, his talent for clowning, coupled with the exposure of television as well as stage, made him the outstanding, for most people, the sole perpetrator of spoof magic. Thomas Frederick Cooper was born, the son of a miner, in Caerphilly, in 1921, but he was mainly brought up in the environs of Exeter and Southampton. After a spell as an apprentice shipwright and seven years with the Horse Guards, he followed the pattern of many of his contemporaries with work in army entertainment and then at the Windmill Theatre. He claimed that stage fright and authentic failure were the grounds for his seemingly chaotic act, but one finds that difficult to believe. He had all the essential traits for becoming the world's most disillusioned illusionist. A lumbering giant of 6ft 3ins, weighing in at 15 stone, gangling and angular in movement, and with madly mobile features, gleaming eyes and gaping mouth, he was perfectly built for the task. The fez, the drooping hands and the much imitated cry of 'just like that' that attended the successively cascading errors in his magic tricks, all added to the picture of a performer who was more clown than comedian.

He gabbled compulsively, shambled convulsively and guffawed maniacally, the visual attack always pre-eminent. When he frightened himself by entering the magic cabinet and pulling the curtain, his trauma was demonstrable, while he wiled the time away with the corniest of gags: 'I found a Van Goch and a Stradivarius in the loft – the trouble is Van Goch couldn't make violins and Stradivarius couldn't paint for toffee'. He was, of course, a brilliant magician, the bungled tricks eventually revealing the conjuring skills that underlay the whole performance.

Nor was magic the only string to his bow, for Tommy Cooper has a further claim to be included in this very chapter as a 'cod' monologuist. Guying the old Thespians who had recited dramatic monologues and essayed changes of apparel for the different characters of their tale, his story, set in a tavern, involved a hamper full of hats, one for each of the cast, the sailor, the policeman, the fireman, and so on. As the stumbling monologue proceeded, the flurry of hats grew ever more frenzied and out of sync. Ron Moody, the first Fagin in Lionel Bart's musical version of *Oliver Twist*, did, in cabaret and revue, a not dissimilar cameo of an ageing theatrical, who, forgetting his rhyming account of *The Face on the Bar-room Floor*, would retrace his steps to the commencement and whisper his way hurriedly to the lost point, vainly hopeful of picking up the flow.

Tommy Cooper made his name in the revue, *Sauce Piquante* in 1950 and at the London Palladium in 1952, before beginning his long TV career with *It's Magic*, the first of ten series that reached into the 1980s. He married Gwen Hanley in 1947, but from 1967 until his death he was romantically involved with his assistant, Mary Fieldhouse. He died in harness in 1984, after collapsing during a television show.

Tommy Cooper was something of a mirth-provoking Colossus who, in the post-1945 decades bestrode the variety stages and the television sets. In no other category of comedic presentation is there so singular a victor; he was far and away the outstanding 'cod' magician of his or any other generation.

Dancers

Few variety programmes failed to include a dance act, usually at the beginning of each half of the bill. It might have been a brave line of high-stepping chorus girls or a couple indulging in tap, adagio, apache, ballet or some other form of dance. Whilst few comedians exclusively set out their stall as burlesque dancers, there were several who included an element within their act.

Two fine examples were Nat Jackley and Billy Dainty. Nathaniel Jackley-Hirsch was a child of Sunderland, born on Wearside in 1909 of a circus and variety background. The stentorian pitch of his father, George Jackley, is said to have influenced the forceful approach of Jimmy Edwards. He began stage life with the Eight Lancashire Lads, did spells in double acts and then went solo, although he sometimes worked with assistants, including his wife, Marianne Lincoln, with whom he enjoyed a volcanic relationship reminiscent of that of Lucan and McShane. A lanky, rubber-necked soul, he danced like a demented ostrich, throwing in a few gags for good measure. He was naturally in some demand as a panto dame. Nat Jackley died in 1988. In later years the engaging Norman Collyer, noted for his disjointed pronouncements through a defective microphone, caught something of the same avian mobility when he adopted the garb of a clucking hen.

Billy Dainty was the converse in style and build. He was born in Dudley in the Black Country in 1927, and, after dancing school and an unresolved course at drama school, he was soon on the treadmill of seaside and pantomime seasons, perfecting his Terpsichorean skills. With the aid of his assistant, Len Lowe, he was pledged to his bill matter invitation – 'Going Mad; Coming?' Tiny, light-footed and smiling, he gently guyed the ballet, both its female and male protagonists, and, like all the best parodists, literary and otherwise, he scored highly with the sheer deftness of his own ability. Arguably, he danced as brilliantly as Tommy Cooper could genuinely perform magic tricks. Billy Dainty's was a joyous act to behold and his premature death in 1986 was much mourned.

A comedian who survived the buffets of misfortune to become something of a cult figure late in his chequered career was Max Wall, a man who founded his comic persona in 'funny walks' a generation before John Cleese and his Pythonesque friends conceived of a Ministry for such activity. He was born in Brixton in 1908, officially, Maxwell George Lorimer. His parents were the music hall entertainers Jack Lorimer and Stella Stahl and his childhood and schooling were confused and destabilising. It was his stepfather, Harry Wallace, who encouraged him to discipline himself for the stage and it was from him that he took the name Max Wall, not just as a stage name but also formally by deed

poll. He concentrated on eccentric dancing, winding himself into the most angular of contortions and whirls, earning for himself the epithets of 'the Boy with the Obedient Feet' and 'Max Wall and His Independent Legs'. Having appeared on stage, kilted, aged two, he made his official debut in panto aged fourteen and his London debut aged seventeen, so that, by the mid 1920s, he was an accomplished performer.

Worryingly, he was invalided out of the RAF with 'anxiety neurosis' in 1943, but he found radio work in such programmes as *Hoopla!*, *Our Shed* (in which he introduced the character of 'Humphrey') and *Petticoat Lane*. He also starred as Hines in the London production of *The Pyjama Game* and in *The Max Wall Show* on TV in 1956. His most bizarre creation was Professor Wallofski, the classical pianist, a construct that embraced Max Wall's musicality as well as his penchant for extraordinary mobility. He would find the piano 'with the help of an AA map and a spirit level'. His spidery figure, clad in black tights, short jacket, enormous boots, the leering face surmounted by a bald wig with extravagantly flowing back and sides, spoke of his obeisance to Grock and to Groucho Marx. He was, at heart, a dancing and musical clown.

He had a very lean phase, in part connected with his colourful private life. His 1942 marriage to Marion Pollachek was dissolved in 1956, the year in which, to tabloid fury, he married the beauty queen, Jennifer Chimes. Divorced again in 1969, he had a third, disastrously brief marriage with Christine Clements, at which point he was playing drill halls and minor clubs. Max Wall rallied valiantly to enjoy a legitimate career in plays like Samuel Beckett's *Krapp's Last Tape* and *Waiting For Godot,* and films like *Little Dorrit,* in which he played Flintwich with beady-eyed venom. From 1974 he also

Away from the bazaar and in quiet mufti – the eccentric sand dancers, Wilson, Keppel and Betty, the quintessence of the variety genre

concentrated on a one man show, where he reproduced the funny gait, coughed and spluttered ('I'll have to get a bed tonight', he would mutter) and deliver a volley of acidic, melancholy comments, often with a shaft of coarseness running through them. In performance, as in career and domestic life, he experienced highs and lows and precious few middles, but in the last ten years of his life he did take on some iconic status. He also earned plenty of money but, avoiding the camaraderie of the entertainment world, he lived as something of a recluse. He died, following a fall, in London in 1990.

There were some comic duos and trios whose motif was burlesque dancing. To take two turns at random, there were Bob and Marion Konyot, a spoof adagio act, and Jo, Jac and Joni, who added musical instruments to their eccentric dancing. However, one speciality dance act stands forth from the motley. This was Wilson, Keppel and Betty.

To the melody of Luigini's *Ballet Egyptien*, arranged for them by Hoagy Carmichael, they offered *Cleopatra's Nightmare*, a carefully synchronised and co-ordinated sand dance. The two men, po-faced, nightshirted, be-fez-zed, spindly-legged, dolefully moustached, stepped and scrabbled in exquisite unison, lost in lustful adulation of the exotically veiled Betty. For once in a commentary on the age of variety, this act was unique.

Jack Wilson was a Liverpuddlian, born in 1894, while Joe Keppel was an Irishman, born in County Cork in 1895. Both were emigrants to the United States, although both served in the British forces in World War I. They were both hard-working dancers in the USA and by 1919 had formed a double act. A few years later Betty Knox, a onetime stage partner of Jack Benny's, joined forces with them, and in 1928 the outline of *Cleopatra's Nightmare* was designed, the Tutankhamen tomb excavations having helped by boosting the interest in Egyptology. Their British/London debut in 1932 at the Palladium was a sensation – and they never looked back. At home and abroad, they were adored. Betty

Knox's daughter, Patsy, took over her part in 1941, and, although there is some obscurity about the count, there were probably eight Betties in all, including Irene Edwin-Scott, Bunnie Bamberger and the last of all, Jean Mackinnon.

Wilson and Keppel retired in 1963, having done the act everywhere from Las Vegas to Leicester for 35 years. Jack Wilson died in Cork in 1977 and Joe Keppel in London in 1967. Like Jewel and Warriss, they were of differing temperaments. Joe Keppel was the careful one, watchful of his money and not seeking the high life, while Jack Wilson liked to spread his largesse and enjoyed partying.

This may explain the story that was certainly circulating in the 1950s that an amorous disagreement, involving the first Betty, had led to their complete estrangement, with them only meeting and speaking on business matters and taking separate digs when touring. Either way, it is remarkable that two men of contrasting character should, for a third of a century, sustain a partnership that was so dependent on precision timing.

If there were the ethereal chance to recreate an ideal variety bill of the immortals, then Wilson, Keppel and Betty, scrunching sand, tinkling cymbals and all, would be high on the list of every aficionado.

12. ARE WOMEN FUNNY? 'COMEDIENNES'

The demographics of comedians in the 'variety' epoch, roughly lasting from the start of radio in the 1920s to the dominance of television in the 1950s, are very male-oriented. Most of the names previously canvassed in this text are men and, even allowing for the decision to pledge a given chapter to women comics, that reflects the reality of the situation. During this era the cant theory was that women could not or should not do stand-up comedy. Either women could not tolerate the ruthless glare of such a public ordeal or, if they were able to do so, it was unfeminine and unseemly. The prejudice was rife among the professionals, the managers and the customers, just as it was in many other walks of life at that time.

The Social Canvas for Gender and Comedy

However, the subject is more complicated than being one of simple bigotry. Paradoxically, the pre-1914 period, when women were even more subjugated to male control than in the 'variety' decades, was characterised by music hall bills on which women were more often then not the stars. Marie Lloyd remains the personification of the old music hall and is fairly regarded as its most glittering star. Besides Marie Lloyd, there were others, such as Florrie Ford, Kate Carney, Vesta Victoria,

Marie Kendall, Gertie Gitana, Lottie Collins and a galaxy of others. It is true that they relied more heavily on song and less on patter than their variety descendants, so a shift in technique to largely spoken comedy may have had some impact, but it scarcely goes near to explaining the pre-eminence of women on the music hall stage.

What is particularly significant is that Marie Lloyd and her colleagues were both funny and sexy, whereas, as we shall see, the women comedians of the following age were mainly funny and unsexy, often cast as dowdy charladies and the like. Moreover, apart from the special case of Gracie Fields, they were rarely bill-toppers like their forebears in the music halls.

One reason for this paradox – as was hinted at in the music hall chapter – may lie in the sexual mores of the time. The social and cultural accent was on domesticity. A massive effect of industrialism was the separation of the working and the home life, for much of pre-industrial existence had found people working in or close to the home. The new convention gave rise to the Victorian ideology of 'spheres', the one 'public', primarily male, and the other 'private', primarily female. That it came precisely at the moment when women were tentatively deciding to seek paid work outside the home indicated the male fear of domesticity being disrupted. The mid-Victorian poet, Coventry Patmore, in the lengthy sequence of poems, *The Angel in the House*, idealised this position, and John Ruskin, the art critic (whose own marriage to Euphemia Chalmers Gray was unconsummated largely because of his unawareness of female physiology) defined the code strictly, in terms of the husband's outgoing and the wife's inward looking roles. 'Domestic fiction' celebrated this dichotomy, not least in the writings of Charles Dickens, although, before, say, David Copperfield and Agnes Wickfield came to make 'domesticity' manifest in the final pages of *David Copperfield*, he had displayed several dysfunctional homesteads, such as the Murdstones and the Micawbers. Victorian fiction also mirrored the moral tenet that non-marital sex was not only illicit but also tending to abnormality and violence

This domestic construct, with Queen Victoria and Prince Albert its titular leaders, and its knock-on effects of a sober propriety that became the by-word of Victorian morality, is no myth, even if it were sometimes honoured in the breach. The social and even legal pressures to enforce its rules were substantial, most certainly in middle class and aspiring working class homes and communities. It was the keystone of bourgeois stability and, for example, one of the reasons why the female suffrage was not contemplated was because politics was a matter for the 'public' and not the 'private' sphere. To some degree, the processes of sexual activity followed these same dictates, with the husband supposedly knowing and dominant and the wife the reverse.

There is research that suggests that this attitude was not wholly representative and there is plenty of evidence of the use of prostitutes, of pornography and of erotic flagellation and other far from homely habits. What this does is to point up the struggle between the variables of nature and the more artificial dictates of societal despotism. The fact that Queen Victoria did not believe that lesbianism existed did not much reduce the incipient incidence of lesbianism, even bearing in mind those women who, sadly, may have been so inclined but, either through their own ignorance or that of their communities, were unable to express these emotions. Ella Westland, an expert in these complex affairs, has written 'societies that are repressive on the surface deal with sex on other levels in ways that can be picked up from a diversity of cultural signals.'

Few cultural norms are comprehensive. The usual outcome is for a larger or smaller accordance with the norm, rather than for 100% obedience to this or that tenet. On balance, then, the Victorian wife was expected to be passive and not proactive in the sex act and the Victorian husband was expected to be considerate – and many probably tried to obey the social law. Incidentally, it is believed that Queen Victoria rather enjoyed sex and that it was her Consort, Albert, who had, doubtless pleading a princely headache, to apply some mild restraint. It was an aspect of the 'medieval dream' that preoccupied many Victorians, with the chivalrous male the knightly guardian of the vulnerable damsel. The inadequacy of even family-based sexual education for most young Victorian women and many young Victorian men may have contributed to the overall climate in which women were supposed to give but not take pleasure in sexuality. In other words, there is plenty of evidence of Victorian women finding a regrettable truth in the theory that sexual delights were not for them.

The music hall may have been one of those 'cultural signals', providing, vicariously, the missing element in the sexual equation.

Along with the burlesques and other musical extravaganzas, produced by managers like John Hollingshead, the music halls supplied a positive and provocative sexual charge. Marie Lloyd and other female stars were the sex symbols of their day. They were saucy, impudent and forward – the complement to the genteel innocence of the domestic hearth. The ultimate in this sexual boldness was the rash of male impersonators on the music hall stage. Vesta Tilley, Ella Shields, Hetty King, Fanny Robina and Bessie Bonehill were probably the most admired – and they were admired for their glamour as well as their talent as masculine portrayers. Often garbed in tight-fitting uniforms and suits, they were bold and assured. The male impersonator more or less disappeared in the post-1918 years. Conversely, that was to be the era, already described, of the female impersonator, often, after the manner of Old Mother Riley, distinctly unglamorous.

The principal boy, buxom thighs in tights, was a mainstay of the pantomime – and many of the music hall stars, most notably, Dorothy Ward, played principal boy. There has been much psychobabble written, some of it of a Marxist tilt, about the place of the insouciant and audacious principal boy, but the truth is probably very straightforward: managements knew that boldly displayed and shapely legs would appeal to the male who would be footing the bill to bring his family to the theatre.

In the coming period, it would be very uncommon for a woman, labelled as a comedian, to play principal boy; she would be more likely to be an ugly sister.

The social changes that arrived with and because of the First World War included some relaxation in the 'private' view of women, including improved educational, vocational and, with the vote, political opportunities. There also seems to have been some greater awareness of the reciprocal delights of married love. This may, in some degree, explain the relatively abrupt switch from the brassy provocativeness of the music hall female comedian to the plain drabness of her variety counterpart – but, once again, there are complications.

Overlying the two periods, roughly from about the 1870s to the 1930s, was another outstanding social factor: the fashion for small families. The birth-rate dropped from about 36 per 1000 population in the 1860s to about 24 by the time of the 1914-1918 War and went on descending. This was driven by the end of family members as an immediate work-force for whatever the family trade or occupation might have been, by the increase of women seeking employment (the numbers of middle class women with jobs rose 161% between 1881 and 1911), by a more beneficent attitude to the personal care of small children and, simply, by different social priorities. For example, it has been said that, in the inter-wars years, 'the garage replaced the nursery', as the aspiration for car-ownership spread, with the 'Baby' Austen perhaps only too pertinently so-called. This was part of a wider desire not to be too tied down by the onus of child-rearing.

Unluckily, this important departure in social conditions was undertaken before birth control was effective, approved of or properly understood. From a variety of evidence it might be provisionally concluded that, around the years after 1918, about one in ten of couples used the sheath method, that the diaphragm was deployed in a few high-class households, that 70% of couples practised withdrawal, that illegal abortion was turned to in working class back-streets and that, in general, abstinence was a major habit. A J P Taylor has pronounced that social historians examining the Britain of the 1870s to the 1930s should recognise that they are dealing with a 'frustrated people'.

In short, there may be some reason for wondering why the vogue for glamorous comedy to titillate the jaded sexual palate of the frustrated might not have been sustained into the variety period. Certainly, the prurient voyeurism of George Formby, no less the crackling innuendo of Max Miller, obviously reached out to this abstinent fraternity in their need, but, apart from the dancing girls, variety before the Second World War, provided little or nothing by way of the sexual frissons that had characterised the old music hall.

There was, however, a new twist in social interplay brought about by the influx of American films into cinemas that had a much more intense incidence of site and custom than ever the music halls or variety theatres could have managed. The cinema, its function a purely robotic, technical one, was truly the leisure offspring of the Industrial Revolution. Where Marie Lloyd could only appear, at best, in two or three theatres each evening, Mary Pickford could appear in thousands. Hollywood films introduced beautiful leading ladies to the public in the same profusion as handsome leading men. Gender equity, at least on the surface of the screen, was observed, and the generations of the 1930s and 1940s turned to the movies for vicarious sexual allure. Some social historians have gone so far as to argue that American actresses taught the callow British male the arts of courtship and kissing or, to give it its then slang identification, 'necking'.

It might be urged, therefore, that the sexual impulse supplied by the music hall was re-sourced by the cinema. The range of screen beauties ran the gamut from the exotic siren to the musically jolly and from the grippingly dramatic to the comically cheery. One measure of this change is that the pin-ups of the 1914-1918 War were primarily London-based theatricals, whereas those of the 1939-45 War were American film stars, with according to the research, Betty Grable beating 'the Love Goddess', Rita Hayworth, by a short head (if that horse racing term is not too inapt) as the most popular.

Relevant to the present discourse is the fact that comedy was an element in all of this, with actresses vying with actors for filmic laughter. Again, the range was wide. From Myrna Loy to Audrey Hepburn, there was the piquant flavour of often flirtatious comedy, while someone like Barbara Hutton could cope with something closer to clowning, at a time when attractive British actresses found it difficult to relax too far from a cool composure. Curiously, it was the American, Bebe Daniels, who was one of but a few to bring this quality to British broadcasting. Thus Hollywood appeared to inherit from the music hall or, more strictly, the American vaudeville tradition, the notion of the funny, sexy woman. The first major icon was the incomparably brazen Mae West – of a 6 ft 7 inch man she suggested 'forget about the six feet; let's concentrate on the seven inches'. In turn, there were to be actresses like Lucille Ball who, on film and television, contrived to combine humour with attractiveness. It was as if the British had exported the gift for amusing charm across the Atlantic. Ultimately, Marilyn Monroe supremely paraded the talent for intelligent comedy and for sexual fascination.

British Comediennes

Meanwhile, the British variety stage made do with mainly downbeat women comics, and they were not even in anything like equal supply. Making do sounds vaguely disparaging, but several of them brought great joy to the stage. To begin with, Nellie Wallace, a Glaswegian, born in 1870, was a superbly comic woman. She bestrode the music hall and variety stages, not so much like a Colossus, as like a gawky, bird-like breed of creature, the erect feather on her bonnet and the button-up boots underlining the image. There were lots of teeth and nose and, preceding Mrs Shufflewick and Hylda Baker, 'me bit of vermin' slung around the thin throat. It was deliberately grotesque – 'the Essence of Eccentricity' – but the message was abrasive and it struck home. Here was an unattractive spinster who could not find and keep a man. Bred in the music hall idiom, she mediated her unhappy communiqués in song, with some patter, all with a measure of self-delusion that somehow matters would turn out more pleasingly.

Gesticulating, winking and sniffing, she confided in fluting ladylike tones to her audiences her ventures around *The Blasted Oak*, location for many of her amorous mishaps, while she always obeyed her mother's advice, *Always Look under the Bed* – 'I always do, but you can lay a bet, it's never been my luck to find a man there yet.' It was a full incantation of the mood captured by the music hall song that ran 'why am I always the bridesmaid and never the blushing bride?' It was a poser Nellie Wallace continued to consider until her death in 1948. It is instructive that she was regarded as one of the best panto 'dames' of her generation in what was principally a male bastion. The comic portrayal of ugliness and thwarted affection may offend some modern sensibilities, but for forty years she was a leading star. She projected a model and maybe she placed a stamp on subsequent stage comedy for women for the next generation.

Over these years the comediennes reflected the styles of the comedians. Mixed gender double acts have already been mentioned and, whilst women were often, like Billie Carlyle, the straight 'man', they also shone as comics, not least in that very well balanced brace of Nat Mills and Bobbie. There were two or three notable all-female pairings. From Scotland came Renee and Billie Houston, the Houston Sisters, who from 1920 to 1935, made quite an impact on the variety stage with some clever and inventive material. They dressed as boy (Billie) and girl (Renee), with their set adjusted in size to emphasise their child-like characters. Renee Houston later re-formed the act with her husband, Donald Houston, until his death in 1965. A pretty, vivacious performer, she furthered her career in musicals, films and on radio. Renee Houston died in 1980, eight years after Billie, who had had to retire because of ill health.

The aping of children, almost like some mirroring of the male work of Georgie Wood and Jimmy Clitheroe, was the key to the success of Revnell and West, who adopted the character of schoolgirls who, in a later era and could their presumably working class parents have afforded it, would have enrolled at St Trinian's. Ethel Revnell (1895-1978) was 6ft 1in in height, while Gracie West (1894-1989) was but 4ft 2in, so their famous billing of 'The Long and Short of it' was perfectly justified. 'The Cockney Kids', full of bubbling mischief and with Ethel Revnell's occasional descent into a gruff voice, were very popular until Gracie West retired in 1953. In regulation gartered stockings, black frocks and straw hats, they were much enjoyed on stage and radio. Ethel Revnell soldiered on and, interestingly, was another female 'dame' in pantomime. Like Jimmy Clitheroe, they had much rapport with children and were, in consequence, to be found in the columns of *Radio Fun*, the children's strip cartoon comic of broadcasting stars. There was also *Film Fun* to celebrate the cinematic heroes and heroines.

There were one or two other acts, such as Lorna and Toots Pound or Beattie and Babs, but the one that is possibly the best remembered is Elsie and Doris Waters, 'Gert and Daisy', the sisters of Jack Warner. In what would later be the Al Read style, they derived their gossiping conversation from the realities of urban life in the 1930s and 1940s, having been hitherto a more musically based duo in concert party. The topics revolved around the iniquities of men, chief among whom were Gert's boy friend, Wally and Daisy's husband, Bert, and other humdrum themes. The tempo was flat and the effect mundane; it was material that evoked the rueful grin rather than the guffaw. They were cockney women, untidily and cheaply dressed, ruminating over their troubles over a cup of tea. They were well suited to radio, especially in the sorrows of the 1930s and the woes of the early 1940s, further evidence, like Revnell and West, of how the 'wireless' loved two voices.

There were other single figures that conveyed the same levels of world-weariness and troubled times, with a tendency to be downcast working class drabs. Suzette Tarri is a good example. *Red Sails in the Sunset* was her well-known signature tune, and, indeed, she had a strong contralto voice, but her comedy routine was the sorrowful doings of a waitress or charlady or other drudge, borne down by domestic troubles. Her voice wavered and cracked – 'it's me, Susie' – as she related these sad yarns. She was another to find radio the ideal vehicle. On stage, as opposed to the more discreet broadcasting studio, Suzette Tarri could get 'near the knuckle', as the saying then went. Commenting on a stoker's tattooed body, she said 'I'd just managed to trace Florrie's journey down to Florida when the foghorn sounded.' She died in 1955.

Jill Summers (1910-1997) followed a short spell as a double act with her brother, Tom E Moss, as a single turn, portraying an artful working class employee and, like Ethel Revnell and Nellie Wallace, competing for the dame role in pantomimes. She found some late fame as Phyllis Pearce in Granada TV's *Coronation Street*. Gladys Morgan (1898-1983), from Swansea, also began her professional life in stage harness with a close relation, her husband, Frank Laurie, but assumed a greater degree of success when she joined Harry Secombe on radio's *Welsh Rarebit*. She combined the toothless mouth of Norman Evans with the manic laughing of Charlie Penrose, and added to the roster of decidedly non-glamorous comediennes. Another Welshwoman, Tessie O'Shea, born in Cardiff in 1914, brought the potency of a forceful and exuberant personality to the frenzied strumming of her banjo and the gusty vigour of her singing of *Two-ton Tessie* and other such cheery melodies, all with some odd trace of an American twang. She died in the USA in 1995. Although more classless than some of her colleagues, there was still the insistence that her fatness, while jolly, was not particularly sexy.

An intriguing example of the genre, who built on her variety and radio work to become a consummate comic actress on legitimate stage and film, was Beryl Reid (1919-1996). Her great radio creations were, in Revnell and West vein, 'Monica', the viperish schoolgirl ('she's my best friend and I hate her'), often to be found with a chocolate biscuit in her knickers, and, looking a little ahead to Victoria Wood's search for her pal, Kimberley, 'Marlene', the Birmingham teenager of blunt opinions and Black Country vowels.

The author saw her, during this formative period for a grand career, as one of Cinderella's ugly sisters, at the Palace Theatre, Manchester, when she somehow managed to combine something of both these amusing characters. Once more, the accent was scarcely on feminine attractiveness.

There were one or two exceptions. Avril Angers, born in Liverpool in 1922, and Audrey Jeans, born in Portsmouth in 1930, were two attractive performers who strove to do light stand-up comedy in many walks of show-business life, while a later example would be the slimline Marti Caine. All three were light-hearted and versatile operators. Another interesting exception was Jeanne de Casalis. A South African, born in 1897, she was entirely the child of broadcasting, courtesy of her friend, the zany 'Mrs Feather', who remained as invisible and unheard as Queen Elizabeth I in Sheridan's play, *The Critics* or as Claude Dampier's Mrs Gibson. She was, like Harry Hemsley, tempted on to the halls, but her disjointed telephonic monologue was solely an aural experience – 'my bell's been tickled', she would gasp, terribly upper middle in class.

There were also female equivalents of the speciality acts encountered in the previous chapter. There were the impressionists, like Florence Desmond (1905-1993), with her *A Hollywood Party* that led to a most fruitful career; or Beryl Orde (Marjorie Stapleton, wife of Cyril Stapleton, the band leader, 1914-1966), who had a strong series of impersonations; the lively Maudie Edwards, from South Wales, and, closer to the modern era, Janet Brown, with her striking take-off of Margaret Thatcher. In later years, there were one or two female ventriloquists. As with the men, the chief consideration was sharpness of technique rather than plain comedy.

★ Hylda Baker – 'she knows, y'know'

There was, however, an outstanding example of the 'sketch' comedian, a queen fit to sit along side some of the kings of that minor art-form, which, in Sid Field, Robb Wilton, Will Hay and Jimmy James, had been the foundation of comedy of an exceptional brand. This was Hylda Baker.

One of the most compelling of British women comics, Hylda – 'she knows, y'know' – Baker

Like Sid Field, Larry Grayson and a few others, she was that show-business curio, the overnight success in middle age. She was born in Farnsworth, Bolton, the daughter of the minor comic, 'Chukky' Baker, in 1905 and made her stage debut in Tunbridge Wells at the age of ten. Quoting a false age, she took the lead, aged fourteen, in *Jingles*, a touring revue, in 1919 and then danced, sang and joked for years, becoming one of the first female 'proprietors' of touring revue companies with, for instance, the wartime *Meet the Girls* and the peacetime *Bareskins and Blushes*, when variety began to include stationary nude posing to boost its own rather than the customers' morale. In 1952 she was taken on board by the Lew and Leslie Grade organisation. They originally were Louis and Lazarus Winogradsky and they, as well as their brother Boris aka Bernard Delfont, became the most powerful impresarios of the post-war years.

They gave her bigger bookings, including the role of Widow Twankey in the 1952 Sunderland Empire *Aladdin*, yet another example of the 'variety' comediennes playing dame, while she enjoyed sudden fame with an outstanding act on the BBC's *The Good Old Days* programme in 1956. For ten glorious years everything prospered. She made her West End variety and legitimate debuts, the latter as the maladroit usherette in the Charles Wood play, *Fill the Stage with Happy Hours*, and she contributed excellent cameos to the films, *Saturday Night and Sunday Morning* (1960, as Aunt Ada) and *Oliver!* (1968, as Mrs Sowerberry). From 1968 to 1972 she partnered Jimmy Jewel as the sister and brother, Nelly and Eli Pledge, owners of the pickle factory in TV's *Nearest and Dearest*, and otherwise enjoyed star billings.

Her marriage in 1929 to Benjamin Pearson had long since collapsed; she was, after three failed pregnancies, childless; she suffered all manner of accidents and ailments, among them enfeebled memory, and her last years were full of disappointment. Having struggled for 40 years to climb what in politics Benjamin Disraeli called 'the greasy pole', Hylda Baker had developed a bristling, aggressive, guarded demeanour, watchful of her rights and repute to the point of self-parody – her raging feud with Jimmy Jewel, for example, became the stuff of legend. It is a mark of such difficulties that, in a profession that is often ultra-extravagant in its celebration of its heroes, there were only five people at her cremation in Twickenham, Surrey in 1986.

Thus she is heavily, but happily, reliant on her professional gifts for posterity's esteem. A feisty lady, less than five feet in height, she strained for respectability in the tradition of the great 'dames'. With her ill-fitting square-checked suit, her weighty handbag, her strapped shoes and her defiantly perched bonnet, there was some of Nelly Wallace's doggedness without her optimistic delusion. Beady of eye and querulous in abrasive tone, Hylda Baker was the epitome of the realistic northern housewife, her commentary on the less than rich pageant of life shrewd and cynical.

Her basic act was a sketch, in that it involved the silent Cynthia, played by umpteen people, most of them men and most of whom scarcely received as much as an 'assisted by' on the theatre programme. Cynthia's was a tall, looming presence of Delphic muteness. Unlike the alter ego of Claude Dampier or Jeanne de Casalis, she was visible, but, unlike the absent wives of Robb Wilton and Al Read, she had nothing to say, but appeared, at least to Hylda Baker, staring adoringly up at her, to be thinking furiously: 'where 'ave ya beeeen?... 'Be soooon', ah said,

The People's Jesters

'be soooon'...but, she knows, y'know.' Few from that era will have forgotten that telling catchphrase.

The exertion required for social propriety was evident throughout. All the worried scrimping, the black-leading of grates, the white-stoning of door-steps and the cajoling of the rent-man were visibly explicit in the taut shoulders, the arched neck, the tense arms, the staring eye and the pursed lip. Most of all was it noticeable in the rasping efforts to talk in genteel vocabulary, leaving Hylda Baker very vulnerable to the disease of Mrs Malaprop – 'the condescension was running down the walls'; 'no one has ever dallied with my afflictions and I can say that without fear of contraception'.

Like Sid Field, Hylda Baker found in middle age a decade of merited fame. Like Sid Field, she is deserving of a high placement in the gallery of British comedians.

★ Gracie Fields – 'Sing as We Go'

Through the years of Hylda Baker's slogging trials and tribulations in the provinces, Gracie Fields was the toast of a nation. As with Mark Anthony, the fates made Gracie Fields, then broke the mould. Her versatility makes her impossible to categorise. It is a question of either a lonely pigeonhole for one or splitting the atoms of this phenomenal talent and slotting them in half a dozen pigeonholes. She would hardly be pleased to be simply docketed as a comedian – but she was, among other things, a decidedly funny woman.

The American dream often used to be portrayed in presidential life-stories with titles like 'from Log Cabin to White House'. Gracie Fields' epic tale might be entitled 'from Chip Shop to Capri', the romance of the mill-girl, born above the aroma of fried fish, who rose to lead a life of rich luxury, from 1933, on the Italian island in the sun, complete, incidentally, with her own restaurant. She was born at 9 Molesworth Street, Rochdale, in 1898 and died in 1979, a Dame of the British Empire, (having also been the first variety artist appointed CBE), on the 'Isle of Capri' that she sang about so touchingly.

Not for Gracie Fields the long grind to stardom and a position described as 'the most famous person next to royalty'. After work with juvenile troupes, she soon took the lead in the 1918-1922 provincial run of the revue, *Mr Tower of London*, and, when it went into London for a week in 1924, she was immediately the talk of the town. 7m people – a sixth of the population – saw her in that show. She found herself invited to the first of her ten royal command performances; she cut the first of over 500 records, and she made a dozen or so films that made her the highest paid woman film star in Britain in the years 1936/39. The movies, beginning with the 1931 *Sally in Our Alley*, the source of her signature tune, *Sally*, all portrayed the never-say-die heroine, determined to battle through against the odds. *Sing as we Go*, another film and another hit song, was another of some dozen or so heart-warming films, with one or two of the scripts prepared by J B Priestley. Her accomplished pianist, Harry Parr-Davis, wrote such memorable songs as *Sing as we Go* and *Wish Me Luck as You Wave me Goodbye*, clarion calls to a public faced first with slump and then war.

She entertained troops on both sides of the Atlantic in World War II and always worked generously for charitable causes, although, necessarily, her career slowed post-war from the energetic rip of the pre-1939 years.

Her twin assets were charisma and a voice of amazing range. A little on the gawky and sharp-faced side of glamorous, she nevertheless commanded audiences with aplomb. The 'our' in 'Our Gracie' was very pertinent. Gracie Fields did not play to, but with ,an audience, the glowing inference always that she was one of them, an example of ordinariness lifted to extraordinary levels. A colossal talent serviced this boundless assurance. There were four facets to her output. There was the deathless hush while she quietly sang *Little Old Lady Passing* by; hearts were moved by her love lyrics, such as *Goodnight, My Love*; she would lift the rafters with a chorus song like *Sing, Soldier, as you March along*; roars of laughter would greet her musical monologues, like the still remembered *The Biggest Aspidistra in the World*.

Like the American stars, Fanny Brice and Judy Garland, she was no sex goddess, but a brilliant entertainer. There have been other British entertainers who have been all-rounders, mixing comedy with song and dance and, especially in the modern era, throwing in show-hosting as a bonus. One thinks of Max Bygraves or Bruce Forsyth – but for all their flair, not even the most devoted fan would pretend they were world-class in one of the bespoke areas. Cricket all-rounders offer an analogy. Most specialise in either batting or bowling, at the very best contributing top-class competence in one and useful endeavour in the other branch. The nonpareil West Indian, Gary Sobers has been alone skilled enough to bat, field and bowl in both fast and slow mode, and all close to world class standards. Gracie Fields was a world-class performer of this genius; an international star in four disciplines. It would have been merely embarrassing if Nelly Wallace had tried her hand at *Dancing with Tears in My Eyes* or if Vera Lynn had recited *Mary Ellen's Hot-pot Party*. To borrow a quartet of males from the Gracie Fields epoch for comparison, it was as if John McCormack, Hutch, Joseph Locke and George Formby had somehow been merged into one. Gracie Fields was a cobbler with four lasts.

The immediate purpose must be to concentrate on the comic element, but the fact that she would switch from the soaring ballad to the croaking monologue is, self-evidently, a significant aspect of her appeal. Husky, resigned and droll, she intoned the comic monologues, half singing, half talking, slightly racing the band or the piano. There are some score of these laments, several of them, from *The Biggest Aspidistra in the World* and ' *E's dead, but he won't lie down* to *All packed up in me little bottom drawer* and *I Took my Harp to a Party, but no one Asked me to Play*, that have entered consciously into the language – 'and I've walked home in me undies, but I'll tell me class on Sundays, that heaven will protect an honest girl'.

Several of them considered the plight of the working class girl left on the shelf, abandoned, like some Austenian heroine in a different temporal and economic league, without much of a meal ticket. Hence the final mournful plea to Walter, the recalcitrant suitor:

> 'Walter! Walter! lead me to the altar; my old age pension's nearly due.
>
> Walter! Walter! lead me to the altar; it's either the workhouse or you.'...

Or the melancholy alternative should the contents of the crowded bottom drawer not be required:

> *If me plans all go to pot, I can sell the blooming lot;*
>
> *All packed up in me little bottom drawer'...*

The People's Jesters

– but always with the final murmured home-spun philosophic fillip of patience:

'you can always do without what you've never had'.

A personal saga of grief that, were it presented fictionally, would be scoffed at and jeered paralleled the theatrical Odyssey from the mill-chimneys of Rochdale to the El Dorado of Capri. The 'Gypsy Rose Lee' syndrome of the pushy, over-ambitious mother, already noted with Frankie Howerd and Sid Field among others, struck once more. Ignoring Noel Coward's arch advice to Mrs Worthington about her daughter's stage-worthiness, Jenny Stansfield was determined – and successfully so – in wishing a stage career on all her children. Thrust into a juvenile troupe as a naïve adolescent, Gracie Fields was apparently sexually abused, with some form of nervous breakdown the result. This was the grim omen for a private life ravaged by sadnesses.

She married her father-figure and Mentor, the autocratic Archie Pitt, in 1923, in the midst of her rise to fame. He attempted to keep a strict control of her life and her work and was possibly more a stepfather than a husband. In 1939 she was stricken with cancer of the womb and underwent two operations that, for the time, indeed, for any time, were horrendous. By now she had fallen for the erstwhile comedian and film director, Monty Banks (Mario Bianchi; 1897-1950). She was divorced from Archie Pitts and married the Italian in 1940. Almost immediately, there was a minor crisis, as, with Italy's entry into World War II, Monty Banks, although he had spent most of his life in the United States, was threatened with internment. Gracie Fields and her husband fled to North America, in order that he might claim USA citizenship, but although she maintained her involvement in war charities and troop shows, this move was misconstrued as a desertion. Questions were raised at the highest levels and it did not help that Gracie Fields relocated her family in America's sunniest climes.

She orchestrated a compelling comeback, when, at the London Palladium soon after the war, she wooed the spellbound audience with her opening number of *Take Me to your Heart again*, but, to a degree, the whiff of treachery was never wholly dispelled. Then Monty Banks died in her arms, as they sped together on the Orient Express in 1950. Soon after, at her villa on Capri, Canzone del Mare, she met and married in 1952 the Bessarabian engineer, Boris Alperovici (1904-1983), who helped her sort out her ailing restaurant business. He proved to be something of a possessive husband, jealous of her celebrity and there were even hinted rumours of marital assault.

The private and public chasm was a wide one. At the time of her drastic surgery in 1939, Gracie Fields received a quarter of a million messages of good wishes. Equally, it was because she was 'our' Gracie that her transatlantic flight at the height of World War II was misinterpreted or caused so much woe. It is the old, old story of the world-class entertainer who could bring happiness to everyone but herself. It has been sagaciously said of Gracie Fields that, a most generous-hearted and outgoing woman, she could love people en masse in audiences, but not as individuals. For all that, she was, when in that mode, one of the funniest women in the canon of British women comedians.

A singer-cum-comedienne who was quick to be compared by knowledgeable critics with Gracie Fields was Joan Turner. Born in 1922, she was in her prime in the 1960s, her dates ranging from the London Palladium to the nightspots of New York and Las Vegas. She starred in *Talk of the Town* at the Adelphi with Tony Hancock and Jimmy Edwards and soared upwards: 'the voice of an angel – the wit of the devil' was her indicative and epigrammatic descriptor. Commonplace chat of showbiz ups and downs fades rather when contrasted with Joan Turner's experience – in 1995 she wowed everyone and stole the show on TV's *Barrymore*; in 2001 she was discovered living destitute in a Los Angeles mission run by nuns for the homeless. She returned to Britain in 2002 and, aged an indomitable 83, she has plans for her future show business career. There is an echo of Gracie Fields, not just in the vocal range and the lightning humour, but in some of the bravely endured white-knuckle ride of her social life.

★ Victoria Wood

To some extent the light comedy actresses, drawn to revue and intimate cabaret, kept flying the banner of female humour during the 'variety' period. They included pert Binnie Hale, often in company with her brother, Sonnie Hale; the very funny Beatrice Lillie, Hermione Gingold, Hermione Baddeley, or the endearing Joyce Grenfell, with her shrewdly observed oral pictures of the nursery teacher or the stately waltzing lady. Later there was Betty Marsden, often partnering that fine impressionist, visual as well as vocal, Stanley Baxter. With her great range of voices, she was intrepid enough to join the cast of BBC's *Round the Horne*, playing, among other mock-Gothic creations, Dame Celia Molestrangler, in the radio programme that, from 1965 to 1969, defied the odds and drew a huge listenership with its breath-taking, sharp-witted innuendo.

They were mostly comic actresses and singers rather than outright comediennes, some of them, like Joyce Grenfell, seizing on the value of radio, or, like Hermione Baddeley, of

film. It is true that they rarely represented the working classes with the consistency of the women variety comics of the period, usually adopting a middle to upper class demeanour, but, unlike their American counterparts, their comedy was not commonly dependent on or related to sexual attraction.

The collapse of variety and, indeed, the cinema as an organ of mass leisure, coincided with some major changes in British society – except that it was not all coincidence, for some of the elements were mutually interlocked. On the gender front, the idea of the contraceptive pill in 1954 was raised, and it was, of course, to be a dramatic sexual liberator, at a time when, through legislative action and cultural pressure, equity between the sexes started to become something more of an authentic goal. As the 1950s turned into the 1960s, the pace and tempo accelerated. The Permissive Society, with its more relaxed and relativist view of morality, prevailed. The abolition of theatre censorship in 1968 was, from the stance of comedy, a great step forward, at least for those who wished to eschew the suggestive and urge the explicit. It was all part of a range of events that constituted 'the swinging sixties'. The Lady Chatterley trial of 1959; the 1963 Great Train Robbery; the Profumo Affair, involving Stephen Ward and Christine Keeler in the same year, the 1966 Moors Murders trial; Premium Bonds and the unshackling of gambling; Beatlemania; Flower-power; libertarian legislation in respect of capital punishment, homosexuality and abortion – all these events, from very good to very bad, contributed to the character of this new age.

There would soon be the first female prime minister. It is true that the 'variety' script was adhered to and Margaret Thatcher, at least to her detractors, was in no way Prince Charming but Mistress Trot, with government

The People's Jesters

something akin to the schoolroom scene in *Babes in the Wood*, with the dame laying down the law with a heavy hand and Revnell and West, as the babes, the emblem of an oppressed nation. There was, however, now no reason, political, legal or otherwise, why women should not compete on equal terms with men as comedians. It was a question of forward to the past, to the late Victorian and Edwardian era when women had strutted their comic stuff and, at least on stage, ruled the music hall roost.

The problem was that, while there were opportunities for women barristers or engineers or politicians, on the variety stage, with its summer concert party and Christmas pantomime adjuncts, and on the radio, for 30 odd years the vocational arena for the stand-up comic, women comics had lost much of their joint impetus. Women comedy players certainly vied successfully with men, as we shall see in a later chapter, as far as television entertainment was concerned – Dawn French and Jennifer Saunders may be cited as splendid provisional illustrations. On the other hand, women, such as Jo Brand, with her forthright opinions on contemporary women's issues, the positive and excellent mimic, Josie Lawrence and the acutely witty Sandy Toksvig, were most welcome on the comedy club circuit and found chances on television. For the most part, however, the outlets, apart from TV, were limited to relatively small scale venues in London and the major conurbations and the opportunity, be it for males or females, to carve out a national reputation as a stand-up comic were restricted.

One interesting development in the post-variety world was the custom of the one-off concert. Sometimes with a couple of supporting acts, frequently as a lone hand, comedians followed the style of pop groups

and singers in embarking on such ventures. Sometimes they would engage in a tour of venues; sometimes it would amount to a once-a-week outing. With the closure of so many commercial theatres, the venues were more often than not civic theatres or municipal halls, a rash of which, either new-build or refurbished, had cropped up in the last third of the 20th century. As far back as the 1950s, the author recalls seeing stars like Lonnie Donegan and his effervescent skiffle group or the biting American satirist, Tom Lehrer, in concert at the Free Trade Hall, Manchester. Morecambe and Wise called these concerts 'bank robberies', in the Jesse James sense of the sudden descent on an unsuspecting town, the quick haul of substantial loot and the fast escape.

As the 20th century closed, it was said that only three performers could be guaranteed to fill the largest such halls in the land. Two of these were Tom Jones and Ken Dodd; the other was Victoria Wood.

Victoria Wood has emerged through the ruck of scores of young bloods, trying their skills in comedy stores and clubs, as the genuine article. Of the post-war vintage of comedians, she must be regarded as the tastiest. Victoria Wood has certainly proved her worth on television, with her own shows, in particular, *Victoria Wood as seen on Television*, with its inclusion of her spoof soap, *Acorn Antiques,* later to be transformed into a stage musical, and her entertaining company canteen sitcom, *Dinner Ladies*. In these enterprises she has been ably assisted by the support of something like her own repertory company, including comic actors like Celia Imrie, Duncan Preston and the doyenne of comedy acting for her generation, the inimitable Julie Walters. She has also shown herself to be an accomplished television playwright.

Nonetheless, her real and lasting worth has been proved on the concert circuit. In writing her own material, of an impressive range and with distinctive insight, in the musicianship of her impishly adept songs, as well as in her amiable delivery of words and lyrics, she has beguiled a nation rather starved of great stand-up comedy. Over half a million people, for example, crowded into some 200 civic theatres and other spaces during her 1997 tour – and this included a spectacular fifteen night spell at a packed Royal Albert Hall. She is fortunate in that, unlike her predecessors, who had access to little beyond records for additional exposure, the video and CD industry has been at her disposal, making her gifts available on an immense scale.

Born in Ramsbottom, Lancashire in 1953, Victoria Wood studied drama at Birmingham University, and knew some of the ups and downs of show-business travail, finally becoming 'a national treasure', as she has been termed, in the 1980s. She was married to the magician, Geoffrey Durham, from 1980 to 2002. Victoria Wood dazzles with the flair of her wordplay, especially perhaps when she sets her teasing homilies to the rhythms of her virtuoso piano accompaniment. There is delight and shock at the intimacy of her targets, just as there is delight and admiration at the acuity of her social observation. Victoria Wood's eye for the minutiae of the modern society and her ear for its sounds and voices is unrivalled among today's comic observers. In this respect she very much resembles the writer and dramatist, Alan Bennett, with his similarly finely tuned understanding of the conversational exchanges of everyday life.

In one of her earlier incarnations, in search of her friend, the elusive Kimberley, there were echoes of Hylda Baker. She similarly began her act, hunting for the lost Cynthia, with 'have you seen my friend? No, she's tall and blonde with aquamarine features...' Victoria Wood's characters, like Hylda Baker, were also addicted to Malapropisms, as witness the pollster, on the street with clipboard in hand, assuring potential interviewees that 'it's all terribly boney fido'; or her Spice Girl type self-constructed celebrity, who is 'becoming known for me big ballads.' This is the very same awfully ostentatious person whose motto is, 'If you think you'll have a shag, pop a Johnnie in your bag'. That couplet alone demonstrates how far the world has shifted either backwards or forwards, according to moral outlook, since the days of variety. Victoria Wood will also play fast and loose with political correctness, contritely amending 'gay frogs' to 'French puffs' on those grounds.

Although entirely comfortable with such creations, Victoria Wood is equally at home as herself, that is, as a suburban mother and housewife, classless, despite the northern overtones, and with a rueful gloss on consumerism, sex, domesticity, child-rearing and other day-by-day concerns. Plump of build, with short crisp hair, unremarkable face and a winning smile, she lies, in the sex appeal stakes, somewhere between Hylda Baker and Marilyn Monroe. Neither grotesque nor sex-pot, she brings something of Gracie Fields' ordinariness to her task. From one angle, it is an update from the Rochdale co-op to Sainsburys (through which Victoria Wood has a man 'running bollock naked shouting "your Jaffa cakes are crap"') from the mill-girl wondering whether she will ever marry, to the modern woman, anxious about her choice of underwear or her child's progress at school. It might be suggested that her bright, witty, explicit songs are today's equivalent of the Gracie Fields' well-crafted but necessarily restrained if slightly suggestive monologues.

Victoria Wood is a lodestone of what J B Priestley called the admass. Aware of and worried by advancing age, she finds that her child can't change schools, because she can no longer thread the needle to sew the name-tags into the new uniform. She turns increasingly to the mail order catalogues: the pleated skirts; the 'easy to open' Tupperware; the wheely-bin cover; the advice to 'microwave your bloomers and keep your kidneys warm'; 'Bladder Alert', with a tiny bell on your braces as an alarm signal. The observation is alert, achingly accurate and very witty.

Whatever the angle, few comedians have enjoyed such superbly clever scripts, the lines often building to a crescendo of audience delirium, and, of course, few comedians have so efficaciously written their own scripts, not, it should be emphasised, the ten or fifteen minutes of a Robb Wilton or a Jimmy James sketch, but the two hours of extended mirth that must be replaced entirely the next time the show-woman takes to the road. Like Max Miller, Victoria Wood sees herself as someone who is only realised professionally when on show; that is, she retreats, when off-stage, into the very placid ordinariness she lampoons on stage. There is no show-biz lavishness of gesture. Pointing out that comedians fall into the two camps of the melancholics and the jolly ones who play golf, she opts for depression – at least, she adds, 'you don't have to wear those check trousers.'

It is particularly gratifying that Victoria Wood is not only the finest woman comedian in the British gallery, but also the outstanding comedian of the ebbing years of the 20th century.

13. THE REGIONAL EFFECT: HUMOUR BY AREAS

The association of comedy with particular regions may be approached in two ways. The first, and simplest, is where comedians have striven to find their material in and base their delivery on the accepted traits of an area. The second and rather more complex approach is the enquiry as to whether particular environments are conducive to specific types of humour – are there, in fact, national or regional typologies of humour and laughter?

Regional Comedians – Scotland, Ireland and Wales

A long established instance of this manifestation of comedy is the grand line of Scottish and Irish comics. The distinctive idiom and dialect of Scotland or, at least, an imagined Scotland, coupled with that nation's reputation, deserved or otherwise, for thrift – 'the streets were as empty as Aberdeen's on a flag day' – and heavy drinking, made for a singular comic posture.

Harry Lauder was the father of Scottish comedy. He was born in Portobello, Edinburgh, in 1870, the eldest of the seven children of John Lauder, a potter. Harry Lauder earned his living as a flaxworker and a miner and tried his hand in local concert parties, but it was only after his marriage in 1891 to

Annie Vallance, the daughter of a Hamilton collier, that he turned seriously to the theatre. Indeed, it was 1895 before he became a full-time professional performer. By due avoidance of too much dialect, he soon found bookings south of the border and reached London in 1900. Henceforward his ascent to stardom was aptly astronomical. In 1913 he was paid £1125 for a week at the Glasgow Empire, the highest such salary paid before the First World War. He was in the inaugural 1912 Royal Command Performance, while he was also very popular among expatriate Scottish communities in the USA and elsewhere. He made 25 overseas tours, a large number for the era. His son, John, was, sadly, killed in action in 1916, but Harry Lauder was knighted in 1919 for his own war service, by way of recruiting, fund-raising and entertaining. He died, a wealthy man, at Lauder House, Strathhaven, in 1950.

Harry Lauder, affable and cheery, established a hearty rapport with audiences and in style he was typical of the music hall, singing chorus songs and interposing a few lines of relevant patter and the occasional rather pious homily. He made famous such happy romantic ditties as *I Love a Lassie* and *Roamin' in the Gloamin'*, which he sang at the 1912 Command Performance, while the more seriously sentimental *Keep Right on to the End of the Road* was another of his winners. Then he would turn to the jollier rhythms of *Stop Your Ticking, Jock* and the even saucier *Treacle Roly-poly*, the treat ostensibly enjoyed by the balladeer and his girl friend when her parents were absent.

Harry Lauder was the first Scot to become an international star. It was a by-product of his achievement that he played a major role in creating the image of the Scottish character. With his sporran, his cromach and his kilt, this physical picture of the mythic Scot was spread throughout the United Kingdom and abroad. To this he added the trait of miserliness, which some say he preserved off as well as on stage, and all presented in a pawky and rather maudlin fashion. It was of a piece with the so-called 'kailyard', that is, 'cabbage patch', aspect of Scottish culture. A school of writers flourished briefly but potently in the last years of the 19th and the early years of the 20th centuries, adhering to homely topics, recorded in something close to vernacular form, and related to the everyday doings of small-town existence in Scotland. It was headed by Ian Maclaren (born John Watson; 1850-1907) and his collection of stories, *Beside the Bonnie Briar Bush* (1894) and the school included S R Crockett (1860-1914), author of *The Stickit Minister* (1893) and J M Barrie (1860-1937) who, in tales like *Auld Licht Idylls* (1888), contributed to the 'cabbage patch' fashion, before gravitating to London to make his name with *Peter Pan* and other plays and books.

Benefiting from a long life and career, the immensely popular Harry Lauder thereby built a strikingly effective configuration of a supposed Scotland. Will Fyffe (1885-1947) came from Dundee and personified the drinking proclivity in *I Belong to Glasgow*, something of a national anthem to intemperance. *I'm 94 Today* was another favourite, whilst there was also *Daft Sandy and The Railway Guard*, the whole done with Glaswegian relish. There were plenty of others, Harry Gordon, with his tales of the 'postie' or the fireman from Inversnecky, Max Wall's father, Jack Lorimer, the deadpan Tommy Lorne, Neil Kenyon and Dave Willis to mention just a sample. Jack Anthony (John Anthony Herbertson, 1900-1962) was a Glaswegian comic who did very well in his native Scotland and played in innumerable Glasgow pantomimes.

Jimmy Logan, born in 1928 in Glasgow, the son of the musical hall partnership, Short and Dalziel, has had a lifetime of solid achievement in variety and in the legitimate theatre, including a one-man tribute to Harry Lauder. In the same tradition was Peter Sinclair, 'the Cock of the North', who lived from 1901 to 1995 and devoted his long life to stories and songs of Bonnie Scotland, not forgetting his role as Jimmy Clitheroe's radio grandfather. Alec Finlay (1906-1984) was his contemporary, an all round talent who, as 'Wee Alec', gained a lot of fans in Scotland. Another minute Glaswegian was Alex Munro (Alexander Horsburgh; 1911-1986), with his catchphrase and radio show, *The Size of It*, a comic who for many years made Happy Valley, Llandudno his stamping ground. Don Arrol (Donald Angus Campbell, born in Glasgow in 1929) was a Scottish comic of sound promise, who merited big television dates, including compering the prestigious *Sunday Night at the London Palladium*, but, sadly, he died, just 38, in 1967. A later popular example who also did some useful work on TV, was Rikki Fulton (1925-2004),

There seemed to be mainly a kilted Lauder highlander and a scruffy working class Fyffe heritage. Chic Murray was another variation, speaking primly in the careful cadences of the Edinburgh bourgeoisie. Charles Thomas

McKinnon was born in Greenock in 1919 and was destined for a career as a marine engineer, when he was persuaded to join in a double act Maidie Dickson, whom he married in 1922 and who was already on the variety stage. His tallness and her shortness made for an amusing contrast, as he proceeded mildly to abuse her, as she plied her instrumental skills, her husband already determined to make the words count. Maidie Dickson, having been on the stage since childhood, tired of the regime and retired; they divorced in 1972. From the early 1960s, he rowed a lone oar and, as his biographer, Archie Foley, remarks, 'self-management was not his strong point'; his career and his health suffered accordingly and in tandem. He later earned plaudits for his acting on film – for instance, as the headmaster in *Gregory's Girl* – and stage – as Bill Shankly in *You'll Never Walk Alone*.

However, his single act became something of a collector's item, a solemn paean of compressed logic. The tiniest and most mundane action, like getting up or waiting at a bus stop, would be subjected to this relentless testing. Roy Hudd quotes as a favourite line, and one that captures the argot as well as the method, the moment where Chic Murray reports being joined on a park bench by a man: 'I thought, 'if he offers me a sweetie, I'm off'.' Arriving on holiday at a hotel, the landlady asks him if he has a good memory for faces; he answers in the affirmative; 'good', says the hostess, 'there's nae shaving mirror in the bathroom'. Chic Murray died in 1985.

The 'stage' Irishman also found plenty of outlets in the variety theatre. Old Mother Riley was but the doyenne of a corps of Irish washerwomen that included the likes of Jimmy O'Dea (1899-1965) with his despairing cry of 'Well, carry me home and bury me dacent.' His eyes fluttered almost as much as his flustered feet, as he faced the slings and arrows of Irish domesticity. Frank Carson and Jimmy Cricket are but the modern incarnations of the Irish comedian, full of the blarney of the accidents and foolishnesses of their race, the fictional land of Erin, where, immemorially, every mother who sends her son a jacket in a parcel, cuts off the buttons to save on the postage – 'PS. You will find the buttons in the left hand pocket.' Harry Bailey (Harry Daniels; 1910-1989) was a son of Limerick, who, as we earlier learned, like Stanelli, Vic Oliver, Jimmy Wheeler and Ted Ray, incorporated the violin into his genial nonsense, often directed at the problems posed by over-large families. Billy O'Sullivan (1912-1987) was a Dubliner, chattering away in much the same style and earning a steady crust throughout the post-war variety period. A fellow-Dubliner was Cecil Sheridan, born in 1910, who raised the laughter in lots of Irish shows, while Terry O'Neil, from Cork, where he was born in 1922, carved out, from the Windmill to the telly, a useful career for himself. Billy Stutt, who came from Belfast and died in 1996, was another solid comedian, guaranteed to tell a good yarn and keep the holiday crowds relaxed.

The ruminative Irishman, philosophising from behind a glass of the hard stuff, was the alternative, although he was more to be found in plays than in variety. The modish version was represented by Dave Allen (David Tynan O'Mahoney) who found a niche in the intimacy of the television studio. *Tonight with Dave Allen* and *Dave Allen at Large* were his chief TV ventures, his approach fuelled by an inner fury about hypocrisy and cruel authority. Quietly, irreverently, if, on occasion, condescendingly, he purred away intelligently, poking fun at taboo themes and, in general, finding a method of telling tales on the telly that older comics with a long stage background failed to emulate. For some he became something of an icon, but, in truth, his thrust was possibly never strong enough to warrant such an appellation. A Dubliner, born in 1936, he died in 2004, aged 68.

Welshness does not quite have the same stagy resonance as its Celtic equivalents. Stinginess and slow-wittedness are marketable comedic commodities, whereas the supposedly Welsh traits, such as dark brooding passion, leant themselves more to the drama. Perhaps the nearest to a comic alternative was in the converse boisterousness and hearty brio of Harry Secombe or Tessie O'Shea or Gladys Morgan. Others of the same breed were Wyn Calvin, 'the Welsh Prince of Laughter', born in Pembrokeshire in 1928; Ossie Noble, 'the Clown Prince'(1901-1975, born in South Wales) his turn based on comedy drumming in the Albert Modley tradition; Ken Roberts (1916-1995), who hailed from the Rhondda and found lots of work in concert party and pantomime, and Stan Stennett, born in Cardiff in 1925 and, according to his bill matter, 'certified insanely funny', a zany, guitar-strumming entertainer who came to prominence with *Welsh Rarebit* and both the TV and theatre versions of *The Black and White Minstrel Show*.

There were hints of a West Indian taste when, in the 1970s, Charlie Williams poked fun at his own mix of exotic birthright and Barnsley breeding, and, in the 1990s, when Lenny Henry waxed exuberantly on television as the beaming immigrant enthusiast. Just after World War II, with a consciousness of a dominions presence in the UK at its height, the Australian, Bill – 'I'm only here for four minutes' – Kerr, amused with his drawling pessimism, worrying, for example, whether the steep incline of the theatre seating might precipitate an avalanche. These apart, there was not much humour of a distinctive nationalist brand, always, of course, excepting the constant flow of potent American comics to the British shores either in person or by way of film or television.

During the 1930s and 1940s there was a penchant for Jewish humour, with an emphasis on financial caution and possessive motherhood. The perceived spoken address, like that of the Scottish or Irish comics, was an important aspect of this form of comedy. Joe Young (Joseph De Yong; born in 1887 in London) was such a 'Hebrew' comic in the days of music hall, although he varied his act after the First World War. Like 'Skeets' Martin (Bernard Martin; born Liverpool, 1886-1970), Joe Young adopted an 'Old Bill' approach, both of them trading on that cartoon figure for many years after 1918. The corpulent Londoner, Max Bacon (1904-1970) was another comic who deployed the drums in his act, which also included musical parodies and mock-fairy tales in a Jewish style. Harry Green and Julian Rose were two others, but perhaps the best known, in the variety era, was Issy Bonn (Benny Levin; 1903-1979), who mixed his stories with schmaltzy tenor ballads, like *My Yiddisher Momma* and *Just a Little Fond Affection*. Round-faced, burly and smiling, he reported for his audiences on the activities of the Finkelfeffer family.

Regional Comedians – the English Regions

Turning to the English regions, there was, inevitably, a Mummerset brigade, a group of yokel hayseeds who dispensed a homespun ideology from over the farmyard gate. They hailed from different parts of agrarian England. Years ago Harry Storey (1825-1870) had sung *I'm the Young Man from the Country* on the early music stage, while *A Naughty Little Twinkle in her Eye* traced the fate of the girl who 'when she left the village she was shy'; Jack Lane (1879-1958) was born in smoky Halifax but appeared as 'the Yorkshire Rustic'. On the post-1945 variety stage the chief protagonist of rural lore was, somewhat surprisingly, Bernard Miles (1907-1991) the celebrated film and stage actor, born in the very suburban haunts of Uxbridge. He thoughtfully chewed a straw and slowly regaled the audience, leaning on a cartwheel, with his by no means innocent references to life in his Hertfordshire village. Attempting to put toilet water behind his ears prior to some furtive assignation, 'the damned seat fell on me 'ead and fetched me such a clout.' The stage yokel or village idiot, beloved of low theatre comedy, would soon be rediscovered on television by the Two Ronnies, in the *Emmerdale* soap opera and in countryside based sit-coms like *The Vicar of Dibley*.

As for specific English regionalism, an intriguing example of the pros and cons of such a manifestation is exemplified by Bobby Thompson, the pride of north eastern comedy for a distinct period from the early 1950s. Robert Michael Thompson was born near Sunderland in 1911, orphaned at eight, in the pit at fourteen and, apart from a spell as a company runner with the Border Regiment in Cumberland in World War II, had precious little stability and nothing much but odd jobs for the next 30 or so years. Thus he had the authentic stamp of Andy Cappery, with a male-oriented and nostalgic view of Tyne-, Tees- and Wear-sides society. Having tried his hand at occasional singing and harmonica playing, he was persuaded to audition and was successful in gaining employment with the localised radio series, *Wot Cheor, Geordie*. This led to theatre work, including pantomime in 1958 at the Theatre Royal, Newcastle upon Tyne and the gainful employ of a Tyne-Tees TV programme, *The Bobby Thompson Show*. His cynical gloss on domestic and working life among the collieries and shipyards of the northeast was appreciated by the many who had shared his sort of upbringing. A flat-capped, shrunken figure, unafraid to break the taboos and tell his honest tale, he breathed fresh air through the stale proprieties of radio and television comedy.

Trying to persuade the doctor to give him a sick note for his hangover, the physician could find nothing wrong with him; 'it must be the drink', he opined; 'alright', said Bobby Thompson, 'I'll come back when yer sober.' His wife had 'gan doon the shop' for a bottle of sauce; 'HP?' - 'No. I'll pay for it.' Of such was his material made up, but, unluckily, he found his skills were largely non-transferable. His thick accent and code of reference were alike incomprehensible to most people outside his native habitat. As 'the Little Waster' and 'Soldier Bobby', he was a rarefied treat for his fellow-denizens of an already changing Geordie-land and, although he continued, after some slippage, to command the loyalty of the working men's clubs of the northeast, he never became a national star. 'I jest canna get a bookin' beyond Rotherham', he once told the press. Patrick Newley was present at one rare occasion when, in the 1970s, Bobby Thompson played to a packed Wimbledon Theatre, the audience almost entirely composed of coach parties of fans from the northeast, almost as if Sunderland (in another sample of rarity) were at Wembley for the FA Cup Final.

His biographers indicate that he was a more complicated man than at first would appear. Although a devout Roman Catholic in an area where that faith has never been as strong as, say, Merseyside or Glasgow, he had a trail of three marriages and a liaison or two that was hardly in line with that stoic endurance in the face of wifely hegemony his theatrical character represented. Off stage he was a dapper dresser with, at the height of his earning power, a personal chauffeur that, again, stood oddly with his espousal of proletarian tradition. His heavy drinking and gambling was a more relevant marker, except that flashy casinos were out of the reach of the majority of his clientele, while he also earned the reputation of being unpunctual and unreliable in terms of engagements. That is not to suggest that the actor or comedian should live his life on and off stage in parallel character, but, unfortunately, the appeal of the wholeheartedly regional artist, flying the banner of the region's culture, does, rightly or wrongly, impose some expectation of integrity.

Bobby Thompson died in North Shields in 1988, adored, and meritoriously so, at home, barely known and understood outside the area. Although the two world wars and some labour mobility had helped the spread of cultural understanding, as men especially had found themselves flung together from all over the nation, particular climes and referential frames were still not so easily absorbed. Liverpool makes for an intriguing illustration. Some of the great comics with Liverpool roots or upbringing, such as Billy Bennett, Robb Wilton, Ted Ray or even the great Ken Dodd himself, never utilised Merseyside exclusively, if at all, to create their comic formulae. Had they attempted to do so, they might have come a professional cropper, for a distinctive 'scouse' ethos, in respect of a national consciousness of it, was a product of Beatlemania, the Cavern and a reputation for militant dockers and chippy football supporters. Only then was it possible to breed a bunch of typically Liverpool comedians, trading on the traits with which the city had become identified.

These have included Jimmy Tarbuck, with his long-serving brand of larky impudence, who sprang suddenly to prominence in 1963 on *Sunday Night at the London Palladium*; Stan Boardman, pulling his lip back over his teeth and worrying about the 'Jairmans'; likeable Tom O'Connor, with his nice line in a sub-Al Read commentary on street life, and Paul O'Grady in his drag version of the frowsy Liverpuddlian madame, Lily Savage. Freddie Davies was another from the Liverpool of the 1960s: with eyes and ears both seeming to be straining to leave his face, he spluttered out his jokes about budgerigars and was known as 'Mr Parrot Face' to his admiring fans, many of them from among the youths who responded so vociferously to the pop groups.

An interesting comparison with Bobby Thompson would be Billy Russell, with his slogan, 'On Behalf of the Working Classes'. Albert George Brown was born in Birmingham in 1893 and first appeared in London music halls in 1905, but it was after the 1914-1918 War that (like Joe Young and 'Skeets' Martin, mentioned above) he adopted the Bruce Bairnsfather's cartoon soldier, Old Bill, to mufti. Ageing himself a generation, he became 'Old Bill, in civvies', still complete with the regulation walrus moustache, but now accompanied by the battered hat, the tied up trousers and the red neckerchief. He lasted until the end of variety and radio's peak years, and then he did well in television plays, dying, in fact, in a television studio in 1972. His targets were the petty obstacles of the workman's everyday life. During the Second World War he was much troubled with the black out – 'I ended up in my own house three nights running last week' – and with officious air raid wardens from the RIP, as he referred to the ARP (Air Raid Precautions). One of them accused him of showing a light, but he claimed every window was covered; 'there's not a blanket left on the beds'. Told that there was a chink of light glinting under the door, he answered belligerently, 'well, you don't think the Germans are going to come on their 'ands and knees, do yer?' Just to underline the point about social class, Robb Wilton might well have been the interfering lower middle class civil defence officer.

Billy Russell had, as one realised when he sang, quite a classless accent, but, of course, he adopted raucous, wheezy gruffness for his act, which, unlike that of Bobby Thompson, represented, even if his tones were hoarsely southern, the universal working man. In consequence, Billy Russell had a general and not immoderate national appeal, whereas Bobby Thompson was worshipped in one locality and scarcely recognised outside its borders. Joe 'Always Jo-King' King (born, Cecil Emmott, in Keighley in 1900; died 1967) had something of the same lugubrious style as Billy Russell, albeit with a northern edge, and he, too, made himself comprehensible in all parts. A smallish figure, with a bowler, a flaming red tie and a ready fag, he had the mordant soul of Norman Evans; his mother apparently borrowed his best shirt, then laid his father out in it. Similarly Bernard Miles, while claiming to hail from Hertfordshire, presented himself as the common-or-garden rustic, who could have been gossiping over a cartwheel in any rural shire in England.

Both types were the lower class converse to the comedians, such as Charles Coborn (who famously broke the bank at Monte Carlo) Gillie Potter or the Western Brothers, who spoofed the nobs. Another of that fraternity was 'the Mad Earl', Norman Caley (born in Bridlington in 1920) who, in forces concert parties and thereafter in the usual runs of pantos and holiday shows, amusingly brought the tweeds, moustache, bow tie and ducal cap of the country landlord to the stage, or Nick Cardello, very much the toff, even if he kept his much-used ash-tray in his jacket pocket.

There was also a great heritage of north country comedians, something of a counterpoint to the cockney and coster comic singers of the old music hall. However, they rarely limited their argot or material to a given location. George Formby Senior, while answering to 'The Wigan Nightingale', or Tom Foy, 'The Yorkshire lad', both starred on the London stage. The plump-faced, cigar-puffing Dick Henderson (1891-1958), born on North Humberside and known both as 'The Yorkshire Comedian' and 'The Yorkshire Nightingale', was another. 'Joke over', he would declare to avert any controversy about his tales, before embarking on a luxuriant rendition of *Tiptoe through the Tulips*. His son, Richard Matthew Henderson, more familiarly known as Dickie Henderson, born in 1922, would become a stylish all-round entertainer, starring in revue, drama and television shows. He never failed to provide a polished contribution in whatever he did.

Albert Modley's descriptor, the vaguely oxymoronic 'Lancashire's Favourite Yorkshireman', gives some idea of that nebulous 'north country' front. Bolton's Ted Lune, 'The Lad from Lancashire', is another example. Gap-mouthed, eyes bulging, skeletal of frame and flat of cap, he rose from the working men's clubs to star in variety, on radio in *Get Lune* and as Corporal Bone in TV's *The Army Game*, until, borne down by ill-health, he retired in 1962 and died six years later. Bill Waddington, although Oldham born, described himself as 'Witty Willie from Warrington', and he, too, kept alive the notion of Lancastrian funniness. Like many another comic, he began in wartime, with *Stars in Battledress*, before being invalided out of the forces and enjoying a solid career in variety, strumming his ukulele and singing his doubtful ditties. He was recalled to the colours from retirement to play the part of Percy Sugden in *Coronation Street*, some-

Thoroughly northern Frank – Frank Randle, very much the regionalised comic, pictured in one of his series of army-based films

thing of a home from home for old variety artists, among them Betty Driver as well as Jill Summers.

It is clear that there were some northern comics who never did well in the south of England, just as the reverse was also true. Frank Randle was one such, for even the ten films he made tended to have a mainly northern circulation. He was born illegitimately in Wigan in 1901 and his resultant chameleon changes of name – Arthur Hughes, Arthur McEvoy and, when he went on the stage after jobs that included being a bottle washer and a tram conductor, Arthur Twist – were but the colourful beginning to a colourful career. Work as a teenage acrobat with the Bouncing Randles suggested his final stage name. From 1928 he was a comic and his series of touring revues, under the generic title of 'Randle's Scandals', scored well in the north of England for 20 and more years.

His chief character was the bibulous, priapic, aggressive old man, seen in the guises of the Vulgar Boatman, Private Sans Grey Matter, the Hiker, Grandpa on his birthday, and others. Drinking, wenching and fighting were the orders of Frank Randle's day: 'byyy, ah've supped some ale toneet; ah'll be glad when ah've 'ad enough'; 'All-slops ale – 36 burps to the bottle'; 't'landlord said 'ah bet you've never tasted our bitter'; ah said 'no, but ah've paddled about in it a bit'; 'ee, ah could warm thee, Gloria'; 'I'll spifflicate the lot of yer'; 'ah'll run 'em, walk 'em, jump 'em, fight 'em and ......play 'em at dominoes'. His was not an act for the reticent or those of a nervous disposition. Calling at the crematorium for his stout aunt's ashes, he is told. 'we've no ashes, but there are three buckets o' drippin' outside'.

Toothless, wrinkled, gaunt, rubbery and with a libidinous eye, his attack was blatant, crude, forceful and undeniably funny. He was assisted for many years by Gus Aubrey (Edward Brown, from Salford, born in 1909), notably a 'dame' character, and also by Ernie

Dale, Dan Young, Arthur Cannon and Stan Stafford, who rejoiced in the appellation of 'The Silver-tongued Navvy.' Frank Randle was something of a monster off as well as on stage and the anecdotes of his exploits are legion, including his setting fire to a hotel after a row with its owner, his collision with a Blackpool tram, and various arguments with theatre managements and police authorities. It may well have been his disputatious nature as well as the defiantly vulgar tone of his shows that restricted him largely to the north of England. Worn down by drink, debts and chronic ill-health, he died in Blackpool in 1957, aged 56, very much short of the years – 'Ah'm 92' – of his stage persona. It is difficult to determine how much was the madness of genius and how much patent ill-discipline, but it is difficult to put a sheet of paper between his role and his self, for both were based on anti-authoritarian rebelliousness. Frank Randle was as likely to wave the two subversive digits on stage or off. Turned down on medical grounds by the RAF in World War II, Frank Randle served with the Home Guard. It would have been worth the price of a theatre ticket to watch 'Granddad's Army' on parade.

The personification of north western comedy in the closing decades of the 20th century was undoubtedly Les Dawson, although it is otiose to add that he enjoyed national affection and fame, as 2000 people at his Westminster Abbey memorial service testified. Leslie Dawson was born in the Collyhurst area of Manchester in 1931. Bred in poverty and bullied at school, he had a number of jobs and fancied himself as a writer, not surprisingly, given his love of vocabulary. He became a pianist in working men's clubs and the story runs that, weary of the horror of it all, he back-chatted trawlermen in a Hull club, and his verbal act was born, even if his off-key piano playing always remained part of his work. After *Opportunity Knocks* and *Blackpool Night Out* he was by 1968 established on television with the *Sez Les* show and later the BBC *Les Dawson Show*; later still he compered the *Blanketty Blank* game-show with heavy – 'good evening, culture vultures' – resignation. He retained the northern connection by living in Lytham St Annes and he was married twice, to Margaret Plan in 1960, after whose death in 1987, he married Tracey Roger in 1989. He died in a Manchester hospital in 1993 at the comparatively young age of 62.

Small, fat and with a 'gurner's' face of multiple grotesque expressions, his depressed manner suited an epoch of social and economic depression. If George Formby and Gracie Fields kept up Lancashire's spirits in the 1930s slump, Les Dawson did his level best to do likewise in the post-1973/4 oil-related downturn in the economy and the brutalist Thatcherite aftermath, with inflation and unemployment soaring and manufacturing industry decimated. However, he did so, not by looking, as his famed predecessors did, on the bright side, but by adopting a doleful view of awful events. It was close to the acquiescent pessimism associated with Jewish wit, while the mournful delivery was sepulchral and gloomy.

The author remembers the first phrases he heard Les Dawson say on TV and live. Switching on the television set one day, there was this dismal countenance muttering, 'I'm not saying our council house is far out of Manchester, but our rent man's a Norwegian'. Dropping in at the Southport Pier Pavilion, first house on a sunny Tuesday evening, there was barely a quorum or, as the old pros used to say, 'you could have shot a stag in the gallery': Les Dawson glanced round lugubriously and opined, 'bloody 'ell; I've seen more in Moscow Conservative Club'.

He paid admiring obeisance to Norman Evans in his duo, Cissie and Ada, with Roy Barraclough, another *Coronation Street* regular, and he was perhaps the funniest old style panto dame of his generation. His hero was W C Fields with whom he shared a relish for verbal flourishes, although something of that same affection for words has already been noticed in the work of Robb Wilton and Jimmy James. A much cited one of Les Dawson's is 'I was vouchsafed the missive from the gin-sodden lips of a pock-marked lascar in the arms of a frump in a Hudders-field bordello.' Other blunt turns of unusual metaphor concern facial features: a face: 'like a bulldog sucking piss off a nettle' or a mouth 'like a workhouse oven'. In the tradi-tion of northern comics, he was merciless in his treatment of mothers-in-law: 'there was a knock at the door. I knew it was the mother-in-law; the mice started throwing themselves on the traps.' It should be remarked that Les Dawson dealt in comment rather than jokes per se. There are also interesting up-datings of conventional northern themes, such as holidays, now in Spain, rather than in Black-pool. Robbed by brigands, his wife consoled him with the news that she had managed to cram all their pesetas in her mouth and save them from the thieves; 'a pity we didn't bring your mother', said Les Dawson glumly, 'we might have saved the luggage as well'. As a sop to political correctness, he was equally tough on himself. He had been an ugly child; when he was born, his parents looked at him, joined hands and ran away; his was the only pram in the neighbourhood with shutters; his ugliness led to such confusion that his mother pinned a nappy round his face – 'God knows what she did with the dummy.'

His mordant demeanour suited the mood of the hour, making him a prime example of the motif of this text that comics, at best, reflect back to their public some annotation of the trials and tribulations of their situation. For 20 years he was, for all his Mancunian dispo-sition, the comedian who most matched the national mood – and it was fortunate that he had the wit and linguistic flair to do that position justice.

There was a further angle on the regional question raised during the 1970s and 1980s when the folk group and folk club movement spawned a set of comedians who identified themselves with particular districts or wider areas. It might not be too fanciful to spot some connection between this and the ris-ing tide of opinion in favour of some level of devolution of power to the three Celtic 'kingdoms' and, later, the English regions. Although one or two of them branched out more into stand up comedy, they each began as guitar strumming singers, with a decidedly comic element. One thinks of Max Boyce, from the mining valleys of South Wales, who revelled in the success of Welsh rugby in that era and charmed with his smiling humour; Mike Harding, 'The Rochdale Cowboy', born in Crumpsall, Manchester, celebrating the ups and downs of the Lancashire urban condition; Jasper Carrott, from Birming-ham, relating tales of the West Midlands, where, he said, there were '5m people with a speech impediment', and moving on to be a much-liked television entertainer with droll opinions on national life; and Billy Connolly, updating the Scottish image with a frighten-ing vengeance. Billy Connolly, born in 1942, Mike Harding, 1944, and Jasper Carrott, 1945, all come from a similar generation, reaching adulthood in the 1960s.

Billy Connolly makes for a fascinating case, not least because, of course, he has matured into an entertainer of global standing and made his mark in film as well, for instance, as John Brown, playing opposite Judy Dench's Queen Victoria in *Mrs Brown*.

From the viewpoint of this analysis what is intriguing is the way in which he switched the regional scenario. Especially in his early and, for some commentators, more telling days, he led a scathing attack on the so-called 'white heather' characterisation of Scotland, typified by Harry Lauder and the sort of TV Hogmanay ceremony associated with the ballad singer, Andy Stewart. He replaced that somewhat effete picture with a red-blooded portrait of Glasgow tenements, their inhabitants spoiling for a scrap and swilling with alcohol. It might be suggested that Will Fyffe had had something to say on these topics, but, in an age free of legal censorship and social censure, Billy Connolly's observations were scatological and profane. For example, in his solo performance in the early and mid 1970s, he offered lengthy sixteen minute accounts on the problems of personal sewage disposal, 'the Jobbie Weecha!!!!', and 'The Crucifixion', with that sacramental event transferred to the outskirts of Glasgow. They were hilarious, cleverly written and performed with buoyant gusto by Billy Connolly. The juxtaposition of the ancient Roman and modern Scottish cultures was well-observed. Jesus, eyeing the spear-carrying centurion with suspicion, tries to engage him in innocent conversation: 'the nights are fair drawin' in then.'

The question remains as to whether the national character reflected by Billy Connolly is more accurate or realistic than that of Harry Lauder. Could it be that national character changes or does not genuinely exist outside the fictions of stage and film or – and here one might recollect the refined Edinburgh voice of Chic Murray over against 'Lauderism' or 'Connollogy' – cannot be encompassed by a single narrow interpretation?

Regional Humour – Myth and Reality

That is a useful introduction to a brief debate about the authenticity of regional humour. There is no doubt that many people believe there is some such phenomenon as Cockney or Geordie or Scottish or Liverpool or Irish comicality and many people probably believe that this is inherited as part of the sharing of some genetic pool. They hold this faith as an aspect of a wider credo, that is, the concept of national or regional character in general. Unfortunately, research into genetics prompts as many thoughts about similitude as disparity. We are told that the human species shares 30% of the genes of the banana, while the genetic sameness of humans and many animals is a salutary reminder of a common rather than a diverse heritage.

To take the example of the Welsh talent for and love of music, especially choral singing. It is unlikely that the Welsh gene bank is at all involved with this or that, indeed, musicality is inherited through the blood-line. What is much more likely is that, for a variety of economic and social grounds, including religious and industrial reasons, music became a matter of esteem in Welsh society, children were born into households and townships where music was revered, and the conditions were conducive to encouraging and rewarding those who engaged keenly with musical concerns. Musicianship is, then, largely an acquired characteristic, not one that is conveyed by nature but by nurture. The suggestion that a child has 'inherited' this or that talent from a parent is usually a distortion of the truth that the child has rather been subjected to a set of circumstances where that talent was viewed favourably and promoted. Yehudi Menhuin, perhaps modestly, stated his belief that there were hundreds of children who, had they been placed, aged two, in his self-same situation, would have become virtuoso violinists. The negative case was put by John Reid, the Scottish trade union leader, who, the day after Roger Bannister ran the first four minute mile in the early 1950s, asked a huge gathering of Clydeside ship-builders how many of them had ever worn a pair of spiked running shoes. Not one hand was raised. Given a shift in early fortune, and there might have been two or three four minute milers in that crowd.

On the broader terrain of national culture, the changing countenance of national identity may only be explained by reference to economic and allied determinants.

Benedict Arnold has used the evocative expression 'an imagined community' to convey the nature of the phenomenon of nationalism. Modern nations have striven to define their separate identity in and through flags, anthems, saints and other heroes, language and literature, sports and other cultural activities. John Bull in 1712, Britannia in the 1750s, the British Museum in 1761 and the Encyclopaedia Britannica in 1768 are varying instances of the mode. In turn, citizens seek to conserve these images and embody them, anxious to present the traits that they believe are integral to their nation-hood. It follows that, because these characteristics are not eugenic, they are vulnerable to alteration and amendment.

The cultural historian, Jeffrey Richards, among other commentators, has argued that the English national character underwent a major sea-change between about 1780 and 1840, when the twin impact of Evangelicalism, with its earnest sense of purpose and 'Chivalry', with its sense of 'decency' and courtesy, caused society to become more orderly and prudish than of yore. In the 17th century the English had been regarded as a rebellious and bloodthirsty lot, killing their

king and having revolutions; the stiff upper lip sort of Englishman only emerged in Victorian times. Similarly, there was another transformation, especially from the 1960s, when the post-war emphasis on affluence and materialism brought a mood of self-gratification and some denial of personal duties and responsibilities. Crime, for example, halved in proportionate terms between 1857 and 1901, remained fairly stable for another 50 years, and then had risen 40 times by the end of the 20th century. There were 791 reported woundings in 1921 and 95,000 in 1980.

From some standpoints, this was not so much a change as a regression back to the rowdy, brutal days of the 18th century, where politics earned the reputation of being 'oligarchy moderated by riot'. A useful illustration is the manner in which the crowd is regarded. In the 18th century and the late 20th century the crowd has been feared, not without cause. In between times the crowd, as at football matches or political rallies, was not seen, again rightly, as unduly dangerous; there would scarcely be a policeman present at events attracting great numbers. Of course, this was not a case of complete adoption of one or other style. Jeffrey Richards suggests that social and cultural features conspire to resolve how the 'smooth' and 'rough' elements in communities, possibly in individuals, are dominant at varying times.

Turning back to the Celtic kingdoms, it was also in the 18th century and after that Irish, Scots and Welsh folk-lorists invented their wild romanticism, largely as a counterpoint to an English sentiment of 'orderliness' that was often observed in its omission. The Irish harp, the Scottish kilt and tartan and the Welsh bardic-cum-druidic lore are traditions that owe much to retrospective history. These English subjects readily adopted them as badges of an incipient nationality to which Anglo-Saxon attitudes were alien, but they certainly owe little, if anything, to any genetic component. They are not, so to say, in the blood.

What we have, at best, is what might be called a persona, a self-belief of groups of regional or national citizens that their 'character' is such and such and the determination to reinforce and demonstrate that image. This is possibly the most authentic explanation of the manifestation of 'national' or 'regional' character.

Ken Dodd: 'The Slide-rule Comedian'

Enter Ken Dodd. Aside from his prodigious talent as the uncrowned emperor of British comedy, Ken Dodd quickly won for himself among the theatre managements a name for making direct and immediate rapport with audiences. First house, Monday night at the Salford Hippodrome – and Ken Dodd knew precisely what material to utilise and how to mould his act. He was, as a consequence, known in the trade as 'the Slide-rule Comedian'. It was the outcome of a careful study of regional humour.

Before investigating how that was achieved, a few brief sentences of biographical introduction: Ken Dodd was born in Knotty Ash, Liverpool, in 1929 and still resides, unlike several Liverpuddlian expatriate theatricals, in the house of his boyhood. It was there that his father, Arthur Dodd, pursued his career as a coal merchant and, even when his son was a big star, the coal lorries lurched and manoeuvred on their lot behind the house. He was also a semi-professional saxophonist, working summer seasons in the Isle of Man, for example, and he gave his son a taste for show-business. Aged eight, he developed a child 'vent' act with his still extant dummy,

Dickie Mint and, as an ex-choir boy of St Thomas' Church, Knotty Ash, he trained as a singer, evolving from 'The Wonder Boy Ventriloquist' into 'Professor Yaffle Chucka-butty, Operatic Tenor and Sausage Knotter'. Having worked with his father for a while, he had opened up a promising hardware venture on his own account, with a string of scout hut, church hall and Masonic lodge engagements in the evenings. It was quite a lucrative combine of interests.

In 1954 he turned fully professional, with an engagement at the Nottingham Empire, and, since that point, he has reigned as the premier stand-up comic of his generation – or maybe of two generations, for he is still working flat out in his late 70s, filling halls everywhere across the country and keeping the audiences entertained until 1.30 and 2.0 in the morning. His Dracula-like den-tistry, the result of a bicycle accident, and his startling quiffs of black hair, were his trademarks, while his material was, at core, burlesque ballads. Early in his career his basic act revolved around the angular, black garbed destruction of *The Floral Dance* and the safari-clad demolition of *The Road to Mandalay*, songs one then heard every day from tenors like Peter Dawson.

Although he rapidly won the prestige of his own radio and television shows, Ken Dodd has, on his own admission, remained a per-former most comfortably at home with the large live audience. He is, to borrow a not inapt religious analogy, the John Wesley of comedians, travelling nationwide to address huge and enthusiastic throngs, an evangelist among comic performers. Ken Dodd's idol, however, is not John Wesley but that other wooer of great crowds, Al Jolson, an uncom-mon choice for a comic, one might think, until one recalls the torrent of energy, the cry of 'you ain't seen nuthin' yet', and the sheer explosive force with which the finest of American entertainers hit every stage. Ken Dodd merits his other appellation of 'The Fireworks Comedian', for it is with that same pyrotechnic vigour that he surges on to the stage, all Punch-like tickling sticks and flamboyant costumes, crackling with gags and bonhomie.

The American illusion is not an idle one. Ken Dodd, with his – hence the 'missis' greeting – back of a van selling experience and his fairground bravura, relates closely to the 'vital entertainer', identified by, F J Turner, the American historian of *The Vanishing Frontier*, as the chief cultural ingredient in the swirling, busy formation of the United States. He mentions Mark Twain (Samuel Clemens; 1835-1910) as a prototype of this dispensation; he might have added to the list J P Souza, Al Jolson, Bob Hope and Elvis Presley, all bringing an immediate, vivid forcefulness to their work. Ken Dodd cites Mark Twain, along with the Canadian humorist, Stephen Leacock (1869-1944), as his literary models. Despite his own 'portmanteau' vocabulary like 'plumptious' and 'titifilarious', Ken Dodd, when a child, found Lewis Carroll menacing. His other influences tend to be comic actors, like Alistair Sim and Cary Grant, while, among comics, he admires the exquisite timing of Robb Wilton and Jimmy James, the outrageousness of Frankie Howerd and the expertise of Will Hay.

He gallops through material like a thoroughbred racehorse, leaving his listeners and watchers breathless and gasping, trying desperately to keep up with the speedy flow, often finding themselves three or four punch-lines behind. Not for Ken Dodd the meditative calm of Robb Wilton, nor yet the carefully timed but never tommy gun delivery of Max Miller. Ken Dodd's is the ratta-tat-tat of the automatic weapon and,

for those faced with dying laughing, just as lethal. Ken Dodd uses as much material in ten minutes as lesser breeds of comics utilise in a lifetime, but the effect is wholly dependent on the full-blooded attack of the confident, perfectly rounded comedic character that he has developed over his own lifetime. People, then, are laughing with Ken Dodd, courtesy of his hundreds of quips.

'What a wonderful day it is' is his conventional opening, followed by a myriad of justifications for the wonderment of the day. 'What a wonderful day it is – for trooping the rentman; for granddad-baiting; stick a rabbit and a ferret down his trousers and see how long it is before his eyes cross; for taking your clothes off, knotting your legs round your neck and shouting, 'how's that for an oven-ready turkey, Bernard Matthews'; for running down the street, sticking a cucumber through the letter-boxes and shouting 'the Martians are coming'. The last is a brilliant example of his triple appeal; sheer daftness for the kiddies; a phallic reference for the mums and dads, and just a hint, with the 'coming', of artful blueness for those who like to regard themselves as knowing.

His gags are as surreal as the rhymes of Billy Bennett, someone Ken Dodd admires and can imitate well, although, as with Billy Bennett, it is the linkage back to a common reality that makes for the humour. For example, Ken Dodd makes amusing play, with the aid of his own quivering fingers and extravagant gestures and expressions, of relocated facial features. There is the eye on the end of one's digit, for easier reading under the bedclothes and goodness knows what other activities. There is the mouth on top of the head, designed for those late for work; you can stick a bacon buttie in, clap on your hat and rush for the bus. There is the mouth under the armpit, extremely use-

The People's Jesters

ful in heated argument, when you might lift an arm defiantly and cry 'I beg your pardon, madam'. Another illustration is the Great Drum of Knotty Ash, which Ken Dodd bangs enthusiastically, carolling *Silent Night* the while. 'Take it to bed with you, missis,' he advises, 'give your hubby a fright'. It is also valuable for those who wake up in the middle of the night and wish to know the time. Open the window, stick the drum out and bang it loudly – and there is always someone who will throw up their window and shout 'who the bloody hell is banging a big base drum at half past two in the morning.' Again, it is the voyage into the imaginative and the return journey to the humdrum.

With hit records to his name, Ken Dodd permits his audience to relax a little with his sentimental or cheery tunes, like *Tears, Happiness* or *Love is like a Violin*, reinterpreted, for nothing is sacred, as 'Love is like a set of bag-pipes; you don't know what to do with your hands.' He is aware of the danger of his audience becoming overwrought with laughter, so he allows them the easement of an unpretentious song. The Diddymen were introduced and profitably marketed to supply another switch of tempo and to ensure that children – an important element in what he calls the 'trilogy' of mum, dad and youngster, were catered for. They were lovingly based on a favourite great-uncle but owe something to Lord Snooty and His Pals in *The Beano* comic. Then, after the lull, he returns to the tempest of gags.

Ken Dodd has suggested that, were he vouchsafed another life, he would be a social psychologist, an interesting outlet for the humorist who has studied his Freud and his Bergson, examined the roots of comedy and pushed his comedy to frontier of his talent and the limits of his beholders' capacity. Ken Dodd has brought a zealous professionalism to serve his natural gifts that led Michael Billington, the *Guardian* drama critic, to write his biography (and Ken Dodd has proved to be a telling Malvolio in *Twelfth Night)* and caused John Osborne to take the Royal Court Players to watch him at the Palladium several times in the mid-1960s, when he starred there in *Doddy's Here* and *Doddy's Here Again*. He makes no mock-academic pretences about his log-books; they are the manuals of his stock in trade and they work for him. It is a rigorous attitude. Asked about P G Wodehouse's definition of humour as 'the kindly contemplation of the incongruous', he remarked that P G Wodehouse had never had to play the Golden Garter Club, Wythenshawe, where what was indispensably required were 'release' jokes, stories dedicated to a packed house, oiled with alcohol and brimming over with testosterone, needful of a liberation of inhibitions.

Guided by the bookkeeping stocktaking necessary when he was a trader, he embarked on a remarkable analysis of every performance he did, with his girlfriend, marking every script with a set of symbols indicative of how well or badly every joke was received. Each script would be headed by the date, the season, whether first or second house, place in programme and time on and off, the size and character (that is, 'fast', 'slow', 'hard') of the audience, and the weather, for, as Ken Dodd was swift to grasp, customers entering from rain or cold conditions are different in mood to those coming in from the sunshine. Eventually, he would be able to gauge his act from a foreknowledge of, say, the likely size or social composition of the audience, while dress was another element. The crowd in dinner jackets and posh frocks has a different expectation to the one wearing open-necked shirts, floral dresses and sandals. He draws the distinction between the jokes he tells at a stag night party to husbands who go home and repeat them to their wives and the jokes he would tell at a hen party for those same wives.

A typical script would be marked in two columns, on one side a brief label for the joke, on the other side a symbol and, afterwards, a final comment from the comedian himself; thus:

JOKE CUE	COMMENT
'country'	went well, but try slower
'docker'	v.g. mimic walk and voice of policeman next time
'Schweinhund'	ex. but re-phrase slightly
H Wilson (Scillies)	political gags need punching more here

Over the years this encyclopaedic knowledge meant that Ken Dodd could resolve that, for example, Wigan was a place for hearty vulgarity without too much overt sex, whereas Brighton fancied weird humour with a touch of spice. One or two sociologists have, in discussion with the author, scoffed at this formula as lacking scientific rationality, but the truth lies in Ken Dodd's success and affluence (does not Ken Dodd boast, in the aftermath of his tax troubles, that he invented self-assessment and the Inland Revenue wish to take the credit?) Given increased mobility and the journeys people are prepared to undergo to see his one-night appearances, some of this wisdom may have been diluted over time, but the professional attitude on which it was predicated, above all, the tremendous respect in which he holds his fans that it demonstrates, remains constant.

Ken Dodd himself would explain much of this in terms of cultural components, such as the Liverpool mix of northern dispassion and Celtic 'talking in pictures', provided by the strong Irish and, sometimes forgotten, Welsh influences on Merseyside. He points out a comparison between the Diddymen and the Manx pixies. However, what is more likely is that the reverse has occurred and that it is in the wake of his great success, coupled with the revival of a Beatle-oriented 'scouse' cult, that the notion of the irreverent Liverpuddlian emerged. In other words, Merseyside has adopted the persona of comicality. Walk, say, across the concourse of Lime Street Station, Liverpool, with Ken Dodd and, at once, would-be gagsters assail him, just as the fastest gun in the west would have been tested by tyro gunslingers, if he had set foot in Dodge City. Frankly, they are no funnier than a representative sample from anywhere else, although there may be something in the cross-currents of compact urban living that make for an irreverent and sharp-witted vein. They were playing at being comic, in the same way that Scots had mimicked the stage miserliness of Harry Lauder and now mimic the stage disrespect of Billy Connolly. The intriguing aspect of most of these examples of regional characterisation is that they are self-propelled; it is the Yorkshireman who claims to be blunt and plain-spoken and the cockney who claims to be chirpy and indomitable.

What Ken Dodd did, at least for that generation, was, through close tabulation and tried practise, to home in on the authentic personality of areas, a character created by the peculiar social compounds of the region or locality. Curiously, it was often alien to the perceived nature of the area, as some of the ensuing summation of Ken Dodd's researches hint. Although Ken Dodd was, as the Wigan/Brighton axis reveals, able to

The People's Jesters

pinpoint districts with some precision, the following is a composite regional précis, dated around the late 1970s.

1. Scotland

Ken Dodd has termed the Glasgow Empire 'the House of Terror'. He reckons that quick-fire artists, full of the one-liners that sustained Bob Hope is the best recipe and he mentions how successful fast-talking Stan Stennett was in Scotland.

2. Wales

Zany off-beat comics are preferred, such as Tommy Cooper, born if not bred in the Principality.

3. The North East

A very class-conscious area, with traits of being frustrated by authority and feelings of anti-pomposity, all making for an enjoyment of dry, allusive, pensive comedians, such as Jimmy James.

4. Yorkshire

Counter to the dour image often propounded on the broad acres, friendly comics are preferred here; hence a keenness for the likes of Jack Pleasants, Sandy Powell and Albert Modley.

5. Lancashire

Although there is some fondness for the warm-hearted approach, there is an affection for a more abrasive, sarcastic flavour, especially in Liverpool and Manchester, as witness Al Read, Eric Morecambe or Les Dawson.

6. The Midlands

Midlanders appear to approve of singing comedians, with Harry Secombe an example of one who made his name at the Coventry Hippodrome. This offers a good illustration of the Doddian method; it is not that he would change his basic act completely, more that he would alter the balance in this or that direction. Thus when playing the Midlands, he would normatively include rather more songs than elsewhere.

7. The South West

There is, or was, a liking for genial and matey comedians here, exuding fun and friendliness; it is perhaps no coincidence that Bruce Forsyth, something of a master of game show hosting, made his early name in this part of the country.

8. The London Region

The next chapter will be devoted to the metropolis and its take on comedy. Ken Dodd's gloss on London humour will form an essential part of that essay.

What, of course, is so surprising is that Ken Dodd has the manifold spread of comic genius to modify and shape his act to these variant needs. Long may his evangelical mission continue to promote what he calls the 'wahoo' factor of sheer exuberance and 'happiness'.

London seems to love comedians with an element of bathos — Norman Wisdom is a splendid example of that tendency

14. LONDON LAUGHS: METROPOLITAN ICONS

London, not uncommonly for a capital city, is not wholly representative of the nation at large. This seeming paradox arises from the very particularity of being the leading city, with all the administrative and cultural apparatus of the country accumulated there. Size is an issue. The 8m or 10m inhabitants, according to the definition used, in the Greater London area, makes it as large as Cuba, Tunisia, Zambia, Ecuador, Cambodia, Portugal or Hungary. It is very cosmopolitan, with, for example, 28% of its population coming from ethnic minorities, as opposed to only 2% in Scotland. Its infrastructure is much more intense than most of the rest of Britain. Parents and patients living in more isolated locales, for instance, read aghast at London-inspired political policies, like having a wide choice of specialist schools or hospitals. Many people are lucky to have one such reachable agency in the neighbourhood – and luckier still if it's an efficient one.

London Lions

So it would not be unexpected to find a slight variant on the national norms in terms of humour. According to Ken Dodd's doctrine, there are two metropolitan proclivities. One is the creation of what Ken Dodd calls 'totems'. This is predictable enough. One may observe the same lionising of notable cultural figures in other central cities, from Paris and Berlin to Tokyo and New York. The opinion-formers and decision-makers, the movers and shakers, form their constellations in these places. It is the ambition of the great stars – political, sporting, literary, journalistic, musical, artistic, as well as theatrical – to strut their stuff in London. It is, in the metaphor of the G &S *Patience* ballad, 'the Magnet and the Churn', a spontaneous coming together of the crowd-puller and the intellectual admirer. How often in this text already as the zenith or the critical point of a career been measured by arrival in the metropolis, especially with a date at the London Palladium, and the heady tributes of the London press? Thus it is hardly surprising that icons are sculpted in London, and, with the heavy presence of radio and then television studios in the region, this did not end with the death of variety.

Dan Leno, Marie Lloyd, George Robey, the Crazy Gang, Sid Field, Max Wall...we have already witnessed in abundance this phenomenon. From Charles Dickens' praise of Joe Grimaldi to John Osborne's laudation of Ken Dodd himself, the glitterati have raised the cultural levels of the critique of comedians from popular to high, from, so to speak, tabloid to broadsheet. It is closely related to the serious criticism disposed on outstanding pop singers or groups, spectacularly talented sportspersons and the like. It is part of a metropolitan scene in which a night-life of often smarter definition than in the provinces enjoyed and lionised the dance bands and cabaret acts. One remembers how, from the bright, clever lyrics of Noel Coward to the sharply funny sketches of Peter Cook, there have been stars, trading on immense comic talent, who have merited the accolade of this type of social singling out. A visit to the Café Royal or the Establishment Club became as important a date on the upper crust social calendar as Royal Ascot or Henley. 'Society' also made gods and goddesses of a discrete few comedians.

A pleasing example of this dispensation would be Lupino Lane. He was born in London in 1892, a child of the celebrated Lupino clan and the great-nephew of Sara Lane, the famous actress and theatre lessee. From her he took his stage name, having been christened Henry William George Lupino. He took to the stage at the age of four and, by assiduous practice, he mastered the falls and tumbles of low comedy and brought a demonic zest to their presentation. He featured in British music hall and American silent film, and he was originally known as Nipper or Nip Lane. The acme of his career and the key to his considerable wealth was his part of Bill Snibson, a role he first played in *Twenty to One* in 1935. He struck gold when the character was revived in the musical play *Me and My Girl*, with a Noel Gay score. Opening in 1937, Lupino Lane played the part over 1500 times consecutively. The show was also the subject of a film and the first TV musical.

The tale of the working class cockney who inherits a country estate and invites his mates to join him in enlivening a pallid aristocracy,

is, of course, the backdrop to the show-stopping popularity of *The Lambeth Walk*. It is difficult to exaggerate the intensity of the craze it produced and, jaunty, quick-footed, Lupino Lane would forever be associated with this achievement. He never repeated that degree of success. He married Violet Blyth and their son, Lauri Lupino Lane, has already been mentioned in these dispatches. Lupino Lane died in London in 1959.

Cockney Capers

There was, to be sure, a strong cockney tradition in the music hall that was maintained in variety. Both the performers, such as Gus Elen, Albert Chevalier and Harry Champion, and the subject matter of the music hall had had close links with London life. One forms the impression, part genuine, part mythic, that the music hall was predominantly a metropolitan phenomenon, whereas the joys of variety were more widely spread across the provinces. There was perhaps what might be called a 'Sam Weller' effect, with the idea spreading, from the model of Mr Pickwick's street-wise and mentally alert servant, of the optimistic, indomitable cockney.

That said, there were cockney-oriented comics who sustained the capital's repute for comicality during the variety era. Some, such as Charlie Chester, we have already encountered on this journey through the environs of comedy. Leon Cortez (Richard Alfred Chalkin; 1899-1970) who could not have been clearer in his intention than in his first foray into variety, as Leon Cortez and His Coster Pals. However, he is now chiefly recalled, on radio as well as on stage, for his throaty cockney interpretations of Shakespearean plots ('now this geezer, 'Amlet...'; 'Mrs Macbeth, just like the cat, crept up to 'is cot, copped 'is clock, coughed and crept aht agin...'). They were amusingly done and with some gusto, while, yet again, we must pay some obeisance to audiences that knew enough about *Henry V* or *Romeo and Juliet* to cope with his lampoonery, just as they could make sense of a Billy Bennett parody. Tommy Godfrey (1920-1984, from London's Waterloo district) was another fruity comic, while Bunny Baron (another Londoner, 1910-1978) brought a cockney flavour to his work in pantos and summer shows.

Arthur Haynes (1914-1966), double chinned and moustached, graduated from Charlie Chester's *Stand Easy* crew to become a stage and television hit as the dogmatic hobo, who knew and insisted on telling all the answers in his crotchety cockney tones to the out-talked Nicholas Parsons. His television career began in 1956 and his character, Oscar Penny-feather, was much appreciated. He also did a skit on stage of a plentifully wounded soldier doing the Josef Locke *Good-bye* number from *The White Horse Inn*.

Arthur English (1919-1996) also took up the cockney cudgels after the Second World War as 'The Prince of the Wide Boys'. Like many others, he began at the Windmill; like many others, he ended his post-variety career as a useful comic TV actor, featuring in *Are You being Served?* and *In Sickness and in Health*, with Warren Mitchell as Alf Garnett regaling the nation with another take on East End personality. 'Open the Cage' and 'Start the Music' were Arthur English's catch-phrases, as, with a tie almost as wide as his padded shoulders, he noisily updated the notion of cockney sharp-witted opportunism with his 'spiv' character. He promoted the Spivs' Union; if offered a job, it would fight your case. 'Don't keep scratching; I've just swept up', was another one of his less than delicate requests.

With the exception of the special case of Max Miller, probably the strongest showing by a London-oriented comedian was by Tommy Trinder, a dominant figure through the 1930s, the 1940s and into the 1950s. Thomas Edward Trinder was born in Streatham in 1909, the son of Thomas, a tram driver, and Jean Trinder. He sprang from being an errand boy at London's Smithfield meat market to, still only twelve, touring South Africa with a concert party and then touring Britain with Will Murray's *Casey's Court*, appearing under the backwards spelling of Red Nirt, akin to the Nedlo of Ted 'Olden' Ray. As the 1930s dawned, he became a single act and worked his assured way forward and upward, until the pantheon of the Palladium was reached in 1939. Not content with arrival, he concentrated on staying, which he did for eleven lively years, figuring and then topping the bill in varied revues, including the long-running *Happy and Glorious*. In 1955 Tommy Trinder, appropriately enough, became the first compère of TV's *Sunday Night at the London Palladium*, a task he undertook until he fell out with the management. As well as this quarter century pre-eminence on stage, radio and television, he was rather more accomplished than some of his contemporaries when transferred to the screen. Older filmgoers will recollect him in films such as *The Foreman went to France* (1941), *The Bells Go Down* (1943) and *Champagne Charlie* (1944).

Tommy Trinder was the abrasive epitome of city street brashness. An adept advertiser, with his ebullient slogan of 'If its laughter you're after, Trinder's the name' committed to posters on the hoardings', his *Tiger Rag* signature tune, and his buoyant cry of 'you lucky people', he wisecracked his way through a career of high attainment. Flippant and disrespectful, he thrust his ski-slope of a chin into the startled face of authority, adjusted the impertinent angle of his ever-present trilby, and grinned disdainfully at everything and everybody, including royalty. During World War II, he mocked the American troops in England as 'over-paid, over-sexed and over here' and, asked (he reported) by a pedestrian on Whitehall, 'which side is the War Office on', he replied 'ours, I hope.' Another of his tales concerned a talk he gave on sex, but which, to avoid embarrassment, he told his wife had been on yachting. When questioned about this, she responded, 'but he's only done it twice; the first time he was sick; the second time his hat flew off.'

Blessed, like Ted Ray, whose style was similarly streamlined if less ferocious, with an elephantine memory, and a sure ear for topicality, Tommy Trinder was something of a marathon runner among performers. Max Miller was noted, to his customers' delight, for hogging the stage, and there are thousands who have groped their way out of theatres after one of Ken Dodd's 'Celebrations of Laughter.' During the London blitz, when audiences were requested to sit tight once the bombs were dropping, Tommy Trinder, based then at the Palladium, toured a burning and hard-hit London, staggering under the violence of the Luftwaffe, and did his act at, unbelievably, seventeen theatres.

While researching the life of Stanley Holloway, the author was lucky enough to interview his widow, 'Laney' Holloway. She told the epic tale of the worst night of the Manchester blitz, just before the Christmas of 1940, when all the guests at the city's Midland Hotel, including a sprinkling of famous artists, were ushered into the ground floor lounge area for safety. Tommy Trinder, with help from her husband, Anne Ziegler and Webster Booth and other stars, entertained those present for thirteen hours, until the 'all clear' sounded at 7.30 the following morning. In parenthesis, it might be recorded how, on that morning, the artists crunched their way over broken glass, past sentries posted at bombed out stores, to their respective theatres for an 11.30 matinee, followed by an afternoon 'evening' show, introduced to counter the difficulties of the bombing. She told how, for the Manchester Palace pantomime, the theatre was two-thirds full for the morning and three-quarters full for the afternoon performance. The mournful loser was Sir Malcolm Sargent: he ventured forth to find the nearby Free Trade Hall destroyed and his Christmas concert with the Hallé orchestra no longer possible.

The writer also spoke years ago to an actor-dancer who had appeared in pantomime with Tommy Trinder. Admiring of his manifest talent and believing him to be the holder of untapped gifts, he had asked Tommy Trinder why he had never sought to extend his comedic horizons. The comedian explained that he had found an approach that suited, that he had played the percentages and had seen no point in risking his career in unnecessary experimentation. Apart from an occasional lapse into drag, usually in a burlesque Carmen Miranda routine, with headgear of fruitful Covent Garden vintage, he stayed steadfast within fairly narrow limits. It is an intriguing detail, the opposite, for example, of Ken Dodd's desire to push out the borders of comedy. Tommy Trinder died in Surrey in 1989. Other fast-talking London-based comics have since presented themselves, such as Mike Reid, who later turned to *Eastenders* with some success, and Jim Davidson, who made something of a splash on television in the 1990s and demonstrated his bluish tendencies in the naughty panto, *Sinderella*. None of them has quite replaced the ever-confident vigour of Tommy Trinder.

Pathos and the City

Tommy Trinder was the absolute converse of Ken Dodd's second 'London' tenet. Tommy Trinder may have been fêted by London audiences, but he never for a moment conceded that there was room in the comedian's make-up for pathos. Ken Dodd reckons that the metropolitan community has a soft spot for sentiment, so that, when appearing in the London region, where he had satisfied the first objective of becoming a 'totem', he relaxed the tempo a little and introduced one or two more of his slushier melodies than he might have risked in Leeds or Newcastle.

Quite why comedic bathos should have a metropolitan appeal is unsure. Possibly, there is an affinity between the creation of idols and romantic sympathy for the same idols in distress. Without being drawn into portentous statements, it is a fact that many of the religious and national figures that are the subject of hero-worship suffer martyrdom and, in consequence, win gushing compassion from their adherents. The blood sacrifice is a common feature of several great faiths, including, self-evidently, Christianity, whilst, from Joan of Arc and Horatio Nelson to Abraham Lincoln and Princess Diana, there is weeping over their deaths as there is exultation at their victories. Maybe that sentiment is somewhat more deep-seated in the political foci of such heroes and maybe the same is true, in minor key, of cultural icons.

Whatever the grounds, it is arguable that London houses have offered theatrical succour to comedians who showed some vulnerability, rather more, possibly, than provincial audiences. On a larger plane, it may touch on the role of the clown, the Jack Point of *The Yeomen of the Guard* and his basic submission that the line between laughter and tears is a slender one. It may

be one of the reasons that the lovelorn role of Buttons in *Cinderella* is viewed by many more thoughtful comedians as the meatiest of pantomime's leading comic parts.

Music hall artists, like Dan Leno, Little Tich and George Formby Senior, earned commiseration as well as laughter. It is, patently, a Chaplinesque concept, interesting in that, although London born, Londoners only really comprehensively knew Charlie Chaplin in his filmic role of the Little Tramp. Lupino Lane played the 'little man', toughing out and making good, like all those folk-tales about tailors and tinkers outwitting giants. There is an analogue here with the 'little man' of H G Wells, writing breezily in his proto-Dickensian vein, about the tribulations of lower middle class existence. Both Arthur Kipps (*Kipps*; 1905) and Alfred Polly (*The History of Mr Polly*; 1910) took on a hostile world and won through to some form of contentment. Sid Field exuded a thin-skinned susceptibility that caused audiences to sympathise with him, while Horace Kenny, who died in 1955, also came across as defenceless in a cruel world, as he tried gamely to persuade managers that his 'trial turn', *The Laughing Policeman*, ('do you want a sword-swallower?') was worth a booking.

In the post-war arena, two or three comedians exerted this kind of appeal. Norman Wisdom, born in London in 1919, did the common round of the army concert party and the variety stage, beginning in 1946 at the Collins' music hall. He consolidated his early grounding with the invention of his simple minded, fragile character, apparently beginning when he supplied a 'volunteer' to tender dubious assistance to the magician, David Nixon. For decades now, he has ploughed the self-same furrow, with the worried frown, the sailor-like rolling gait, the over-sized cap and the under-sized jacket. Tormented, intellectually challenged and frail, he has enjoyed unusual success in the cinema, with, peculiarly, special reference to communist Albania, where his characterisation was regarded, not surprisingly, as ideologically neutral. He made the song *Don't Laugh at Me 'cause I'm a Fool* his very own and has ably pursued obtuseness as a career qualification well into older age.

It was another song – *Confidentially* – that boosted the calling of Reg Dixon (1915-1984). Born in Coventry, he was a biggish man who wore his trilby as defensively as Tommy Trinder carried his belligerently, and his gentle, rather dim-witted manner was quite well suited to radio. Like the elder Formby, he made a point of his ill-health – 'I'm proper poorly' – and, like the elder Formby, his professional life was shortened by illness. Ironically, it was the poor health of the younger Formby that gave Reg Dixon the chance to woo the London crowds, which he successfully did when he replaced the stricken George Formby at the Palace Theatre, Shaftesbury Avenue, in *Zip Goes a Million* in 1952. Reg Dixon made a Formby-type plea to audiences and went down well as Percy Piggott, required, in a musical version of *Brewster's Millions*, to squander a million dollars in quick time. Was it merely the linguistic difficulty and the off-stage tantrums that drove Frank Randle, emanating boisterous antagonism, from a London theatre-land that lauded the kind-hearted feats of Reg Dixon?

A third contender in the same stakes is Charlie Drake, minute and squeaky-voiced, shrilling 'Hello, My Darlings' and, like those others, hoping for sympathy amid the smiles. It is worthy of remark that Charlie Drake (real name, Charles Springall, born London, 1925) founded his career in children's television, before making a hit in revue and on film.

Several of these comedians of milder mode have made manifest a child-like quality, itself something of a cry for compassion. As he has tumbled and squawked on stage and screens, small and large, Charlie Drake, like George Formby and Norman Wisdom, has presented that trait, one that Michael Crawford was to milk in TV's *Some Mothers do 'ave 'em*.

The Incomparable Max

Max Miller was certainly an idol of the London music hall and variety fraternity and, if in a mocking way, he pleaded with his adoring fans for understanding – 'what if I am, lidy, what if I am?'; 'nahhhhhhhhh, listen' there was precious little bathos. Whatever the reasons, he remains the outstandingly great stand-up comic of his generation, challenged only by Ken Dodd as the premier exponent of that type of comedy in the 20th century. Moreover, his London credentials are impeccable, for it was in the capital and the Greater London environs that he carved out his glittering vocation for what Ernest Bramah called 'mirth-provoking' action. If there were northern comedians who shunned the south or were uninvited there, he was certainly one – Sid Field was another who was reluctant to travel far northwards. Asked about playing Glasgow, Max Miller pointed out that he was a comedian, not a missionary.

Although his accent had the nasal intonation of the Londoner, he was born in Brighton. The year was 1895. His parents, James and Alice Sargent, named him Thomas Henry Sargent, and, with his father a jobbing builder's labourer, he knew poverty in his childhood and, for all his acute intelligence, he never enjoyed a proper education. Like George Formby, he remained semi-literate all his life. He tried odd jobs and some amateur entertaining, before enlisting with the Royal

Field Artillery in the 1914-1918 conflict. He found himself in army shows and he was temporarily blinded by shellfire in Mesopotamia, but, after the war – and with a hint of the regular army about his brassy diction – he opted for the professional stage, starting out with Clifford Sheppard's concert party, and then joining the Rogues CP on tour and later the Merrie Arcadians.

He married Kitty March, a fellow artiste, in 1921 and she it was who persuaded him to change his name to the more biddable Max Miller. Kitty Marsh, while never a domestic Gauleiter after the fashion of Beryl Formby, managed his career effectively and, shielding him from his lack of schooling, answered his fan mail and signed the requests for autographs. From the 1930s Max Miller formed a more loving relationship with Ann Graham and she, not without a degree of self-parody, was entitled his 'organisational secretary'.

It was about 1928 that he adopted the garish, multicoloured garb, along with the white shoes and hat, by which he would be long recognised. If Al Jolson was to be Ken Dodd's favourite model, Max Miller regarded G H Elliott as his idol. He was no more a comedian than Jolson, but the explanation makes sense. He always admired the well-groomed, white rig of the singer-dancer and the chic style of his movement. Max Miller was much taller than the moderately sized G H Elliott. Max Miller was a good 6ft in height, with a well-built frame, but he moved as easily and as deftly as the older artiste, sang his lusty ditties clearly and tunefully, as well as strumming the guitar. 'Just give me a touch up with the wire brushes', he would ask the pit drummer, as he moved into his soft shoe routine, ending with the splits. Half way down he would pause; 'that's yer lot; 'alf tonight; 'alf tomorrow night.'

By 1929 he had made it to the London Palladium and in 1931 he was included in the royal command variety performance. Until the death of variety, he was its brightest shining luminary. For 25 years he bewitched audiences with his audacious, boastful ways, like a commercial traveller, full of reprehensible yarns, with a fascinated theatre audience, rather than a sniggering bunch in a bar parlour. His 1940 revue, *Apple Sauce*, had an apt title, while he also made a few films, the best of them being *Educated Evans*, distributed in 1931. He was not too keen on the restrictions of cameras and, like Ken Dodd, was at his most efficacious on stage. As for radio, the BBC banned him in 1944 for five years. His description of a sixteen year old girl who swallowed a pin but didn't feel the prick until she was twenty-one was not acceptable to the broadcasting authorities.

Max Miller was blue eyed and pleasant looking. He leaned over the footlights, casting conspiratorial glances to left and right as if afraid of officious eavesdroppers, as he drew the theatre-goers into his confidential web of intrigue and innuendo. Commentators have mentioned the feeling of 'danger' as he came on stage. There was certainly an air of expectancy, for Max Miller was proficient in the art of threatening his listeners with impending vulgarity. Some of his pygmy imitators resorted to crass blueness and floundering velocity of delivery. Max Miller was cleverer than that. His pace was impeccable. There were silences that spoke volumes; there were nods and winks of expressive clarity; there were repetitions of key phrases to guarantee understanding; there were the naughty punch-lines that were left knowingly unsaid; there were constant appeals to the better nature of the waiting hosts – all in all, it amounted to the most effective attack ever of any British front cloth comic.

The sexual ambiguity, underpinned by the gaudy garb, was patent. It was curious but effective. Here was a braggart of sexual athleticism. Taking a girl into the woods, he asked her if she believed in the 'hereafter'; she asked for a definition; 'if you're not here-after what I'm hereafter, you'll be hereafter I've gone'. And yet women were on his side. Listen carefully to recordings of his live performances in variety theatres; having made women his primary target, there is a genuine sense of women laughing first, with the men following suit. Both genders were sinners in the 'blue' and 'white' books of Max Miller. His wife, he explained, had had six babies, and he threatened to kill himself should she again become pregnant. She inevitably did, and he rushed to his bedroom and made a noose of his ties; then, just as he was about to commit suicide, he paused: 'wait a minute; I might be hanging the wrong man'. Finding his wife in bed with the coalman, he was so mad, he went outside and kicked his horse. This was the wife whom he always took everywhere with him, as he preferred that to kissing her good-bye.

Wartime bombing was but another mask for nefarious habits. The bombs frightened him so much 'he would run in anyone's house', while, during an air raid, he bumped into a man running down the street in his night-shirt: 'where are you going?' – 'ome...'ere'. Finishing his song and dance and professing tiredness, he would sigh, 'blimey, I'm ready for bed now'...the perfectly adjusted pause, then... 'anybody?'

'There'll never be another' was his by no means unjustified cry, and it is often said that as he finished, and as he prophesied, 'the game was up', and variety tottered on its last legs. He did not parade the same bonhomie off-stage and is said not to have been over-popular with other theatricals. Despite the aid he gave various charities, he had some reputation for meanness, and, much as he enjoyed golf, breeding parrots and horse riding, he was a solitary figure. He made the point that his was a profession like any other. He would put on his raincoat and go for a stroll along Brighton promenade and not be recognised. Why should he be? The bus conductor does not wear his uniform when off duty.

Nonetheless, one cannot help noting that he was born in Brighton and he died there in 1963; Brighton, for his mid-century genera-tion, the prototypical location for the dirty weekend, the correspondent shoes and what George Formby might have called 'hanky panky'. Max Miller was the startling voice of that rather prurient, rather seedy itchiness and covetousness. The catchy notes of *Mary from the Dairy* heralded his entry on to the stage and, for any length of time, he would captivate his devotees with a cheerful, robust, if questionably moral, recapitulation of his many adventures, as if he were a pirate on the high seas of sexual activity.

Of all London's beloved comedians, none satisfied more fulsomely and lasciviously than Max Miller.

The People's Jesters

15. COMEDY ALPHABET: SINGLE COMEDIANS

It is time for the application of a fail-safe mechanism. Proceeding by style and construct of comedy has the slight disadvantage of omitting some comedians. Either they do not fall neatly into one of the categories or it is judged that sufficient examples of a specific class have been included. There have been hundreds of comedians, many of them honest-to-goodness professionals, making people laugh for a sometimes precarious living, from pier end to panto scene and all points in every direction. Before venturing further into the post-variety, critically, the television age, say, from about the mid-1950s, it is intended to conduct a sweep of the comic territory and provide an alphabetical register of some, by no means all, of the missing funny persons. Many of them were, and there is no fault in this, straightforward funny men, keen to tell a few tales and entertain the folk, without maybe ever striking it especially rich or attracting the adulation of the serious critics. They range from the well remembered to the partially forgotten – and not the least fascinating aspect of this roster is that those labels will vary according to the reader. The hope is that memories will be jogged and former laughter will be recalled with pleasure and that, beyond that, this study will make good its implicit boast to offer a fairly comprehensive log of British stage and allied comedy from 1918 to the end of the 20th century.

Bolton, Reg – 1884-1955, he was born in Eccles and first appeared at the nearby Rusholme Pavilion in Harry Leslie's concert party; from about 1909 he gravitated for umpteen years between Ernest Binn's summer shows and prestigious Francis Laidler pantomimes; a lanky, humorous character, he was known as 'The Laugh Salesman'.

Bolton, George – known as 'The New Gagster', George Bolton was born in Portsmouth in 1895 and he enjoyed, from boyhood, a long career along many show-business avenues, relying on a speedy delivery after the manner of Ted Ray: 'what about the Scottish chemist who sat up all night to keep an eye on the vanishing cream'. He was married to the singer, Freda Gardner, and he died in 1981.

Cantor, Terry – nicknamed 'Toby Jug', although his real name was K E Macnaghton (from Sheffield, 1912-1979), he was an expansive, smiling comic of wide experience, and with a son, Kerry Cantor, who carried on the family tradition of stage comedy.

Church, Joe – a Londoner, born in 1919, he was one of the most affable of wags, befriending audiences from his start in armed forces' concerts through to a wide range of work, including being a supporting act at the Palladium.

Connor, Kenneth – quite a celebrated name, he provided radio's *Ray's a Laugh* with Sidney Mincing, confronting Ted Ray with officious dignity, and also the diffident individual who really irritated Ted Ray – that was the stock character, with the trembling voice, that he later portrayed in many a 'Carry On' film.

Dale, Jim – originally James Smith, born in Kettering in 1935, here was a Carroll Levis 'discovery', who earned his billing as 'Britain's Youngest Comedian', until he successfully switched tracks and became a well-known pop singer and film actor.

Dallas, Johnny – Peter Ross, of Leicester, born 1929, he started with Brian Michie and went on to do lots of work on television as well as at the seaside, notably at Rhyl, and in pantomime. Unbelievably, he began his career by being put under contract by Don Ross for 25 years, a wondrous piece of optimism for an impresario.

Danvers, Billy – a plump and joyous Liverpuddlian, born 1889, who rejoiced in the name of William Mikado Danvers, he emerged from the old-time music hall, a Fred Karno apprenticeship and George Hall's *Merry Japes* at Morecambe to be an affectionately regarded variety and seaside comic until his death in Manchester in 1964. His material, delivered from behind a cheeky grin and a check waistcoat, was much to do with drink and women; he described his eyes as 'brown behind the settee'.

Darnley, Albert – Albert Dennis Darnley McCarthy, born in London in 1898, was a comedian from his teenage to his very senior years; he came from music hall stock and enjoyed a lengthy career in pantomime and variety.

Dowler, Cyril – another Liverpool-born comic, 1906-1986, who worked with Kay White, Sandy Powell's wife, and then his own wife, Rhoda Rogers, in concert party, panto and touring revue.

Doyle, Bunny – Bernard Doyle, born in Hull in 1898, died 1955, he was billed as 'The Minister for Idiotic Affairs'; he started off in seaside shows as a youngster; was decorated for bravery with the West Yorkshire Regiment in World War I; and did lots of pantomime and radio work as well as variety dates thereafter. He offered homilies on life in Giggleswick, where, he claimed, they 'played tiddlywinks with manhole covers'.

Fields, Tommy – 1908-1988; another of the Rochdale Stansfields, pushed on, like his sister, Gracie, by a stage-struck mother; he turned out to be a personable comic, who did well in musical comedy and revue as well as in the usual round of variety, panto and summer shows.

Francois, Jack – Edinburgh born, Jack Francois (1911-1997) came from a theatre family and, a good looking light comedian, he proceeded to find a niche in touring revue, panto and summer show that provided him with a steady living.

Gay, Jimmy – this Liverpool comic was born in 1906, and, like Jimmy James, he smoked incessantly, as, in a good suit and a trilby, he ruminated on life's passing parade, maintaining a stillness, where many comedians jibbered and jigged

Glen, Archie – and another cross-reference to the great Jimmy James, for Archie 'Blotto as Usual' Glen (born Manchester; 1889-1966), made his name as a drunk in evening dress and enjoyed some success in that role between the two world wars.

Goodwright, Peter – light-hearted and well-liked, he has enjoyed a lot of success as comical impersonator and affable entertainer. So accurate was his impersonation of Max Wall that Max Wall claimed this was the only way his name was kept alive as he struggled through the 1970s. Max Wall also added Freddie Starr, and his Wallite impression, to his list of benefactors.

Hearne, Richard – a famous name among children's entertainers, his 'Mr Pastry' was made immensely popular by television. The gaping jaws, the thick spectacles and the white moustache masked an agility developed during his childhood circus years, while he also featured a one-man old time dance item, often seen on the BBC *The Good Old Days* TV programme. He was born in Norwich and lived from 1909 to 1979.

Kaye, Davy – another comic who, although he turned his hand to most things, including musical comedy, is most particularly recalled for one cameo; this was his one-man band routine to the tune of *Macnamara's Band*, a riot of drums, cymbals, wind instruments and acrobatics. Of minute build, this Londoner could never be doubted on grounds of gusto.

Learmouth, Jimmy – he was born in Gateshead in 1891 – and died, aged only 30, in 1921. Moustached and garbed in an ancient fur coat, he is reported as having been very funny, but heavy drinking foreshortened his potentially sound career. J B Priestley, no mean judge, reckoned he was 'the funniest comic in Britain' around the time of the first world war.

Lester, Alfred – something of a precursor of Robb Wilton with his sketch *The Village Fire Brigade*: the firemen were inefficient, it was confessed, but they made quite a show in the annual procession between the dustcart and the Ancient Order of Foresters.

Lester, Claude – (born Stafford, 1893-1955; real name, Claude Forrester); a lanky, skinny comic of a potential ruined by booze and one who, in his curtailed hay day, had played very good dates.

Lester, Roy – this bespectacled Blackpool front-cloth performer was best known for his catchphrase 'Hiya Pals!' He was married to Paula Lee, daughter of The Great Cingalee, and was, in fact, an accomplished magician in his own right. He encompassed being both a burly panto Dame and ringmaster for the touring Roberts Brothers.

Lockwood, Johnny – a Londoner, born in 1920, John Sidney Lockwood had an early radio start as a Brian Michie discovery, and, buoyant in manner and topical in material, he worked for ENSA during World War II and in variety thereafter.

Long, Norman – this toothy, plump pianist (1893-1952; born in Deal, Kent) deserves a mention for his bill matter: 'a smile, a song and a piano' was genuine enough, and, especially on radio, such melodies as *I'll Never Love a Barmaid Anymore* and *Never have a Bath with your Wrist-watch on* were really jolly.

Lotinga, Ernie – born on Wearside in 1876, died 1951, his first wife was Hetty King; he created the character 'Jimmy Josser', which he featured, inter alia, in his own revues, for he became noted as something of an impresario. 'Jimmy Josser' did the rounds from about 1911 to 1925.

Lyons, Jimmy – rather after the fashion of Jimmy Edwards in political vogue, he did a rousing 'member of parliament' routine with some forceful intent.

Martin, George – George Frederick Martin (1921-1991; born in Aldershot) did, after being one of the Martin Brothers musical trio, a lengthy stint at the Windmill Theatre, before enjoying loads of radio and variety engagements. Known as 'The Casual Comedian', he concentrated on very topical reference for his jokes, delivering them with quiet aplomb. His younger brother, Bill, born in 1927, was one of the Martin trio (the third was a brother-in-law, Bob McGowan) and he, too, became a stand up comic, trading as Bill Vinden.

Matchett, Billy – 1890-1973, born in Liverpool; he was another hard-working comic with a flavour of the old music hall about his honest-to-goodness nature; he did the usual full gamut of concert parties, variety and pantos, but was also often heard on the 'wireless', especially in the 1940s.

Maynard, Bill – although he was later to make a name for himself as a TV comic actor, Walter Frederick George Williams, a native of Surrey, born in 1928, was quite a star as a shining comedian in holiday shows and revue. Many will recollect his telly series with Terry Scott, *Great Scott – It's Maynard*, in the 1950s.

Mennard, Tom – this Nottingham born comic (1918-1989) was a reflective observer of human activity, who made his mark on radio as well as in revue and variety; he was one of several variety artistes to find a part in *Coronation Street*.

Monty, Hal – originally Albert Sutan, he was noted for his balloon routine and, heading up his own touring shows, he was something of a name during the 1940s at local variety theatres.

Murgatroyd, Joe – this Rotherham born actor, accompanied by his assistant, called 'Poppet', turned to the variety stage and to pantomime, although he never forewent the legitimate theatre altogether.

Nelson, Bob – he was born, Rupert Lambert, in Burnley in 1893, and his was a slapstick act, mixed with philosophic reflections, plus the ineluctable but Delphic utterance, 'aren't plums cheap' – another of those nonsensical catchphrases that people cottoned on to and couldn't stop repeating.

Oates, Chubby – the rotund Bermondsey born Arthur 'Chubby' Oates did clubs and army bases and became well known as a bonny panto dame. He worked for years in Paul Raymond revues, such as *Pyjama Tops* and took some straight roles as well. Irrepressibly jovial, he has recovered from the serious stroke that beset him in 1997 while appearing at the Butlin's Variety Theatre, Margate, and he is busying himself as funnily as ever.

Parsons, Charlie – visitors to Blackpool would invariably bump into this cheery little comic, who was born in 1906 in Kirkham, not far away from the Golden Mile; he always seemed to be in a summer show on the Fylde coast.

Platt, Ken – 1922-1998, another of the gormless brand of Lancastrian drolls, of whom a lot was heard on radio, for instance *Variety Fanfare*, and in a couple of television shows, *Wild Wild Women* and *Our Kid*. His opening line, 'ah woant tek me coat off – ah'm not stopping', was yet another saying that melted into the public consciousness.

Pleon, Alec – born in London of theatrical kin in 1911, he was the southern equivalent of a 'gurner' à la Les Dawson, adding some Alpine yodelling to his 'Mr Funny Face' contortions in revue and variety.

Plummer, Sid – born in London, 1901-1967, he was one of musical comedians, making extensive use of the xylophone as a complex comic prop, in an act of circus-like dimension.

The People's Jesters

Randall, Alan – (1934-2005), the Warwickshire musician who has made a profession of being the most prolific and impressive George Formby mimic there has been – in a world where there is a George Formby society, not just of fans, but of imitators of all ages.

Reindeer, Eddie – born, named Reinhardt, in South Wales, he was full of life and jokes, doing the rounds of the variety theatres and clubs, coming on strong without any finesse, but always getting the laughs.

Sales, Freddie – (Frederick Harry Walker; 1920-1995; born in Hull); a good all-round entertainer from a theatre background, who worked all over the world; most variety goers will recall him for his well observed take off of a baby.

Starr, Freddie – Frederick Fowell was a wartime Liverpool baby, who recovered from a troubled childhood to base his crazed, madcap career, plus some ballad singing, on the back of his native city's Beatle-inspired swinging image. His big break was inclusion in the 1970 *Royal Variety Performance*.

Saunders, Don – more of a musical clown than a comedian per se, but he trod the variety boards with some panache, blowing and hooting and doing lots of strong visual japes.

Seltzer, Harry – this tiny Hull born comedian was another who began with Will Murray's Casey's Court and then had a long, chequered career in and out of show business, performing in all manner of fashions.

Shiels, Harry – he was born in Birmingham in 1906, the son of a music hall comic, and he worked as dame, as a musician, as part of a double act and as part of a group, as well as being a solo comedian.

Stein, Joe – born Joseph Shipper in Manchester in 1904, he enjoyed a long career in comedy; he will be most remembered as being a leading member of the *Soldiers in Skirts* drag revue of the post-war years.

Trafford, Tommy – a typically clothcapped Northern comic, as betokened by his 'Laughs from Lancs' catchphrase, he began his career with Mildred Crossley's *Happiness Ahead* at Cleveleys and was a noted Dame in the Norman Evans tradition. He appeared with Jimmy Clitheroe on radio and, with his partner Ronnie Parnell, he presented summer shows and pantos for many years at New Brighton, Southport and Blackpool. He died in 1993 aged 65.

Turner, Tubby – Clarence Turner (1882-1952), from Great Harwood, Lancashire, with the trousers and blazer all at full stretch over the portly frame, and the little bowler and striped socks fore and aft, stuttered and stammered his way through a sound career, falling fatally ill in harness at the Halifax Palace. He was normally assisted by his wife, Florence Revill, in such routines as the collapsing deckchair: 'there's no bottom in that deckchair' – 'w-w-what do you c-c-call this?'. His famous catchphrase, still occasionally overheard in the north of England was 'if it's ho-ho-ho kay with you, it's ho-ho-kay with me.'

Varney, Reg – another southern based comic, with lots of experience in seaside shows, who went on to be a well-known TV comedy actor in knock-about programmes like *The Rag Trade* and *On the Buses*.

Walden, Harry – a pallid face, surmounted by a kiss-curl, was the countenance presented by Harry Walden (1887-1955), 'the anaemic footballer', of music hall and concert party note; he really was a footballer and he played for Great Britain in the 1912 Olympics in Stockholm.

Williams, George – this Liverpool born comic, with the droll patter and the exquisite timing, adopted the white face of the Auguste clown. He began his career proper in 1944 at the Shepherd's Bush Empire and graduated to *Variety Bandbox*, where his catchphrases 'I'm not well' and 'I'm proper poorly' led to some conflict with Reg Dixon, both comedians claiming they were the originator of the lines. He was imprisoned for a minor homosexual offence in the 1950s and this was a major setback, but, championed by such notables as the great mime, Marcel Morceau, and by Sir Anton Dolin, he found his way back on the pub and club circuit in the 1970s.

Willis, Denny – Dennis Williams, 1920-1995; of Scottish descent and the son of comedian Dave Willis, he may immediately be identified to all TV viewers of a certain age from his several appearances on *The Good Old Days*, where he was the odd one out in the 'Quorn Quartet' where three huntsmen were united in song and dance – and Denny Willis wasn't.

Wise, Vic – David Victor Bloom, of Southampton, 1900-1976; he graduated from a couple of double acts to be a smart, engaging comic with somewhat of a transatlantic twang, and he did quite well on radio and television in his later career.

London 1952; with a programme, full of incidental detail, starring the immortal Jimmy James - and the always diverting Nat Mills and Bobbie are coming soon in Mother Goose

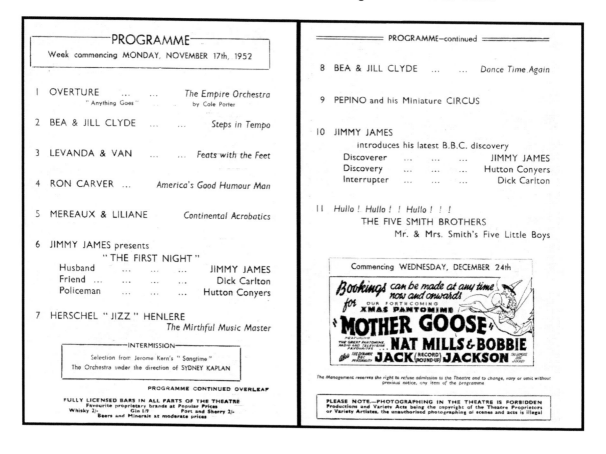

The People's Jesters

16. TELEVISION: BOX OF DELIGHTS

The last chapter's grouping of 50 and more comedians range from the fringes of the pre-1914 music hall to the popularity of television comedy in the last half of the 20th century. Comedians make for a hardy breed. Nonetheless, the closure of the variety theatres and the growth of television viewing was a contextual change of inordinate importance in the story of British popular comedy.

The Social Canvas

It was, of course, part of a greater sea change, one that has been called 'the miniaturisation of society'. This amounted to technological changes, amid rising standards of material life, which placed an emphasis on a less collective and a more private life-style. Its motivators were the motorcar and the TV set. People retreated from the conglomerate habits of bus, tram and train travel, often geared to visits to the theatre and the cinema, to the personal usage of cars and the enjoyment of leisure within the home. The public wash-house or commercial laundry and the ice stores were fast becoming the individual washing machine and the refrigerator and freezer, while the concert hall and bandstand were rapidly being reproduced in miniscule form in the living room, as music centres graduated from LPs to CDs. The television,

later supported by video and DVD, was the centrepiece of this domestic technical revolution, but, quite quickly, the personal computer, the mobile phone and other electronic accessories completed this amazing refurbishment of personal life-styles.

In its turn, personalised transport liberated families from a reliance on cinemas and theatres within easy walking or public transport distance, and people began to stretch their leisure wings. Aeroplane travel carried thousands away from the British holiday resorts to the sunny shores of Spain and elsewhere, with immediate affects on summer shows. All in all, the 1950s and 1960s shook up the world of entertainment and tossed it into a different context.

A few random figures might illustrate this major point. By the end of the 20th century there were no more than 500 professional theatres, of all kinds, left in the United Kingdom, whereas at the end of the 19th century there had been close on that number, counting all the singing rooms and so forth, just in the London region. Moreover, two-thirds of the cinemas had closed by the 1960s and only 11% of people visited a cinema at least once a month, a far cry from the near religious rite of the weekly turn-out a decade or so before. With the advent of multi-screen complexes, the numbers steadied and revived a little but never looked like emulating those massive congregations of the 1940s.

20.5m people gathered around 5m bought or rented TV sets to watch the fuzzy images of the Coronation in 1953, properly regarded not so much as the beginning of an impressive monarchical reign but as the commencement of the television age. By 1959 there were 15.5m sets and, assisted by the coming of colour in 1967, 90% of households had television by 1970. It is now close on 99%. Average viewing is well over 20 hours a week – with the over 60s age echelon it rises to 38 hours, whilst radio listening has declined accordingly from its 1940s prime to something much less than an average of ten hours weekly. In 1948 there were 2m private cars in Britain, the same as in 1939. By 1960 the figure was 6m cars – and in 1959 the first modest piece of motorway came into use. By 1970 there were 12m cars. In 1950 traffic travelled 30bn miles on British roads; in the year 2000, it was 300bn miles, a tenfold increase. As for foreign holidays, these rose from 2m in 1950 to 10m by 1980.

In the dying years of variety, that is the larger part of the 1950s and the early years of the 1960s, some of the efforts made to save the genre were embarrassing. Some theatres were transformed into supposedly continental-style clubs with meals and drinks, with the variety show offered as a cabaret, but this seemed to have little or no resonance with audiences. The other attempt to lure in the customers was the 'girlie' shows, with the notorious stationary nudes (for at that time the Lord Chamberlain's diktat was that poseurs must remain still), with the overtly brazen titles, such as The *Bareway to Stardom* or *Strip, Strip, Hooray*. One or two of the striptease artistes were well-known. They included Phyllis Dixey (born in Wales; 1914-1964) who, managed by her husband,

the comic, Jack 'Snuffy' Tracy, essayed to be Britain's equivalent of America's Gypsy Rose Lee; and the Daily Mirror's famed cartoon girl, Jane, the model for whom, Crystabel Leighton-Porter (born in Hampshire; 1913-2000), toured with her dachshund, Fritz, also courtesy of the newspaper. However, most of the performers were anonymous, promising more than they delivered. It is said that the Queen's Park Hippodrome, Manchester, a theatre, it must be said, among those frequented in his youth by the writer, once presented two volunteer nudes.

One often sees claims that these rather tawdry, tired shows destroyed variety by driving away the family audience. However, Paul Raymond, for one, profited from it; at the height of this craze in 1956 he had no less than ten 'nude' revues on tour, all making money, enough for him to invest in his gainful Raymond Revuebar in 1958. It is perhaps truer to assert that the game was up for variety and that the 'girlie' shows could not save it from collapse. Changing social habits, helped by car usage, meant that a range of leisure pursuits was competing with the theatres, many of which, in response to the times, became bingo halls. The 1960s also saw the culmination of a gradual process, ongoing since the 1880s and 1890s, whereby shopping was more regarded as a pleasure than a chore, while innovations like floodlit football and bowling alleys were other rivals for the people's leisure intentions.

The club circuit, especially in the north of the country, rallied and stood up well, and what had been a nursery for budding comedians and other entertainers became a major source of income. Some clubs developed a goodly reputation for having a top-class variety show. The expansion of the cruise ship trade, part of the new tendency to take foreign holidays, was another ideal opportu-

The People's Jesters

nity for performers to provide cabaret for the passengers. It is true that clubland, notoriously boisterous, was not attractive to every type of comic, for there was a premium on tough, no-holds-barred gags and the need to handle drunken hecklers with bold bravado, while there was plainly a limit to the number and type of artists who could work the holiday boats.

Later the 'comedy clubs' developed, offering chances to budding young comedians, but these were limited by location to the larger conurbations and by generation to student and young middle class adult audiences, often catering for an interest in the so-called 'alternative' wave of comedy. So, even with these outlets, it must be pressed that the variety profession, including dozens of comics, felt the pinch very much as the halls closed one by one. On the side of the customers, it became more and more unusual for families to make regular trips to the theatre; often youngsters were reduced to maybe a Christmas show and, dependent on whether their traditional vacation was sustained or they had been flown out to the Spanish coast, perhaps a summer show as well.

The Knocking of Opportunities

What, then, did television provide by way of opportunities for comedians?

This may be analysed under three heads. One was the use of TV as a straightforward showcase for comics, in the same sense that the stage, the radio microphone and, if less successfully, the cinema screen merely allowed the comedian to project himself. These were frequently programmes hosted or fronted by one particular comedian, who often gave his name to the title, so that 'the Joe Bloggs Show', or its equivalent, became a rather overused identity tag.

The second was the incursion of a strong revue and cabaret element, avowedly of a satiric nature, but where it became more difficult to label the performers as comedians in any traditional sense. Typically, they were, to rework an Elizabethan coinage, 'university wits', and, although one or two deployed themselves as single acts, they tended to remain inside the revue sketch format of the Cambridge Footlights convention.

Thirdly, there was the development of an important branch of comic acting on television. One's impression is that this was more powerful in incidence on television than on radio. A genre of comedy drama, often excellently written, evolved, so much so that television's 'funny men' were more likely to be actors specialising in comic roles than old style comics, although, of course, there were instances where comedians turned their hand to such parts with relish and dispatch.

The upshot was that, overall, television was not too generous to the kind of comics that had paraded on the variety stage or in front of the BBC mikes. At best, it might be urged that the distinction between the comedian and the comic actor became much more vague and less clear cut. It is proposed to look briefly at each of these three brands of comedy.

Somebody's Show

From its onset as a national vehicle, television attempted to provide comedians with a colourful format, more revue than variety in style, with some accent on dancing girls and musical interludes. A host of comics had shows named in their honour, several of them not enduring for too long. Some deserve a more fulsome mention than others. Bob Monkhouse (1928-2004), for instance, sustained a good rate of success over many years. Drilled, through his association with

Dennis Goodwin, in script writing as well as performing, he became the consummate cracker of up-to-date topical gags, rather after the manner of Bob Hope. Slick, grinning, self-assured, this was a sophisticated and self-aware approach, if slightly oleaginous for some tastes. One should note his parallel conquest of the club circuit, where, in saltier mode than on the telly, he was in great demand. Not least of his assets was a devastating execution of the hapless and usually drunken barracker, to the point, where this supremely confident artiste would openly provoke heckling to demonstrate his masterly skill, something after the model of those now much fewer politicians, such as the agile minded Harold Wilson, who revelled in the cut and thrust of a rowdy meeting.

In private life a more serious-minded man, who devoted much of his time to charitable activity, Bob Monkhouse's very final quip on his death-bed may serve as a suitable encomium to a highly professional performer: 'I've decided to take a course in reincarnation; it's very expensive, but, what the hell, you've only got one life'.

Alfred Marks (Alfred Edward Touchinsky; 1921-1996) has a very varied career, the consequence of being able to sing in a rich baritone voice and act competently, as well as tell funny tales. The usual chain of action – RAF shows in the Middle East in World War II; the Windmill; radio broadcasting – led eventually to his own TV programme, *Alfred Marks Time*, which, with his commanding build and luxurious range of voices, he handled very well indeed. It was based on the sketch formula and this ideally suited him. He was also an excellent pantomime villain, say, as Abanazar in *Aladdin*. He was married to the comedienne, Paddy O'Neill, best remembered perhaps for her appearances with Libby Morris in the John Jackson

Record Round-up shows on television, where pop records were played over displays of comical mime.

The television concern about the 'talking head' prevailed against the salience of the monologue comic, rather favouring the sketch pattern, which broke up the dominance of the one face one voice, adding not only extra actors to the changing scene but also involving switches of costume and the like. Even brilliant stand-up comedians like Les Dawson found themselves participating in rather banal sketches. Performers like Dick Emery, Russ Abbott and Kenny Everett were more attuned to this modus operandi. Dick Emery (1930-1993) had the classic career – show-business family background; concert party; Ralph Reader RAF gang shows; post-war radio in *Variety Bandbox* and *Educating Archie*; then with Michael Bentine in TV's *It's a Square World*. Thus on to his very own The *Dick Emery Show*, where he introduced the earnest middle-aged lady, bespectacled, a little frumpish, but ever hopeful of masculine attachment. 'Her' interview normally ended with a coy slap and the expression, 'oh, you are awful'.

The tall clown, Russ Abbott, also showed up well as a serious actor, for instance, as Ted Butler, playing opposite Michael Williams, taking the role of a comic, in TV's *September Song*. Born in Chester in 1947, his real name Russell Roberts, he led a manic assault team in a series of insane sorties that owed something to the Crazy Gang and to Tommy Cooper. Having worked with the equally wacky Freddie Starr, notoriously accused by the tabloid press of eating a hamster, and also as a member of the Black Abbotts group, he went on to front *Russ Abbott's Madhouse* and *Russ Abbott's Show*, creating such lunatic characters as Basildon Bond, CU Jimmy the Scot and Cooperman. Large and

Television made Tommy Cooper, the manic magician, a familiar figure to millions

looming maniacally, he won the title of 'The Funniest Man on Television' no less than five times. Like Dick Emery, Kenny Everett focussed on drag, with his garishly dressed young woman insisting against verbal and visual testimony that it was 'all in the best possible taste'. Kenny Everett, sadly, died at a young age, but it is likely that his comet was already exhausted.

This typified a serious problem for television comics. On the one hand, there was little chance of an apprenticeship. With the death of the variety theatres, and with even panto-mimes and summer shows in much smaller numbers, there was no place to learn the trade and hone the act. The club circuit was available, but it basically only sustained the hard-hitting, thick-skinned comic of the Bob Monkhouse breed, so that anything gentler, scenically more elaborate or more experi-mental was at a discount. On the other hand, television consumed material rapidly and in gargantuan quantities. The comparison has been drawn by many commentators of the old-time comedians, hawking the same turn around a hundred and more theatres, improving and varnishing as they travelled, with the young comic suddenly thrust in front of the television camera and finding his flimsy supply of material discharged to the waiting millions and squandered forever. When *King Lear* was first shown on televi-sion, before a not oversized audience, it was seen by more people on that one occasion that all who had ever seen it professionally produced since it was first written four cen-turies previously. Not for nothing did Bob Hope assert that 'television was the box they buried entertainment in.'

Morecambe and Wise, as has already been analysed, surmounted this obstacle with unique observation, superb technique and excellent writing. Another sketch comedian to enjoy a popular success, without ever appealing, as did Morecambe and Wise, to the critical echelon, was Benny Hill. Born Alfred Hawthorne Hill, in Southampton, in 1924, he was in concert party in Margate and elsewhere, at one time stooge for Reg Varney. Benny Hill moved on to West End revues, like *Paris by Night* and *Fine Fettle*. He has been described as the first comedian to be made completely by the television screen and, from the mid 1950s and for the better part of 20 years, he discovered a winning streak that was lasciviously rude, in the sense that our grandmothers would have used that censori-ous adjective. He rarely then went back to the stage, for, like Tony Hancock, he was never too keen on a live audience. Moreover, he proceeded to make a killing in the United States, where so often English comics had had nightmarish trips. The overall result was that this rather solitary figure died in 1992 and left £7m in his will, one of the big-gest fortunes piled high by a British comic entertainer.

The basis for his characterisation was the leeringly twinkling eye, set in the simper-ing, fully rounded countenance. With the assistance of the costume and make up departments and a full battery of effects, he cleverly deployed this fundamental charac-ter in a range of guises, stemming from Mr Chow Mein, whose 'blessed with two nippers' was conveyed as 'breast with two nipples', and the sly, lisping Fred Scuttle, finding chances of voyeurism and the like in his various enterprises, to a Cavalier folk-singer of randy wordage that rivalled Kenneth Wil-liams' *Round the Horne* lyrics, and a blonde bombshell called Primrose Hill. The humour was unremittingly smutty, with scarcely a word or phrase included that could not have its entendre doubled, and with the whole scenario reminiscent, in word and picture, of the Donald M'Gill postcard. It has been concluded that what made the series such a hit in America was 'the Jiggle Factor', the surrounding of Benny Hill by a bevy of pneumatically voluptuous showgirls, the constant cause of his tell-tale smirks, gloating glances and saucy asides.

So it continued. Year on year, young comedians came and went, unto the days of Bobby Davro, Ben Elton, Harry Enfield, Lenny Henry, Harry Hill, Eddie Izzard, Julian Clary and others, with the sketch motif dominant, so much so that older viewers may have bethought themselves transported back to the seaside promenades of yesteryear, where the bright and breezy concert parties placed a heavy premium on the black-out sketch with a saucy punch-line. Sometimes the departure was for different and even better things. Ben Elton, having toured the nation with his highly politicised one-man appraisal of British society, then delivered it in high octane vein to the television audience in his *The Man from Auntie* series, before moving on to a successful career in writing for theatre-goers and readers alike.

One programme, however, was brutally unequivocal in its emphatic determination to pose the stand-up comic on the dais. This was *Comedians*, a project of Granada Television, whereby an edited version of a line-up of comics told 50 jokes in half an hour, less what was available to the credits and to Shep's Banjo Band. It began in 1971 and drew contributors from the club and pub circuit. It included, for example, Johnny 'Goon' Tweed, whom the author watched at his brother's local doing a very funny mime to an extravagantly compiled tape of sound and verbal effects, a turn that was really only viable in a club or pub.

The comedians simply stood, mike in hand, and told jokes, many of them pushing at the frontiers of the non-PC. It is said that some of them saw their nightly fee soar from £50 to £1000. Russ Abbott appeared once or twice, as did the fast-talking cockney comedian, Mike Reid. Others were Belfast's Roy Walker, giggling Lennie Bennett, cheery Duggie Brown, another who moved over to the legitimate stage, Charlie Williams who has already been mentioned, and the burly figure of Merseyside's George Roper. One of the most luminous was Ken Goodwin, who could manage a very passable George Formby imitation, and who had some of the other's innate daftness. 'Settle down', he would murmur to a hushed throng, as if all was hullabaloo and rumpus. Then he would tell silly tales, like the one about the two elephants that robbed a bank, but he wouldn't be able to identify them because they had pulled tights over their heads. His very quietude and assumed diffidence set him apart from the almost gruesome assurance of his confrères on *Comedians*.

There was a spin-off in 1974 into *The Wheeltappers and Shunters Social Club*, again a naked expression of the reality of clubland as the source of much of the day's stand-up comedy. Little Colin Crompton, from Manchester, was the chairman – 'we've had trouble with the acoustics, but we've set traps.' Ciggie dangling, his harsh treatment of Morecambe '('they don't bury the dead; they stick them up in bus shelters wi' bingo tickets in their hand') attracted municipal protest. His fellow artiste on these occasions was Bernard Manning, and it was his own profitable club, The Embassy, in North Manchester, that was the location for the show.

Tubby and combative, Bernard Manning, a onetime singer with the Oscar Rabin dance band, was one of the few performers on Comedians to build a national repute. Not that it was all sunshine and flowers, for social commentators often vilified him for his racist cracks ('if you dial 999 in Bradford, you get the Bengal Lancers' – 'heard about the Jewish Kamikaze pilot who crashed in his brother's scrap yard?'), but he remained impenitent. He endured and was unyielding, while, over against the usual often smarmy bonhomie of showbiz, he was decidedly censorious about fellow-professionals. Commenting on Max Bygraves's son's disastrous attempt to launch himself into the world of entertainment with a summer season on the Channel Islands that, apparently, lasted but one night, Bernard Manning remarked. 'the people in Jersey said, if it comes to a toss-up, we would rather have the Germans back.'

Several of those who starred in *Comedians*, such as Jim Bowen and Roy Walker, became game show hosts, and – Bruce Forsyth, Jonathan Ross, Bob Monkhouse, – this sort of role suited the amiable comic, always ready with a joke up his sleeve. From Tommy Trinder onwards, telly-show compering was another line of business for the likes of Bruce Forsyth, Larry Grayson, Des O'Connor and others. Norman Vaughan, born in Liverpool in 1923, took over the prestigious Palladium show on Sunday evenings from Bruce Forsyth. He had had experience in concert party and other spheres since adolescence, but this was his big break. Pleasant and unthreatening, his catchwords 'dodgy' and 'swinging' soon took on a vogue of their own, whilst, such were the times, many will recall his 'Roses will grow on you' chocolates advertisement.

Then, it seemed, he was gone. Another star of those Palladium nights was Dave King. Tall, dark and with a quiet line in comedy and a decent sideline in balladry, he was a regular headliner in the late 1950s and early 1960s. He also went into straight acting and was lost to the world of comedy. The Gargantuan

appetite of *Comedians*, wolfing down material and perforce, the performers, was but one token of the effect of television on the old-style art of comedianship. Only a few seemed to find a feasible niche or last the pace.

One such exception was, in the first decade of the 21st century, Bolton-born Peter Kay, who, eschewing the swish argot of the modernist brigade, appeared to be, in crude terms, a throwback. Having captivated audiences over an arduous 200 night tour, he made his mark on television, with the almost obligatory cameo on *Coronation Street* and an advertising spot, and won the hearts of the northern club audiences, he seems ready for extensive success. A rather corpulent young man, with a slow Lancashire burr and a deprecatory line in softly spoken jokes of deliberately banal connotations, he may well be destined to be one of the greats. The naked man, giving a piggy-back to a naked girl, turns out to be going to a fancy dress party as a tortoise; asked about his Godiva-like burden, he explains 'that's Michelle; 'me shell', he underlines the meaning with some emphasis, as if his listeners are as slow on the uptake as he pretends to be. He tells of a mobile library that knocks over a man, who lies groaning heavily in the road with agonising injuries. Out steps the librarian; 'Shhhh', she whispers. There is a decided element of character here, alongside and complementary to the material, that somehow sets Peter Kay off from the ordinary run of present day young comics.

Cabaret

On the 10 May 1961 *Beyond the Fringe*, having been tried out with success and amid some controversy in Edinburgh and Brighton, opened in London. It is not too farfetched to assert that it changed the face of British comedy. The inventive wit of Peter Cook, the prodigious mimicry of Jonathan Miller, the sly observation of Alan Bennett and the clownish as well as musical talent of Dudley Moore combined to present a cabaret or revue style of entertainment that was, as one critic suggested, like being 'tickled with a sharp scythe.' The format of sketch, monologue and song was not unlike the normative fodder of years of university 'smokers' and revues, the sort of offering that had levered the likes of Claude Hulbert, Jack Hulbert, Richard Murdoch and Jimmy Edwards towards the stage. The formula was, by the same token, not too far distanced from the cabaret approach of Noel Coward or Joyce Grenfell, the revue approach of Betty Marsden and Stanley Baxter and the concert approach of Michael Flanders and Donald Swann.

What lifted *Beyond the Fringe* on to a higher plateau was the simplicity of the technique – four young men basically black-garbed on a near empty stage – the artistic discipline – all the material was strictly of the highest standard – the sheer intelligence of the enterprise and the razor blade sharpness of the attack. Many of the targets were old butts. The church, xenophobia, the monarchy, the political establishment, pretentious art-forms, advertising, sex, race and class – most of these had been skitted at for generations. What distinguished the show was that every Aunt Sally was felled with clinical ease, with taboos falling to left and right, and with a genuine sense of purposive demolition. It was more than guying; there was a feeling that real flaws were being exposed. There was something of the American acuteness of the transatlantic satirists, Mort Sahl, Lenny Bruce, Mike Nichols, Mel Brooks and Bob Newhart about the proceedings. Above all else, it was immensely funny. Audiences rocked with laughter. The author regards his hearing and watching of Alan Bennett's famed Anglican sermon of stupefying blandness as one of the three or four funniest items he has ever witnessed in live performance.

That brilliant quartet were not in the traditional sense comedians. Each member became famous in his own right: Jonathan Miller the scintillating polymath; Alan Bennett (after a sharp-witted TV series in 1966, *On The Margin*) the finest comic dramatist of his generation; Dudley Moore the unlikely Hollywood sex-god; Peter Cook the founder of the Establishment Club for satirical performance. Peter Cook and Dudley Moore did combine on television in *Not Only...But Also* in the mid-1960s; their 'Pete' and 'Dud' working class duo, with Pete pestered by the naked arrival of Greta Garbo, became a huge hit, as did Peter Cook's E L Wisty character, a figure of earnest pedantry.

Beyond the Fringe had a marked effect on the comic culture, although it did give rise to, if not a problem, an issue. Nothing that came thereafter outdid it for style or basic funniness. Most inventions begin primitively and are refined and sophisticated to a higher ideal. Not so with so-called 1960s satire. The first remained the best.

Apart from isolated and often metropolitan instances, such as Peter Cook's Establishment Club and journalistic endeavours, such as the launch of the magazine *Private Eye* in 1961, the chief effect, as far as the public was concerned, was on television comedy. It may have helped the progress of 'university' humour (few even of its proponents saw the genre as fundamentally satiric) that, by the 1960s, the percentage of the relevant age-group at college had risen from a pre-war 3% to over 8% and was rising steadily to its current total of over 20%. The student audience enjoyed the flavours of undergraduate irreverence. *That Was The Week That Was*, broadcast in 1962/1963, was the flagship for the cult. Fronted by David Frost, it presented a range of topical sketches and songs each Saturday night, generally culled from the week's events and news. Young artists, writers and critics, such as Ned Sherrin, Millicent Martin, Eleanor Bron, David Kernan, Willie Rushton, Bernard Levin, Ken Cope and Lance Perceval were heavily engaged in *TWTWTW*. Necessarily a hastily thrown together show, it made a feature of its improvised format, although, truth to tell, it thus sometimes conveyed a sense of self-indulgence, indiscipline and amateurishness. Nevertheless, it made contact with a massive following, who delighted in its cocking of a snook at politicians and other authoritative figures. It was widely seen as 'the death of deference'.

In the wake of the mould-breaking success of 'TW3', a number of programmes and a crop of ex-university types brought supposedly satiric comedy to the airways. *Not so much a Programme, More a Way of Life* (1964/65) featured a mixed bag of would-be cabaret satirists, like David Frost, John Fortune and John Bird, alongside Cleo Laine, Roy Hudd and Michael Crawford. *Not the Nine O'Clock News* (1979/82) assembled the talents of Mel Smith, Griff Rhys Jones, Pamela Stephenson and Rowan Atkinson. In sit-com vein, the cleverly understated interplay of Nigel Hawthorne, as the controlling civil servant, and Paul Eddington, as the bewildered politician, made a hit of *Yes, Minister* and *Yes, Prime Minister* (1980/88), a show updated and copied in 2005 with the spin-doctoring capers of *The Thick of it*. The work of impersonators like Mike Yarwood (*Mike Yarwood in Persons*, 1976/81) and of Rory Bremner (still going strong with *Bremner, Bird and Fortune*, from 1997 onwards and the new *Mock the Week* in 2005, with the up

and coming comics, Frankie Boyle and Dara O'Briain) has already been discussed. Other satiric news shows have been *Drop the Dead Donkey* (1990/98), *The Day Today* (1994), *Brass Eye* (1997/2001) and *11 O'Clock Show* (1998/2000).

The sketch and revue style of these politicised programmes was also incorporated into other comedy shows. The pick of these was undoubtedly *Monty Python's Flying Circus*. Leaning on Michael Bentine's *Square World* activities, it experimented vividly with the possibilities of surrealism on television, introducing a glowing range of visual gags in support. The punctuation of the show was deliberately uneven, with dialogue abruptly terminated and events left dangling tantalisingly in midair. Whether it was the conclave of cardinals or the Ministry for Funny Walks, there was a hectic, excitable verve and pace to 'Python', some of which was transferred to two or three Pythonesque films, such as *The Life of Brian*, a hilarious rehash of the story of Jesus and an apt example of how deeply the non-deferential knife had slit into social values.

It is perhaps an oversimplification to assert that 'Python' was televised Goonery – and intuition suggests that public affection for the Goons was possibly a little higher than for the Pythons – but such a comparison offers a crude trademark of the series' worth. From one angle, the Python format recalled the old-style stage groups, like those of Fred Karno or Harry Tate, with, of course, the craziness sophisticated through technological process. John Cleese, who had already made his name in political 'sketch' programmes like *The Frost Report* (1966) with, among others, Ronnie Barker and Ronnie Corbett, led a team of talented players, including Michael Palin and Eric Idle. Other post-university cabaret performers found a corner on television, not least Dawn French and Jennifer Saunders, who were, in *French and Saunders*, to contribute, with the technical aids of wardrobe and make-up, a telling series of clever if somtimes repetitious mimicry.

One fascinating side-product of this mighty productivity was the artistry of Barry Humphries. In the 1960s the Australian comic actor created the monstrous character of Dame Edna Everage, a woman of genial self-absorption and tasteless buoyancy. He also added Sir Les Patterson, a cultural attaché of uncultivated practices that bordered on the obscene. Dame Edna made so powerful an impact that 'she' passed triumphantly into that gallery of entertainment icons that resides in the folk-memory of the populace. As a male study in female characterisation, it deservedly must stand with and against the great 'dames' such as Norman Evans and Danny La Rue. Two Englishmen presented, about the same time, the prissy duo of Hinge and Bracket, a spinsterish pair of outmoded musical buffs, all lace and spite. In quieter mode, this, too, was well observed. It was intriguing to remark how age-old techniques, such as female impersonation, could be deployed in the modern service of social comment.

During and just after the era of Margaret Thatcher's administrations, from about 1979 to 1997, there were several interesting by-products of the satiric boom of the 1960s and early 1970s. One was the puppet show, *Spitting Image*, in which cartoon sculpted models of well-known politicians and celebrities were relentlessly teased. It was if the ventriloquial profession had chosen mass ridicule for its weapon. As with both ventriloquists and impersonators, the problem was the inconsistency of the scripts, most of which were pretty woeful, at least compared with the lethal quality of the puppets. It often ended, as with a second-rate Punch and Judy show, with everyone knocking one another over.

Of the several university or cabaret style performers who attempted solo concerts and appearances, Rowan Atkinson perhaps had particular weight. His dark, leering, saturnine looks, not unlike a 'cod' Olivier as Richard III, gave him a literal head start on television in sketches like the one where, as the devil, cigarette in one hand, clipboard in the other, he allocated sub-groups of miscreants their places in hell, subsequent on the Last Judgement – 'atheists over here; you must be feeling pretty stupid this morning; bankers...Americans; lavatory? You should have gone before you came.' Such cameos were of classic standard. He went on to create the characters of the grossly incompetent and unaware Mr Bean and the despicably cynical Blackadder in a set of mock-historical dramas.

Were the satirists satirical? It is a moot point. It is significant that the top-class experts, such as Jonathan Miller and Alan Bennett, never really claimed the honour, and that it was the second string of artists who self-styled themselves thus. There is also a chicken-and-egg argument. The last third of the 20th century certainly witnessed less formal and less respectful behaviour patterns, so that irreverent humour could be estimated to be both a cause and an effect. Admirers of the Greek dramatist Aristophanes or of Jonathan Swift, author of *Gulliver's Travels*, would mildly suggest that 1960s satire was too soft-centred and self-regarding to be a realistic weapon of ridicule, in the connotation of its being directed towards subversion and disruption. It was rarely that savage or malicious.

The prime minister, Harold Macmillan, went smilingly to the Fortune Theatre to chuckle over Peter Cook's amusing representation of him as the outmoded Edwardian statesman trying to comes to terms with the telly age. That recalled William Gladstone's like enjoyment of Gilbert and Sullivan's *Iolanthe*, wherein the Lord Chancellor was supposed to be modelled on the Grand Old Man. Patrons drew quickened breath on both occasions, but the combine of sharp-witted but not malevolent disrespect with politicians bright enough to understand voters would think better of them if they rode with the punch and did not make a fuss, implies that the mix was not too explosive. Margaret Thatcher's favourite TV comedy was *Yes, Minister*; that says it all.

It has also been urged that that *Beyond the Fringe* and its successors were against 'trendiness' rather than in favour of revolution. The absorption of a be-knighted David Frost into the old-fashioned establishment – an age-old device of the top drawer when faced with rebellious but ambitious adversaries – summarises the discussion concisely. Perhaps all eras are ready to indulge in minor but relatively harmless shocks to the social system. The Gilbertian sortie against the peerage in *Iolanthe* was regarded with much the same shuddering frisson of insubordinate delight as was the abuse of Harold Wilson and other politicos on '*TW3*'. We are back where we began; with the comedian as the diverter of dissidence through moderate scorn.

In society, comedy provides the exhaust pipe for the excess steam of public indignation. The purportedly seditious material on stage and television from the 1960s onwards obviously changed contextually, particularly following legal and cultural changes in the laws of censorship and in social mores. One consequence might have been a contribution to a scepticism, indeed, an indifference to the political process that marked the last

decades of the 20th and the opening of the 21st centuries. All the media combined to degrade the governmental process, although it must be added quickly that there was a generation of politicians that did little to disabuse the public of the frailties and corruption of the political process. From satiric cabaret artists to sarcastic political diarists, the constant deflation and rubbishing of politicians, without the occasional word of praise for the many hard-working and honest men and women working in the governmental and allied services, may have paid that price of a public resolve to regard politics with diffidence and disrespect. General election turn-outs of just over 50% at the opening of the 21st century compared badly with those of 80% soon after the Second World War.

Nonetheless, it is again difficult to disentangle causes and symptoms. In the end, the witty antics of the satiric brigade were probably no more and no less damaging to the establishment than, say, the word-play of *ITMA* and the lugubrious reminiscence of Robb Wilton in World War II.

As was previously remarked, a further aspect of the wholesale seismic shift in social mores from the 1960s onwards was the construction of 'comedy clubs' and the beginnings of 'alternative' comedy, some of whose exponents made their way on to the television channels and gained broader public access. It was not easy to define. Sceptics inferred that the comedy was 'alternative' in so far as it was not funny. It claimed to offer a commentary on previously taboo themes, many of them of a sexual or physiological nature, and there was an especial welcome for women stand-up comics, such as the quietly observational Jo Brand, in this respect. Some of these young comedians took well to the telly, among them Julian Clary, Eddie Izzard and Paul Merton. These were brightly intelligent young people, although it was possible, and by way of compliment, to view them as latter-day incarnations of, respectively, Larry Grayson, Frankie Howerd and Tony Hancock. Indeed, Paul Merton reconstituted, not altogether convincingly, some of Tony Hancock's material, although the younger man certainly beat Tony Hancock, a slave of the script, in quick-wittedness. In politically aware shows like *Have I Got News For You*, where much depended on speed of reaction, he showed himself to be a consummate master of free association, divergent thinking and droll digression.

Comedy Playhouse

That mention of Tony Hancock is sufficient introduction both to him and to the third component of television comedy, viz, the comic sit-com, series or drama. It is generally accepted that, the rule-proving exception of Morecambe and Wise apart, Tony Hancock made the transfer from variety stage to television screen with greater facility than any other comedian. Some managed pretty well: Arthur Askey, with his ready eye for camera positions, was probably as funny on television as on summer show stage and radio. We earlier observed how Benny Hill certainly came over more buoyantly on screen than on stage. Others found the shackles of the TV studio too restrictive. However, of Tony Hancock it can be fairly said that he was better, that is, funnier, on television (and on radio) than on stage, where he sometimes seemed awkward and ill at ease. He himself said that his theatre audiences met in Hyde Park, dressed in mackintoshes, prior to his performances, to decide on what sort of negative crowd they were going to be.

Anthony John Hancock was born in Small Heath, Birmingham in 1924. The son of a hotelier to, and semi-professional member of, the variety profession, he had a good schooling at Durlston Court and Bradfield College, Reading. Amidst the artists staying at the family hotel in Bournemouth, he fostered theatrical ambitions and found other employment irksome. Initially, his progress was unremarkable. He made his stage debut in 1940; worked with the Ralph Reader *Gang Show*, having joined the RAF in 1942, went on to the books of the Entertainments National Service Association (ENSA) and did a stint at the Windmill, along with intermittent radio appearances on *Workers' Playtime* and *Varity Bandbox*. His stage act included an ageing pop singer and a number of 'cod' impersonations, such as Quasimodo ('Sanctuary; sanctuary; sancs you very much') and – 'here's one for the youngsters' – the old actor, George Arliss.

Following his major breakthrough into radio via *Educating Archie*, as one of that errant puppet's tutors, he introduced his famous 'half hours' in 1954, establishing the faded address of 23 Railway Cuttings, East Cheam into the public consciousness and drawing around him other gifted players such as Sid James, ever the rugged opportunist Sancho Panza to his Don Quixote, the drawling Bill Kerr, Kenneth 'ooh, do stop messin' about' Williams, the bristling Hattie Jacques and the much put upon Hugh Lloyd. An appropriate example of the series might be the portrayal of the tedious Sunday afternoon, itself an echo of the opening scene of John Osborne's *Look Back in Anger*, with Tony Hancock enduring with some frustration the longuers of the gloomy 1950s Sabbath.

With the sparse beauties of its Ray Galton and Alan Simpson scripts, *Hancock's Half Hour* was transferred to BBC TV in 1956. The radio ham, the blood donor, the soldier's reunion, the search for a television set to watch the end of a serial...these, and other polished nuggets, were acclaimed alike by Joe Public and broadsheet critic. The jury room skit on Henry Fonda's *Twelve Angry Men* had Tony Hancock swerving violently from verdict to verdict, with Sid James craftily stacking up the expenses; in one piece of demagoguery Tony Hancock cried, 'What about Magna Carta; did that brave Hungarian girl die for nothing?' During the 1950s he also appeared at the Adelphi Theatre, in the *London Laughs* revues with Jimmy Edwards and others, while in 1958, at the televised *Royal Command Performance*, he presented his cameo of a caged and bored budgerigar, his classic answer to the joint calls of stage and screen.

There were films, such as *The Rebel* (1961) and *The Punch and Judy Man* (1962), but they were no more than moderate, and Tony Hancock's attempts to become a global star were not too successful. A tortured soul, he cut away his props – his fellow artists; even his writers – first to do single-handed Hancock episodes and second to do an unsatisfactory ITV series. There was a sense in which his hollow bravado – the blood donor, boasting Viking streams of gore, who was terrified of even a pinprick – was almost too neatly a personification of Britain in the 1950s. Exhausted by the war but thrilled by their achievement, the British people and its politicians veered between vaulting thoughts of greatness and desperate scramblings of pettiness. The Suez fiasco of 1956 was Hancockian to the life.

One might argue that Tony Hancock never really survived the 1950s. The radio series ended in 1959 and the television series was concluded in 1961. From about 1952 Tony Hancock drank heavily (twice did the author visit the Adelphi Theatre in the 1950s to see him, only to find the comedian 'indisposed').

His two marriages to Cicely Romanis, 1950-65, and to Freddie Ross, 1965-68, were scarred by inebriation and domestic violence, and, whilst visiting Australia to discuss the concept of a TV series about a disappointed 'pommy' emigrant, he committed suicide in Sydney in 1968.

A troublesome colleague and tense perfectionist, Tony Hancock was, as Kenneth Williams confided to his diary, 'incredibly destructive' – of self and of others. Comedians are self-made men and women. They have to stand up and be counted, alone and unprotected, night after night. This may be one reason several have offered some support to the Conservative Party, on the grounds that they have had to fight the good fight as a form of comic private enterprise. Jimmy Edwards, Eric Morecambe and Kenny Everett spring to mind, although Ken Dodd's attachment – 'when you go abroad, tell them you're British; play on their sympathies' – may have been determined more by the chance of yet another stand-up gig than incipient Toryism. Tony Hancock is one of the few great comedians of whom much is known of their politics to remain persuaded by Socialist ideals. How this connected with his struggle to be the perfect comic artist is hard to assess. Certainly he disdained the 'funny voice cardboard characters' of average comedy and sought a truth in his work, rather as the leading and profound dramatists seek to utilise comedy as a thoughtful and revealing tool.

Tony Hancock's models were Sid Field and the French droll, Jacques Tati, whose film *Monsieur Hulot's Holidays* (1953) was so fondly received by middlebrow British audiences. The tart comments and ambiguous personality of the former and the accident-prone earnestness of the latter were what marked them out for Hancockian attention.

In the decade of his prime, Tony Hancock moulded a comic creation of Falstaffian proportion. Outwardly brazen, inwardly tentative, the rakish overcoat and Hombourg hat and the half-educated oratory – ' 'it is a far, far better thing that I do than I ever done': Rembrandt' – the braggart mask for the basic unsureness, it was a devastating portrait. Possibly only George Formby Senior has approached close to this extremely difficult representation of dual characterisation.

Its television appeal was emphatic. Tony Hancock buttonholed his listener/watcher on his or her own settee and held them bewitched in one-sided conversation. It was like a priestly confessional, or, to deploy political analogues, it was like Stanley Baldwin on the 'wireless' with his fireside chats in the 1930s or Tony Blair's engaging informality on television in the 1990s. It was not the evangelist, the Billy Graham, or the demotic statesman, the William Gladstone, crying forth to the huge outdoor multitude. It was not, for example, Ken Dodd, rarely, on his own admission, at home on TV, but explosively brilliant faced with a horde of thousands.

In creating and presenting this monstrous figure, the source of laughter but also of sympathy, Tony Hancock (to say nothing of Galton and Simpson) helped to define what TV comedy would become. By his utilisation of the plotted playlet, especially when surrounded by a small troupe of attendants, he served notice that television would find its main seams of humour in the comedy play. There is even some reason to believe that, by his very success, Tony Hancock made it even more difficult for the straightforward comic to find opportunities to perform simple stand-up on the box.

To a large extent, the comic actor rather than the comedian has ruled the world of TV com-edy. Ray Galton and Alan Simpson did for television comedy what their mentors, Denis Norden and Frank Muir (who, in reciprocally admiring terms, admitted this) for radio comedy. Denis Norden reckoned that their *Steptoe and Son*, with Wilfred Bramwell and Harry H Corbett the bickering father and son totters, should be studied as a classic piece of Eng Lit. Assuredly it had shades of *King Lear* in its searing saga of the parent-child love-hate relationship. Its chief concentration on two main characters was not to be too typical of the TV comedy play. That was much more a radio device, and television writers soon realised they could spread themselves a little, for, self-evidently, TV watchers could identify types more readily.

Several of the best television comedy series, while sometimes centred on a couple of salient figures, have progressed well by the adoption of a surrounding team. Examples include *Dad's Army*, with its file of Poujadiste shopkeepers; the not too soldierly concert party of the India-based *It Ain't 'Alf Hot, Mum*; the ill-assorted entertainment staff of Maplin's holiday camp in *Hi-de-Hi* (those three from the same David Croft and Jimmy Perry stable); the eccentric management and assistants of Grace Brothers' department store in *Are You Being Served?*; the oddball cons and screws in *Porridge*; the mixed bag of residents in the grotty lodgings of *Rising Damp*; the quartet of John Cleese, Prunella Scales, Connie Booth and Andrew Sachs running the grim fortification of *Fawlty Towers*; the customers in the Nag's Head, Trigger, Boycey and so on, as well as the Trotter brothers, in *Only Fools and Horses*; the discordant parish council members around Dawn French as *The Vicar of Dibley*; Victoria Wood's *Acorn Antiques* cast and her eponymous *Dinner Ladies*, both of those troupes boosted by the exceptional comedic gifts of

Julie Walters, and extended dysfunctional families as in Alf Garnett's *Till Death Do Us Part*, the Liverpuddlian *Bread* and Caroline Ahearne's *The Royle Family*.

In this regard they recall the expanded sketch format of the old variety stage, after the fashion of Fred Karno, Harry Tate and Duggie Wakefield, although the Will Hay formula is probably the closest approximation. The TV comedies might also be viewed as extended versions of revue or concert party sketches, in part because they tend to end with a punch-line, rather like a dramatised shaggy dog story. The opposite way of seeing them is as contracted farces, with a repertory of characters playing out a shortened version of something like a Ben Travers/Ralph Lynn/Robertson Hare/Brian Rix frolic.

They do seem to owe more to theatrical than to cinematic precedents. This has much to do with the tighter focus of the television screen, as opposed to the more spacious area of the cinema screen, and, even more importantly, the contrast of the two or three, not the two or three hundred, viewing together. This change in the psychology of the experience places a premium on the verbal exchanges, closely observed, with much emphasis on facial expression. The frenetic Michael Crawford just about got away with the physical excesses of *Some Mothers Do Have 'Em*, a programme that owed a debt to variety slapstick like the 'slosh' decorating of Laurie Lupino Lane and George Truzzi and even the enraged crockery demolition of Lucan and McShane, as well as the more obvious antics of the circus clown. However, television comedy has never been so successful as the cinema in the expansive visual and physical humour of Charlie Chaplin, Harold Lloyd, Laurel and Hardy and the Marx Brothers.

Thus, where the visual gags are happily completed on television, they tend to be more specific and quick-fire, like David Jason, as Del Boy Trotter, leaning nonchalantly sideways on to a bar top he had not realised had been lifted and vanishing from sight – an item voted by viewers the funniest single item witnessed on the medium. Often where there are more corporeal scenes, it is the verbal comment that elevates them from the mundane. For example, Leonard Rossiter, as Rigsby, the seedy landlord in *Rising Damp*, whilst trying to talk down a would-be suicide from his roof top, asks, 'while you're up there, could you, could you just adjust me television aerial?' What most people remember are the funny exchanges: when the captured German naval officer demands of Private Pike, Ian Lavender's callow youth in *Dad's Army*: 'vot is your name?', Captain Mainwaring orders, 'don't tell him, Pike.' When Warren Mitchell's monster proletarian bigot, Alf Garnett, is sounding off about the nativity and how Jesus was born in the stable because the inn was full, his dim wife, Dandy Nicholls, opines 'well, it would have been crowded, what with it being Christmas'. When the doctor asks Del Boy Trotter, 'do you have trouble passing water', he responds, 'well, I did have a funny turn going over London Bridge last week'. It is the pure, harvested corn of variety, but no worse for that, and beautifully served by accomplished actors.

It is often the case that, when the characters break away from their normative surrounds and engage in more extensive visual exploits, the results are gauche and awkward, again a reflection of the limitations of the small screen and the different thought-processes of a tiny audience. It as if the big screen may offer big visual gags to big audiences, while the small screen calls for a much more intimate, Hancockian technique. If one were to seek a further common denominator of successful television comedy, the single keyword might be claustrophobia. Where the

Marx Brothers might have sought the open spaces of the wild west or Laurel and Hardy, in legionnaire guise, the drifting sands of the desert, TV comic actors are at their best when locked claustrophobically in some social or cultural closet.

The illustrations are plentiful: the Steptoes in their miscellaneously furnished den; Captain Mainwaring, Sergeant Wilson, Corporal Jones and company secured within the parish hall; the effeminate John 'I'm Free' Inman, the blowsy Mollie Sugden and colleagues in their department store; the Trotters' flat and pub; the dinner ladies cabined in the factory canteen; the suffocating lodging house of *Rising Damp* and the ghastly jail of *Fawlty Towers*; the fenced in holiday camp and the smothering jungle heat of *Hi-de-Hi* and *It Ain't 'Alf Hot, Mum*; more recently, the brilliant pastiche of David Brent's *The Office*, with its harrowing rake over modern working conditions; the Garnetts and the Royles stuck, without chance of social or cultural escape, in their unbearable living rooms, the ultimate irony being the Royles constantly watching the telly on which we are watching them malfunction. This inward-looking concept, of tightly bonded groups of characters communing, from social penitentiaries, with ones and twos, themselves couch potatoes, in part or whole, trapped in their own living rooms, is perhaps best illustrated by the prison theme of Ronnie Barker's *Porridge*.

At its best, this genre has produced for millions, who might never have had the opportunity or inclination to visit the legitimate theatre in search of dramatic comedy, successive treats of comic artistry, most of it created and expressed by gifted comic actors. It has meant, that apart from the exceptions already noted and in the aftermath of Tony Hancock's fluent success, the funny men of television have been comic actors rather than comedians. It has been their sayings – Private Jones' 'Don't Panic'; Captain Mainwaring's 'Stupid Boy'; Mrs Fawlty's 'he's from Barcelona', apropos Manuel, the 'dumb'waiter; her angry husband's 'don't mention the war' – that have found their way into the public discourse, as those of Tommy Handley or Robb Wilton had in a previous generation. Arthur Lowe, John Le Mesurier, Warren Mitchell, John Cleese, David Jason and Leonard Rossiter are just a few who have created the comic characters that are discussed and laughed over the following day in schoolyard and office. The nearest approximation to their style of mastery from the previous age may be Will Hay, who, on stage, radio and film, was the salient figure in the sort of comic play in which television excels – and Leonard Rossiter included in his ingenious bag of acting tools a prolonged double-take of which Will Hay could have been proud.

The career of Ronnie Barker makes for interesting analysis. Ronald William George Barker was born in Bedford in 1929. He died, to be feted with fulsome and much merited obituaries, in 2005, aged 76. Initially a repertory actor, he gravitated from radio comedy in *The Navy Lark* and television revue (*The Frost Report; Frost on Sunday*) to a bisected existence. On the one hand, his vocal skills brought him success as a comic actor in *Open All Hours*, as the grasping, stuttering northern grocer, and as the street-wise cockney convict in *Porridge*; on the other hand, he joined with Ronnie Corbett, more after the fashion of the typical comedian, in *The Two Ronnies*, a magazine programme of coruscating wit, rather like a televised version of radio's *Take It from Here*, even unto the parodic song-chainer that ended each show on the high that '*TIFH*'s concluding cinematic skit did. The show ran from 1971 to 1987, and there have been 21st century replays and refurbishments, and, at peak, it claimed high audiences of 17m viewers. Ronnie Barker, who also did much of the writing, brought exquisite dexterity to a range of parts, from yokel and honest toiler to snotty-nosed toff. Exceptionally for this kind of programme, the wit of the scripts was deliciously well maintained – 'the toilets at a local police station have been stolen. Police say they have nothing to go on.'

The moot question that best summarises a discussion of laughter on British television is: should one regard Ronnie Barker as a comedian or a comic actor? From George Robey to Sid Field, 'genuine' comedians have assumed characterisations, with added costume and altered voices, but maybe they have, at base, preserved their intrinsic identity. The comic TV actors of the last 50 years have created an amusing gallery of faces, but that is not necessarily their fundamental rationale. Warren Mitchell, rightly, refuses to answer to or be personally identified with Alf Garnett, although the part contributed much to his fame. It is probably correct to argue that, when one had seen Robb Wilton play the role of the fire chief in his famous sketch, one would afterwards discuss what Robb Wilton, rather than the fire officer, had contributed. The same is possibly true of Will Hay.

It is the fate of the modern comic actors to be recollected in character. The merits of Sergeant Wilson, not of John Le Mesurier, may be debated. That does not in any way distract from the admiration for the actor, rather is it a compliment to his comprehen-sive embrace of the role. And, just as actors like Richard Wattis seemed to find a decent niche in practically every British film comedy of the 1940s and 1950s, a similar breed of skilled, artfully underplaying actors have assisted at the banquet of TV comedy; Richard Beckinsale both in *Rising Damp* and *Porridge* or Roger Lloyd Pack both in *Only Fools and Horses* and *The Vicar of Dibley* are good examples, but, given the dozens of fine supporting players, it is near invidious even to cite instances.

There can be no doubt that comic actors have largely replaced comedians on television over wide stretches of the comedy show on offer. It leads to the final comment that herein there is some reversion to an older convention. We began this analysis around the time of the Great War, when the descriptor 'comedian' was deployed usually to label those actors who were, to define it negatively, not 'tragedians'. The title of 'comedian' was then more broadly bestowed on those who did stand-up or sketches in variety and later on radio. It is a usage that has been current for almost a hundred years, but, over the last few decades, it has come under some pressure from the usurpation of comedy by fully-fledged television actors in the popular culture. It may be necessary to start thinking whether or not the recently knighted David Jason (*Porridge* and *Open All Hours*, as well as *Only Fools and Horses*, but also the comedy drama of *The Darling Budds of May* and the serious crime drama of *A Touch of Frost*) should be re-styled a 'comedian' of the old, old Victorian dispensation, that is, the complement of the 'tragedian'.

The Comic Era

Comedians are less publicly visible than of yore. A current weekly television guide was randomly selected and the listings for the hours from 6 o'clock in the evening until midnight were examined for the four main terrestrial channels. That amounts to 168 hours prime viewing time. There was not one slot for a comedian to do what comedians customarily do, that is, tell jokes or act out comic sketches and characterisations.

The closest approximation was Paul Merton in his regular spot on *Have I Got News For You*, the topical news quiz show. Hereon he waxes amusingly, drawing out comical threads and sustaining running gags. Of course, this is reliant on the balance of the two teams and the material to hand; occasionally, he is relatively dormant. It is not a typical comedian's turn. One or two comedians may be found hosting quiz and talk shows of varying kinds or appearing on them, whilst, occasionally, they may turn up in a play or a soap opera but the showcasing of comedians has practically ground to a halt on television.

Television is by far the most used vehicle of entertainment and communication. The average weekly viewing among the population, four years old and over, is 26 hours,

that is, a quarter of the waking hours. With no variety theatres to speak of, live comedy is, as was noted, to be found in good heart in clubs of varied descriptions and in one-night gigs in large civic and other halls. This is encouraging but engages chiefly with specialised audiences, of, for instance, the student or younger generation type. Apart from the panto (where 'soap' characters rather than comedians often star) and the very occasional summer show, it is unlikely that many children or, for that matter, middle aged and older people, get to see or hear a comedian performing in the acknowledged sense of comedian-ship.

In retrospect, one begins to comprehend how much the radio had offered opportunities to comedians, the more especially after its relaxation of restriction with the passing of John Reith as Director-General of the BBC and the advent of World War II. It is true that, with first houses and a Saturday matinee, the variety theatres had provided succour for a family audience, but, in the central decades of the late 1930s, the 1940s and the early 1950s, there were comedian-oriented shows on radio day in, day out. From Arthur Askey and Tommy Handley, via Jimmy Edwards, Ted Ray and Jimmy Clitheroe, through to Tony Hancock and the ever enjoyable Roy Hudd, the flag of straightforward comedy was flown. Now the personal ten hours weekly average listening time is devoted chiefly to music.

The cinema was another outlet. Even if one missed George Formby, Gracie Fields, Frank Randle, Old Mother Riley or Will Hay, one might have seen one of the American comedians in filmic action, such as Bob Hope, Abbott and Costello or the Marx Brothers. Now only a tenth of the population visits the cinema as much as once a month and not many comics on either side of the Atlantic are making many movies.

Thus the public exposure to comedians is now quite low. That does not mean that there is no laughter on television, merely that it is provoked by other means, notably, as was described in the foregoing chapter, by the brilliance of comic actors. They have largely replaced the old-style comics as 'the People's Jesters', persuading people to laugh at the foibles of the hour and distracting them from overly much consideration of the horrors of the day.

This leads to the contention that the comedian, as popularly recognised, has been a manifestation that has enjoyed a main circulation of some 50 or 60 years. Emerging from the end of the old-time music hall, about the time of the 1914-1918 War, it flourished on the variety, pantomime and summer show stages, and was given particularly weighty support by the radio in its golden age and, less dramatically, by the cinema, reaching something of a climax with the counterfactual success of Morecambe and Wise on television in the 1970s.

As with much social history, these are assessments about pools of emphasis, not absolute divisions. Several music hall stars had the attributes commonly associated with comedians, while, of course, comedians are still

very active: Ken Dodd lives! It is more a question of impact and opportunity. For a half a century or so comedians were in dominant mode on stage and across the airways; they were much more part of the common coin of everyday converse and understanding than was or is now the case.

Tops of the Bill

So, by way of finale, it is proposed to assess those five or six decades of comedians and draw up a championship list of 'the best in show'.

There are a few ground rules. First, this has been a study of British comedians, men and women born and bred in the United Kingdom and who mainly made their comic way in this country. This immediately raises a few pedantic questions to which expedient answers are supplied. Eltham-born Bob Hope is ruled out on the grounds of his being brought up in the United States and being an essentially transatlantic entertainer. Charlie Chaplin is included, his having grown up, initially in grim conditions, and learned his business in England, before heading off for global stardom. Similarly Stan Laurel is included, and for the same reasons, although it should be added that, self-evidently, he makes his premier appeal in concert with the American, Oliver Hardy.

For the most part, and by token of the chosen parameters, most of the contenders have either died or retired. Just a few are still in gravity-dispersing activity. Another critical aspect of the time-factor is the vintage or longevity of a comedian. In the past, some have made what seemed to be a hit, only for it to transpire that they were, in fact, one-joke or one-gimmick operators, too two-dimensional to develop a fulfilling career against a canvas of constant acclaim. It is this proviso that

Arguably Britian's best ever stand-up comedian in the second half of the 20th century, the invariably effervescent Ken Dodd makes it difficult to judge some contemporary comics with any degree of perspective; several may come to be enduring household names, but, as yet, it is impossible to guess.

The great majority of them have been seen or heard by the author, usually through more than one medium, but, crucially, in the medium – stage, radio, cinema, television – where they are normally believed to have produced their optimal work. The major criterion has been the simple one of funniness, the extent to which these men and women moved one to laughter. That said, there are degrees of laughter, and there is a critical element here in terms of the originality, the profundity and style whereby the laughter is raised. That patently links with the previous point about constancy, for, plainly, it is mainly the comedians who have developed a three-dimensional persona for their comedy who have survived to tell their tales and bring comic value to audiences over longish careers.

Although the choices are inevitably personal and guided by individual likes and dislikes, some authorial attempt has been made to take into the reckoning the public and cultural impact of these figures, some of whom have been the subject of cultural adulation and have been hailed as comic icons. Nonetheless, at the last the personal preference must perforce remain dominant. It might be mentioned, by way of example, that the writer numbers among his less favourite kinds of comedians those who might more readily be labelled 'entertainers', that is, those who have mixed other skills, such as singing, with their jokes and relied heavily on a charming rather than on an amusing personality. The other possible prejudice is against those comedians who have introduced an element of bathos into their performance, this often producing, unless very subtly presented,

something of a mawkish streak that sits ill with genuine comedy.

One might do worse than proceed by order of categories, rather after the Crufts dog show manner of 'best in breed', utilising the formats and styles that have been used to rationalise the chapter contents of this book.

Firstly, there were one or two great music hall performers who either overlapped profitably into the post-1918 era or whose special genius demands that they might be considered. Marie Lloyd, Gus Elen, George Formby Senior and George Robey might thus be short-listed for selection. Then there were the 'dames' associated with the pantomime season, from whom Norman Evans emerges with particular merit, but this group also yields up, on the glamorous side, Danny La Rue, on the sleazy side, Mrs Shufflewick, and, on the boisterous side, Old Mother Riley. Close to this group might be the famed gossips of comedy, notably, Frankie Howerd and Larry Grayson. The summer shows are more difficult, in that most stars played the concert parties at some part of their career. Three who deserve special mention are 'Mr Eastbourne' aka Sandy Powell, Blackpool's Dave Morris and Morecambe's Albert Modley.

Radio was the preserve of another set of all-time greats, among them Arthur Askey; Tommy Handley, as the maestro of *ITMA*; the inimitable Al Read, Ted Ray and Jimmy Edwards. A 'Goon' delegate, such as Spike Milligan, should probably be added to the roster, in part because he achieved some cult status, in part because Peter Sellers evolved into more of a film star proper. Cinema was the particular medium perhaps of Will Hay and George Formby, although both had enormous success on the stage and radio, whilst, of course, Stan Laurel and Charlie Chaplin are, from the stance of this study, almost exclusively film stars. Television was the home for Tony Hancock's genius, but Benny Hill cannot be discounted in this respect.

Turning to the 'styles', as opposed to the media, the finest sketch comedians have been Harry Tate, Jimmy James and Robb Wilton, while Morecambe and Wise top the double acts, followed perhaps by Jewel and War-riss. Certainly if one had to cast the all-time pantomime, one would immediately turn to Jewel and Warriss to play the robbers or the broker's men, over against Norman Evans as dame and Ken Dodd as chief comic. Flanagan and Allen might be added to the possibilities, not least in recognition of their Crazy Gang membership, but also because they earned some special and affectionate identity with the British public. There is space, too, for the eccentric oddity of Nat Mills and Bobbie.

In the regional stakes, the honours might go to Billy Connolly and to Chic Murray of Scotland, with the likes of Frank Randle and Les Dawson appearing as strong northern representatives. Billy Russell should be included under the banner of his own bill matter, 'on behalf of the working classes'. Of the London based comics, with their slightly totemistic flavour, Tommy Trinder and Max Wall come to the fore. Among the women comedians the chief entrants might be Nelly Wallace, Gracie Fields (one of few entertainment all-rounders whose comedy is of classic proportions), Hylda Baker and Victoria Wood. Among the speciality acts one finds and is pleased to choose the manic magician, Tommy Cooper; the essence of variety, Wilson, Keppel and Betty; the pick of the comedy dancers, Billy Dainty, and the supreme monologuists, Billy Bennett and Stanley Holloway. Finally, in the key spotlight of the genuine front cloth stand-up comedian, Max Miller and Ken Dodd make their glittering entry.

That provides 40 or more 'turns' as candidates, out of perhaps many scores that have been gazetted, at shorter or longer length, in this text. Gazing anew over those somewhat synthetic pigeon-holes into which these gifted stars have been pushed, one would, if pressed into a corner, have to choose one or two from each set for the top honours. From the music hall rivals, one would opt for George Formby Senior, on the grounds of puristic comedy and acknowledging the sheer scintillating glory of Marie Lloyd as an entertainer per se. Norman Evans would be the pick of the dames and gossips; Sandy Powell the choice among the summer resort comics; Al Read the doyen of the airways; Tony Hancock easily the greatest of the TV comedians. Cinema is intriguing, given the international repute of Charlie Chaplin and Stan Laurel, but the former has perhaps lost a little bit of his sheen in the less sentimental days since his peak and there always hangs over Stan Laurel the notion that his fate was entwined with that of Oliver Hardy. Given his like command of stage and radio, Will Hay emerges powerfully, although, once more, the undoubted appeal of George Formby can never be neglected in this sort of assessment.

Morecambe and Wise would be most people's selection from among the double acts, while all the regional and class-oriented contenders – Billy Connolly, Chic Murray, Frank Randle, Billy Russell and Les Dawson – must be in with a shout. Victoria Wood is maybe the finest of that very funny female foursome, while, for all the zaniness of Tommy Cooper, it is hard to ignore the definitive clout of Wilson, Keppel and Betty. Finally, it is difficult to separate Max Miller and Ken Dodd, each the best stand-up comic of his generation, just as it is near impossible to distinguish between the genius of Jimmy James and Robb Wilton.

Ultimately, the choice is very subjective. A friend of the author uses the '£1000' yard-stick, as in 'I would give £1000 to see A, B or C...'. If, then, this approach were adopted, the following would be the programme in order of 'wishability' – the sequence denoting how much the writer would dearly love to see and/or hear each of these acts for about 20 minutes apiece. At the close, an unrequited affection for the great sketch and stand-up comedians of the period are finally revealed.

1. Jimmy James
2. Robb Wilton
3. Ken Dodd
4. Victoria Wood
5. Max Miller
6. Al Read
7. Wilson, Keppel and Betty
8. Morecambe and Wise
9. Stan Laurel
10. Norman Evans
11. Will Hay and 'boys'
12. Tony Hancock
13. Gracie Fields
14. Les Dawson
15. Charlie Chaplin
16. George Formby Senior
17. Tommy Cooper
18. Billy Connolly
19. Sandy Powell
20. Billy Bennett
21. Chic Murray
22. Larry Grayson
23. George Formby
24. Jewel and Warriss
25. Frankie Howerd
26. Billy Russell
27. Hylda Baker
28. Frank Randle
29. Jimmy Edwards
30. Dave Morris
31. Arthur Askey
32. Mrs Shufflewick
33. Stanley Holloway
34. Marie Lloyd
35. Nelly Wallace
36. Tommy Handley (plus *ITMA* cast)
37. Old Mother Riley and daughter, Kitty
38. Albert Modley
39. Danny La Rue
40. George Robey
41. Ted Ray
42. Harry Tate and company
43. Max Wall
44. Tommy Trinder
45. Flanagan and Allen
46. Billy Dainty
47. Nat Mills and Bobbie
48. Gus Elen
49. Spike Milligan
50. Benny Hill

The People's Jesters

For those many, if not all readers, who find this order singular and controversial, why not attempt to make your own list of those comedians who have reigned at the court of the public as 'the People's Jesters'?

Let the connoisseur's comedian, and the author's favourite, Jimmy James, have the last words. More than anyone, he illustrated the genuine comedian's ideal of integrating a comical persona with reflective and amusing use of language. Like Robb Wilton, the second in the writer's list, he sustained his joy of language and droll character offstage. The tale has been several times told of Jimmy James and his compadres being approached, in somewhat condescending mode, by an assistant producer, who demanded, prior to some TV show, to know of what exactly his act consisted. This rather patronising young man apparently grew more and more perturbed, as Jimmy James, his cigarette revolving and the smoke issuing randomly from his mouth, spontaneously and immediately replied:

'now I'm glad you asked me that, because we've been a bit worried about it – well, you were worried, weren't you, Eli? You see, when we open on the trapeze and we're hanging there upside down – in the Chinese costumes, of course – we swing, and as we swing we sing *By a Blue Lagoon she's Waiting* in three part harmony. Now that'll be alright, because the camera can move (Eli, it can move with you, you see). But it's the finish that has got us worried, sir, when we get the bowls of goldfish on the strings and we spin 'em on our teeth and they go right out – it's what you call centrifugal, Eli, centrifugal – will the trapeze be wide enough...and, by the way, have the Chinese costumes arrived yet?....

FINSBURY PARK EMPIRE

PROGRAMME Price 3º.

Index

Individuals are listed by stage or most commonly known name; double (and other) acts listed together

The People's Jesters

Preece, Richard 17
Presley, Elvis 174
Preston, Duncan 157
Priestley, J B 45,77,153,189
Prince, Arthur 131

Quaintesques,The 45

Rabin, Oscar 199
Raffles, Mark 139
Randall, Alan 191
Randle, Frank 33,65,79,123,168-9,184,212-216
Ransome, Arthur 93
Rawitz and Landauer 123
Ray, Ted 58,81,85-7,116,121,166,181-2, 187-8,205-7,211-216
Raymond, Paul 190,194
Read, Al 15,89-90,129,132-4,150-2,166,177,214-16
Reader,Ralph 88,97,196,205
Rees, Phil 93
Reeve, Ada 22
Reid, Beryl 133,150
Reid, Mike 182,199,211
Reid, John 172
Reindeer, Eddie 191
Reith, John 56-9,62,79,211
Revill, Florence 191
Revnell and West 149-150,157
Revnell, Ethel 129
Rhys Jones, Griff 202
Richard, Cyril 137
Richards, Jeffrey 172
Riley, Old Mother (Lucan,Arthur) and Kitty McShane 37-40,103,115-6,147,163,208,212-216
Roberts, Ken 164
Robertson Justice, James 133
Robey, George 9,24-8,35,41,49,85,179,210,214-216
Robina, Fanny 23,147
Robinson, William 139
Rogers, Rhoda 188
Rogues Concert Party, The 185
Roper, Vera 83
Roper, George 199

Rose, Clarkson 3649
Rose, Julian 164
Ross, Jonathan 200
Ross, Don 188
Rossitter, Leonard 208-9
Rowson, Harry 109
Roy, Harry 101
Roy, Derek 83
Royal Pierrots, The 45
Royle, George 45
Rushton, Willie 202
Ruskin, John 146
Russell, Billy 25,166
Russell, Fred 131

Sachs, Andrew 207
Sahl, Mort 201
Sales, Freddie 191
Saunders, Jennifer 157,203
Saunders,Don 191
Savage, Lily 40,166 (O'Grady, Paul)
Saveen 131
Scales, Prunella 207
Scott, Terry 190
Scott and Foster 120
Scott and Whaley 113
Seaforth, Victor 134
Seamon and Farrell 115
Secombe,Harry 88,133,150,164,177
Segar, Elzie 87
Sellars, Peter 52,78,86-9,106,134,214
Seltzer, Harry 191
Sennett, Mack 71,92
Service, Robert 136
Seven Little Foys, The 93
Sewell, Bob 92
Shadwell, Charles 66-7,120,123-4
Sharman, John 58
Shellfire Concert Party, The 138
Sheppard, Clifford 185
Sheridan, Cecil 163
Sheridan, Mark 23
Sherrin, Ned 202

THIRD AGE PRESS

. . . a unique publishing company

. . . an independent publishing company which recognizes that the period of life after full-time employment and family responsibility can be a time of fulfilment and continuing development . . . a time of regeneration

Third Age Press books are available by direct mail order from Third Age Press, 6 Parkside Gardens London SW19 5EY . . . or on order through book shops

Email: dnort@globalnet.co.uk   Website: www.thirdagepress.co.uk

All prices include UK p & p. Please add 20% for other countries.   UK Sterling cheques payable to *Third Age Press*.

Dianne Norton ~ Managing Editor

Third Age Press books by Eric Midwinter

. . is a series that focuses on the presentation of your unique life. These booklets seek to stimulate and guide your thoughts and words in what is acknowledged to be not only a process of value to future generations but also a personally beneficial exercise.

A Voyage of Rediscovery: a guide to writing your life story . . . is a 'sea chart' to guide your reminiscence & provide practical advice about the business of writing or recording your story.   **36 pages   £4.50**

Encore: a guide to planning a celebration of your life   An unusual and useful booklet that encourages you to think about the ways you would like to be remembered, hopefully in the distant future.   **20 pages   £2.00**

The Rhubarb People . . . Eric Midwinter's own witty and poignant story of growing up in Manchester in the 1930s. Also on tape including useful tips on writing or recording your story. **32 pages   £4.50**   **~ audio cassette   £5.00**

Getting To Know Me . . . is aimed at carers and families of people in care. It provides the opportunity to create a profile of an older person ~ their background and relationships, likes and dislikes, as well as record the practical information needed to make the caring process a positive experience for all concerned.   **24 pages   £2.00**

Best Remembered . . . a hundred stars of yesteryear

. . . presents a galaxy of 100 stars from the days before television ruled our lives. These cultural icons achieved lasting fame through radio, cinema, stage, dance hall, theatre, variety hall and sporting field between 1927 and 1953 – a quarter century rich in talent, innovation, humour and unforgettable melodies. As a trigger for reminiscence or a rich but light scholarly text on social and cultural history, its lively style and fizzing illustrations cannot fail to please.

168 pages   £10.95

Novel Approaches: a guide to the popular classic novel

Oh for a good read and an un-putdownable book! Despite the lurid blandishments of television, there are still many of us who turn, quietly, pensively, to the novel in leisure moments. This short text is aimed at such people whose interest has been kindled sufficiently to permit some extra contemplation and study.

Novel Approaches takes 35 novels that have stood the test of time and embeds them in historical and literary commentary – a combination of social background giving scientific objectivity, and the author's artistic subjectivity.   **180 pages   £9.50**

As one ^ stage door closes . . . The story of John Wade: Jobbing Conjuror

As one stage door closes . . . is a study of the way the entertainment world has changed over the past 50 years by shifts in the social and economic fabric, as personally witnessed by John Wade, who, over that period, has successfully plied the ancient craft of magicianship in every possible show-business outlet. In the course of his personal journey, he crosses paths with a sparkling array of stars. This book contrives to look both in front of and behind the scenes – and then locates both in social context. From the dingy theatrical lodgings and dreary train journeys of the 1950s to the sumptuous environs of luxury liners and Hollywood glamour 40 years on, this show-business saga unrolls. **176 pages   £12.50**

500 Beacons: The U3A Story

The British University of the Third Age, launched in 1982, has proved to be one of the most successful exercises in social co-operation, radical adult education and older age citizenship since World War II. This is the tale of the origins, the development, the current position and the future aspirations of this unique pioneering of the principles of mutual aid. While closely analysing the national and regional elements in this dramatic success story, the book's focus is also on the many local stories of individuals battling to make the U3A ideal work amid the homes and streets of their own town or community. **320 pages   £12.50**

Other books from Third Age Press

On the Tip of Your Tongue: your memory in later life

by Dr H B Gibson . . . explores memory's history and examines what an 'ordinary' person can expect of their memory. He reveals the truth behind myths about memory and demonstrates how you can manage your large stock of memories and your life. Wittily illustrated by Rufus Segar.
160 pages   £7.00

A Little of What You Fancy Does You Good: your health in later life   by Dr H B Gibson

'Managing an older body is like running a very old car - as the years go by you get to know its tricks and how to get the best out of it, so that you may keep it running sweetly for years and years' . . . so says Dr H B Gibson in his sensible and practical book which respects your intelligence and, above all, appreciates the need to enjoy later life. It explains the whys, hows and wherefores of exercise, diet and sex ~ discusses 'You and your doctor' and deals with some of the pitfalls and disabilities of later life. Illustrated by Rufus Segar. **256 pages   £7.00**

Buy both the above books for the special price of only £10.00

The Play Reader: 7 dramas by thirdagers

Seven one-act plays ideal for reading in groups, rehearsed readings or performance. Their rich variety is certain to challenge and stimulate as well as provide entertainment. Now available in A4 format, hole punched (binder not included ~ may be photocopied). Includes: a mystery set in 1900s Paris; a psychological drama; all-woman play set in Roman Britain; Greek holiday setting; the Third Age of the future?; family drama; comedy duet for two women. **£10.00**

Our Grandmothers, Our Mothers, Ourselves: A century of women's lives

Charmian Cannon (Editor). . . Eleven women who met through a U3A group exploring women's hidden social history talked, and then wrote, about their grandmothers, their mothers and their own lives. Their stories spanned the whole 20th Century, encompassed two world wars and many social and political changes affecting women. Through their discussions they crossed class and ethnic boundaries and exchanged their experiences of education, work and home life. They shared intimate family recollections honestly ~ uncovering affectionate as well as painful memories.

The book includes a section on the increasing use of life histories as a way of linking personal lives and public events, and a list of sources and further reading.

200 pages   £9.95

For details of all Third Age Press publications visit our website at www.thirdagepress.co.uk